LYNDON'S LEGACY

LYNDON'S LEGACY

A Candid Look at the President's Policymakers

by Frank L. Kluckhohn

The Devin-Adair Company
New York, 1964

Canadian Agents: Abelard-Schuman Canada, Ltd., Toronto
Library of Congress Catalog card number: 64-23751
Manufactured in the United States of America

To

My wife, June, without whose

help this book would not have been possible

v

ACKNOWLEDGMENTS

Special gratitude is due Don Ackerman for his expert research and his contacts and experience, which assisted considerably in the preparation of this book. Publisher and author also wish to thank the publishers of *National Review* for permission to quote extensively from James Burnham's article in the May 7, 1963 issue of *National Review*.

CONTENTS

CONTENTS

Introduction

Introduction

THE HERITAGE of President Johnson must be examined. For it is he who insisted that he would follow the domestic and foreign policies of his predecessor soon after he took the oath of office in a plane which was to take him from Dallas to Washington. It is he who is saddled with precisely the same advisers, speech writers and pundits who urged President Kennedy to change traditional American policies in speeches at Yale, at Philadelphia, and at American University in the nation's capital. They even wrote the speeches to put in words like "accommodation," "diversity," "interdependence" and "disarmament," which if divested of their professorial touch would have been anathema to thinking Americans. Whether they were spoken in New Haven, in Philadelphia, or at the American University campus, an examination in detail of these and other pronouncements reveals a dangerous trend for every American —doubly dangerous because, while the man who spoke the words has passed from the scene, the men who wrote them and thought them up still write, think and advise his successor today.

President Lyndon Johnson must decide in what direction he will lead our nation and the free world. Will it continue to be toward goals urged by the men around Kennedy who today are Lyndon's legacy? Or will it be more toward the Right?

Thus far—in paying personal tribute to controversial nuclear scientist Robert Oppenheimer, in calling Congress back during the 1963 holidays to give a "Christmas present" of U. S. taxpayer-subsidized wheat to N. Khrushchev, and in appointing a host of leftwingers to the highest federal office— the Man from Texas has followed the course set by the men around Kennedy. Moreover, his own record in a long political career does not give a definitive answer.

The nation, wishing him well in the light of the tragic way he assumed the powerful office of President, senses the depth of the current crisis and the importance of its outcome to our future and that of other free peoples of the world. His actions are being watched and weighed with expectancy; it is still too early to render final judgment.

The record does show that Lyndon Johnson entered public life as Texas director of the radical National Youth Administration and that he first ran for Congress supporting Franklin D. Roosevelt's controversial Supreme Court "packing" plan. During the Eisenhower Administration, Johnson was widely regarded as a Conservative, but in analyzing Johnson's voting record, the nonpartisan *Congressional Quarterly* asserts that "as Majority Leader, Senator Johnson found himself in the company of Democratic moderates most often, Liberals less often and Conservatives least often." The Kennedy years found Johnson enthusiastically supporting the JFK program, speaking out for the Kennedys' race proposals and lambasting those who warned of the dangers of the Soviet arms build-up in Cuba.

Lyndon Johnson, as President, has already paid lip service, at least, to the policies of the Kennedy advisers he has inherited. He has promised to continue and even surpass John F. Kennedy's disarmament plans and his "world safe for diversity" policy. When Khrushchev opened 1964 with an interview promising "the development of relations of peaceful cooperation, good neighborliness and friendship between the peoples of the United States and the Soviet Union," Lyndon Johnson met him more than halfway. LBJ held "peace talks" with new West German Chancellor Ludwig Erhard and promised to explore all opportunities for improvement of East-West relations. This was followed by a statement of a "White House spokesman" that Mr. Johnson was determined to wage "an unrelenting peace offensive" to end the tensions of the Cold War.

The climate of cordiality advocated by Lyndon Johnson seems not an iota different from John F. Kennedy's "relaxation of tension." Will LBJ lean as far toward "accommodation," and away from opposition to communism?

The rulers of the Soviet Union believe that they are

gaining from this policy of "accommodation"; for reasons best known to themselves, John F. Kennedy's advisers have favored such a policy, have held that victory in the struggle with communism is impossible. Now, as Lyndon's legacy, they continue to influence American policy in the direction of disarmament and peace at almost any price.

There are many Americans who wish that Lyndon Johnson would cut free from his legacy; others who think he cannot or does not wish to do so. Let us take a look at the men who compose his unusual legacy, see who they are, and how they developed their ideas. One or two have left, but most are still at hand and plan to stay.

JFK sometimes went to the lowest echelon to determine how a decision had been made. In this way, he sometimes saw through faulty reasoning by the Pentagon "Whiz Kids" or by State Department officials down the line where policy was so often made.

With Lyndon Johnson it is different. Johnson goes right to the top in an effort to get a short, snappy, definite recommendation from the Rusks or McNamaras or Taylors rather than from the Yarmolinskys or Bundys. This could be dangerous; by not knowing where a decision originated or how it was made, President Johnson might very well have less control over his legacy of advisers than did President Kennedy, who bequeathed them.

In addition, some in Washington see the advent of a "government by crony" regime under the new President. While John F. Kennedy frequently consulted twenty or thirty advisers or officials on an important decision, which meant a choice of alternatives, it is evident that recommendations received by LBJ will offer no minority views, but will be passed on by the top-level Kennedy "hangers-on" or perhaps by new additions like William Moyers or Abe Fortas—surely a shaky foundation for major decision-making. Under Kennedy, the American people never knew who was responsible for recommending liberal policies and unwise moves in both domestic and foreign areas; under Johnson, not only the American people but even the President himself may never know.

Access to Lyndon Johnson is more limited than it was to Kennedy. LBJ is not interested in presenting an image to the American people through televised press conferences with mundane but amusing questions and answers. Neither is he interested in parading a stream of Boy Scouts, state soil-conservation experts or party fund-raisers through the White House for precisely timed two-minute conferences. Some of this he will have to do, but fundamentally Johnson's interest is in identifying the problem, consulting with the top experts on the situation, and making instant decisions based on briefings. It is up to the top experts, he believes, to consult with under-lings in order to collect and evaluate related evidence. And in this lies the possibility that the men around Kennedy will become even more influential with Johnson.

Lyndon Johnson moved to the left in 1960, when he tried to capture the Presidential nomination as a Westerner, rather than as a Southerner. He had to continue to move left as Vice President to a President who was committed to the cause of the ultra-liberals and leftists. Now, as President in his own right, he has shown that he will continue the program of his predecessor, as well as his predecessor's policy of accepting advice from the Clevelands, the Bundys, the Rusks, the Ros-tows, the Yarmolinskys, and the rest of a strange crew.

Perhaps the most revealing description of LBJ's political beliefs came from his own lips. In an interview with Columnist Robert Spivack of the N. Y. *Herald-Tribune* syndicate, Johnson said:

"You say I am not a liberal. Let me tell you I am more liberal than Eleanor Roosevelt and I will prove it to you. Franklin D. Roosevelt was my hero. He gave me my start."

Again, as reported in the *Tribune's* Evans-Novak column in December of 1963, LBJ showed his true colors with these words: "No matter what you may think, I'm a Roosevelt New Dealer."

CHAPTER ONE

What Breed of Men
Is Making Over America?

*"The power of the crown, almost dead and rotten
as Prerogative, has grown up anew, with much more
strength, and far less odium, under the name of
Influence."*
. . . Edmund Burke—THOUGHTS ON THE CAUSE
OF THE PRESENT DISCONTENTS

WHEN PRESIDENT JOHN F. KENNEDY declared in his commencement address at Yale on June 12, 1962, that "mythology surrounds us everywhere" in our American life; when he urged Americans to forsake the "stale phrases" and the "clichés of our forebears" in favor of "a more sophisticated view" of "reality," he advertised the fact that he accepted the thinking of the narrow segment of his advisers from Harvard and from a few other academic seats.

Speaking before a distinguished audience and to the nation, the late President gave voice to the muddled, upside-down thinking which is commonplace in nations opposed to us. It is a "myth," the President claimed to the American people, that deficits are bad. It is a "myth" that the national debt is growing at a dangerously rapid rate. It is a "myth" that federal deficits create inflation. It is a "myth" that government is big. It is a "myth" that the federal government is big and growing steadily bigger.

In fact, he characterized most of our traditional American thinking as having been built on "myths." We must free ourselves, he said, from these "myths," from the "stale phrases" and the "clichés of our forebears." even though they have made our nation great.

Whose words are these? Whose thinking is this? A national magazine reported that Walt Whitman Rostow, McGeorge Bundy and Arthur Schlesinger, Jr., had written the

1

Presidential address, and that Theodore Sorenson, who drafted *Profiles in Courage* for Mr. Kennedy, had smoothed the rough edges.

Since Arthur Schlesinger, Jr., for example, had earlier made use of the word "myth" to characterize American traditions, this report seems to have some validity. And when had Schlesinger made use of the term "myth"? In eulogizing "the capitalistic death wish" and "the advance of socialism in the United States."

Just prior to this speech, State Department Policy Planning Council Chairman Walt Rostow had proposed an "end of nationhood," and Assistant Secretary of State Harlan Cleveland had told us publicly that we cannot defeat communism in a cold war or in any other kind of war.

On April 18, 1962, two months before President Kennedy's Yale speech, Ambassador Arthur H. Dean had laid before the Geneva disarmament conference, together with a letter of approval from the President, the "outline of a Treaty on General and Complete Disarmament in a Peaceful World," a treaty to be accepted and made binding by the United Nations. It was the formalization of a Presidential proposal for a three-stage program for the disarmament of the United States under United Nations control, which Kennedy made in a speech before the United Nations in September 1961. That same month, the State Department published—as the official policy of the United States Government—its Department of State Publication 7277, entitled "Freedom from War. The United States Program for General and Complete Disarmament in a Peaceful World," which details the complete disarmament of the United States within approximately ten years, as our nation's part in this three-stage program for world disarmament under United Nations control.

Sending Arthur Dean to horse-trade with the Communists at Geneva on a matter of life-or-death importance to every American seemed a trifle incongruous to many observers, in view of Arthur Dean's public record since at least 1927. But we shall see more of Arthur Dean in the next chapter.

In his first press conference of the Kennedy Administration, Secretary of State Dean Rusk announced that Dean had been named by President Kennedy as U. S. Ambassador to the Geneva disarmament conference, where he subsequently presented the Presidential-U. S. State Department proposal for a three-stage program for disarmament under United Nations control.

And from whom had the world received the blueprint of this Kennedy-State Department-Dean *three-stage program* for disarmament *under United Nations control?*

From Nikita S. Khrushchev.

On September 15, 1959, in a speech before the United Nations, Khrushchev presented the Communist plan "for world peace and security." The proposal which Khrushchev specifically outlined was a *three-stage program* for world disarmament *under United Nations control.*

Communist schemes to disarm the free world are nothing new, of course. In fact, Khrushchev was simply enunciating the original Communist blueprint for "General and Complete Disarmament" which was first given to the world in 1927 by Litvinov.

The Kennedy-Johnson dismantling of the props for U. S. disarmament is discussed fully later on. It is sufficient to say here that the Presidential-State Department-Dean disarmament proposal is a virtual carbon copy of the "world disarmament proposal" first promulgated by Litvinov in 1927, pushed by the Communist Party throughout the non-Communist world during the 1930's, 1940's, and 1950's, and again enunciated by Nikita Khrushchev before the United Nations in 1959.

Three weeks after his Yale speech, President Kennedy chose the Fourth of July to consign our Declaration of Independence to the scrap heap; to declare that the Constitution of the United States—the immortal document written to guarantee individual liberty and our independence—stands "not for individual liberty," and "not for *in*dependence, but for *inter*dependence" on other nations; and that the proud sovereignty and independence of the United States of America is a thing of the past.

Standing on the steps of Independence Hall in Philadelphia where on July 4, 1776, our Founding Fathers issued our Declaration of Independence, Mr. Kennedy proclaimed that both our Declaration of Independence and our American Constitution are now outdated. They stood merely for "the old American Union found here 175 years ago. Now we have reached the end of that era.

"I will say here and now on this Day of Independence," he proclaimed to the world, "that the United States will be ready for a Declaration of *Inter*dependence. . . . All this will not be accomplished in a year, but let the world know *it is our goal.*"

If there is any cornerstone upon which the United States of America rests, it is on the gospel of the individual liberty of every citizen, and that our *nation* is *indivisible* and *independent*—nor *inter*dependent on other nations, as Mr. Kennedy tried to tell us.

In fact, the late President compared the nations of Africa and Asia—those backward nations which, for the most part, are actually emerging from the jungle straight into the Soviet orbit—with our nation of civilized men which threw off the tyranny of the English monarch in 1776. He said that we look forward to *inter*dependence with these emerging nations, and as a prelude to this, he promised *inter*dependence soon with the "more perfect union" now being formed in Europe.

Praising the emerging nations of Africa and Asia, President Kennedy declared that "with the passing of ancient empires, less than two per cent of the world's population live in territories *officially* termed dependent."

The fact is that today, in the Communist empire, which is not "passing," but rather growing steadily every day, one-third of the entire world—almost one billion human beings

—groans in Communist bondage; and furthermore, the great United States of America was created to bring people out of the bondage of tyranny and into the free air of *in*dependence —not into the bondage of *inter*dependence on other nations.

Exactly one hundred and eighty-six years before, on the same hallowed ground, on July 4, 1776, our nation was born with these stirring words:

> The Representatives of the United States of America in Congress assembled, appealing to the Supreme Judge of the World for the rectitude of our intentions do, in the Name, and by the authority of the good people of these Colonies, solemnly publish and declare that these Colonies are, and of right ought to be, Free and *Independent States. . . .* And for the support of this Declaration, with a firm reliance on the protection of Divine Providence, we mutually pledge to each other our Lives, our Fortunes and our Sacred Honor.

The light of liberty, the torch of human freedom, the shining beacon of man's dignity as a free creature of Almighty God, was kindled in the world. And to our shores for 186 years thronged the huddled masses of Europe to breathe the air of liberty and to work out their destiny as a free people. And for 186 years, millions of human beings lived and fought and died to preserve the greatest nation ever shaped by the mind and spirit of man in all of human history—the sovereign, proud, independent nation of the United States of America.

But now it is all over.

Standing on that same ground in 1962, John F. Kennedy gave voice to the grand design of the handful of "advanced thinkers" who surrounded him, and with not a mention of "appealing to the Supreme Judge of the World for the rectitude of our intentions," he declared that now we have reached the end of our independence. Now, we are no longer to be a single, *independent* nation, but *interdependent* on other nations.

A clearer statement of the "end of nationhood"—preached by Walt Whitman Rostow and the men surrounding the President—than that contained in this speech, this perversion of the immortal testaments of our American freedom and independence, could not be presented to the American people.

But on no occasion to date has the influence of the men of the New Frontier been more shockingly bared than on June 10, 1963, when Kennedy delivered the commencement address at American University in Washington, D. C.—a speech which shook Democrats and Republicans alike throughout the nation. This speech was received by many as signaling a new, unparalleled era in naïve attempts to appease the Communist juggernaut in its primary and unyielding purpose of conquering the entire world for communism.

In that speech, President Kennedy announced his subject as "the most important topic on earth: world peace." The President summed up his attitude by saying: "In short, the United States and its allies, *and the Soviet Union and its allies,* have a *mutually deep interest in a just and genuine peace.*"

To transmit the heart of this speech to readers of this book, it is best to let the Presidential words speak for themselves:

> Some say it is useless to speak of world peace or world law or world disarmament and that it will be useless until the leaders of the Soviet Union adopt a more enlightened attitude. I hope they do. . . . But I also believe that we must re-examine our own attitude . . . for our attitude is as essential as theirs . . . every thoughtful citizen should begin by looking inward—by examining his own attitude toward the possibilities of peace, *toward the Soviet Union.*
>
> Let us focus instead on a more practical peace . . . *on a series of concrete actions and agreements* which are in the interest of all concerned.
>
> *World peace . . . requires only that* [all men] *live together in mutual tolerance,* submitting their disputes to a just and peaceful settlement.
>
> By defining our goal more clearly . . . we can help all people to see it, to draw hope from it, and to move irresistibly toward it.
>
> *Let us re-examine our attitude toward the Soviet Union.* It is discouraging to think that their leaders *may actually believe* what their propagandists write.
>
> . . . a warning to the American people . . . not to see only

a distorted and desperate view of the other side, not to see conflict as inevitable, *accommodation as impossible,* and communication as nothing more than exchange of threats.

But we can still hail the Russian people for their many achievements—in science and space, in economic and industrial growth, in culture and in acts of courage.

Among the many traits the people of our two countries have in common, none is stronger than *our mutual abhorrence of war.*

Today, should total war ever break out again—not matter how—our two countries would become the principal targets. All that *we* have built, all that *we* have worked for, would be destroyed in the first 24 hours.

And even in the Cold War . . . our two countries bear the heaviest burdens. . . . We are both caught up in a vicious and dangerous cycle in which *suspicion on one side breeds suspicion on the other . . .*

In short, both the United States and its allies, and the Soviet Union and its allies, have a mutually deep interest in a just and genuine peace.

. . . let us also direct our attention to our common interests and to the means by which those differences [*sic*] *can be* resolved. And if we cannot end now our differences, at least *we can help make the world safe for diversity.*

It is our hope . . . to convince the Soviet Union that she, too, should let each nation choose its own future, so long as that choice does not interfere with the choice of others.

This will require a new effort to achieve in world law a new context for world discussions. It will require *increased understanding between the Soviet Union and ourselves.**

One of the best analyses of this stunning speech was written by a man who understands communism better than most Americans who have never known it first-hand, ex-Communist Frank S. Meyer, now a vigorously anti-Communist editor of *National Review* magazine.

To the Communist mind, Mr. Meyer points out, "it would be heresy to 'let each nation choose its own future,' " and it "is pathetic to hope, as President Kennedy does in his speech, that 'if we cannot end now our differences, at least we can make

---

* Emphasis supplied unless otherwise indicated, here and throughout the book.

the world safe for diversity.'" Diversity, Mr. Meyer points out, "is just what the Communists, with their vision of a collectivist, controlled, engineered and Utopian world, strive by every means at their disposal to eliminate.

"To posit 'diversity' as the basis of a possible compromise with communism," says Meyer, "is the historical equivalent of a Norman Crusader proposing to a Moslem leader acceptance of the doctrine of the Trinity as the basis for agreement between them."

The "differences" between the United States and the Communists, to which President Kennedy alluded in his speech, are in fact, says Meyer, "the principled devotion of communism to the destruction of Western civilization (the civilization of the free person and of the transcendental moral law) and of the American Republic . . ."

Mr. Meyer sums up the President's speech: "This radical failure to understand the historical significance of communism as an alien and inimical force bearing down upon the West is central to the suicidal program which Kennedy presents in his address."

The crux of President Kennedy's proposed program was enunciated in his speech: "Our primary long-range interest in Geneva, however, is *general and complete disarmament, designed to take place by stages . . .*"

Then the President announced—translating his intentions into actions—first, the signing of "a comprehensive test-ban treaty," which, the President assured, "would increase our security—it would decrease the prospects of war," and which, he proposed, "will help us to achieve disarmament." Will these intentions reach fruition under President Johnson?

On August 5, 1963, the Moscow Treaty, for a "limited" nuclear test-ban, was signed in Moscow by Secretary of State Dean Rusk. The treaty was ratified by the U. S. Senate on September 24, 1963.

Little realized by Americans is the fact that this "test-ban" treaty is, as President Kennedy asserted in his speech, the first step to disarmament. The preamble to the treaty states that the signatories "proclaim as their *principal* aim the speediest possible achievement of an agreement or *general and complete disarmament* under strict international control in accordance with the objectives of the United Nations."

How many Americans believe that America will survive the Communist onslaught if we carry out "general and complete disarmament" and entrust our lives to a UN "peace army"; if we liquidate our Army, Navy and Air Force; destroy our planes, ships, tanks and nuclear weapons; and entrust our lives to the United Nations army (whose strategy is mapped by the Assistant Secretary General for Security and Political Affairs, the UN post which, by secret agreement made by Alger Hiss, is always held by a Communist from the Soviet Union or the Soviet bloc of nations—the same UN army which mutilated and slaughtered men, women and children in the Congo and destroyed the only anti-Communist government in all of Black Africa)?

In the light of America's rush to disarm completely and to be friends with the Communists in order to foster "increased understanding between the Soviet Union and ourselves," as Kennedy termed it, it seems fitting to recall the chilling prophecy made 30 years ago by Dimitri Manuilsky, later Chairman of the UN Security Council, in a lecture at the Lenin School of Political Warfare in Moscow:

> War to the hilt, between Communism and Capitalism, is inevitable. Today, of course, we are not strong enough to attack. *Our time will come in 20 or 30 years.*
>
> To win, we shall need the element of surprise. The bourgeoisie will have to be lulled to sleep. So we shall begin by launching the most spectacular "peace" movement on record. There will be electrifying overtures and unheard-of concessions. The Capitalist countries, stupid and decadent, will rejoice to cooperate in their own destruction. *They will leap at another chance to be friends.*
>
> As soon as their guard is down, *we shall smash them with our clenched fist!*

John F. Kennedy had not voiced previously the kind of
talk he enunciated in these speeches—certainly not while running for the Presidency in 1960.

But the goals enumerated by President Kennedy in these
speeches are exactly the same goals, openly expressed, of the
men advising President Johnson—Rostow, Schlesinger (until
he resigned), Ball, Cleveland, Yarmolinsky, Jerome Wiesner,
Richard Goodwin, Dean Rusk, and their intimate associates
and subordinates. Their goals publicly acknowledged, but so
little dreamed of by the average American, which I have delineated in this book by direct quotes, by documented evidence
and by reproducing speeches, statements and official papers
of New Frontier advisers are:

General and complete disarmament of the United States,
trusting that the Soviets will also disarm; destruction of our
military weapons; liquidation of our armed forces; entrusting
of our lives to a United Nations army; replacing our American
courts of justice with United Nations courts; and finally, "an
end to nationhood"—the end of the United States, and of all
countries, as independent, sovereign nations. As this book is
written, the goals of the men who guide President Johnson
are speeding toward fulfillment, unrealized by the majority
of Americans.

These men are advocates of Big Government, Big Spending—international and national—and their objectives are a
cause for worried speculation. What they are attempting is
far more important than what they have accomplished to
date. They have become the faculty which has taken the place
of a Cabinet. They are the Inner Circle of advisers, and can
be accurately described as "the backstairs bosses," in contrast,
for example, with the "kitchen cabinet" of Andrew Jackson's
era.

Except for Dean Rusk, who was somewhat known but
had never been prominently mentioned in connection with
Cabinet speculation, none of these men was very well known
to the average American before they suddenly began to steer

the course leading the United States into new, uncharted and troubled waters. While we boast that we are a democratic model for the world, none of us ever had a chance to vote for any of them. Half were never approved by Congress. Who are these men and who are their faceless associates and helpers?

First, they are the men who advocated the spending which led to a deficit of more than $6 billion for fiscal 1962; more than $8 billion for fiscal 1964, leaving us with a national debt of $320 billion by June 30 of a Presidential election year. These are the men in charge of adding one new federal employee to the public tax bill every two minutes, 24 hours a day, during the first year of the New Frontier.

And the New Frontier is accelerating its hiring of federal employees. In June 1963, 21,469 civilian employees were added to the federal payroll *during that month alone.* This tops even the federal hiring rate of 1961. In addition to this stepped-up hiring rate, President Kennedy asked for 46,000 extra (non-defense) federal employees for fiscal 1964. Senator Harry F. Byrd's Committee on Reduction of Non-Essential Federal Expenditures estimated that approximately 2.6 million Americans would be on the federal civilian payroll by June 30, 1964.

Next, these Presidential advisers are the men who have induced the New Frontier to demand, in effect, "all authority for the President." During the first four and one-half months of 1962, between January 10 and June 1, President Kennedy demanded of Congress 27 new Executive powers and 68 new federal spending authorizations. And during the first six months of the 88th Congress (1963) his requests for new federal funds and additional Presidential powers far exceeded his requests for all of 1962: 207 requests for new federal funds and 70 requests for new Presidential powers. By May 1963, Kennedy had sent 23 major messages to Congress, on subjects ranging from District of Columbia Home Rule to

Mental Illness and Retardation; and from Foreign Aid to Public Defenders.

Then, these policy makers are the men responsible for the avalanche of legislative requests included in the million-plus words President Kennedy addressed to the 87th Congress. FDR's first 100 days are regarded as the legislative blizzard of all time, but compared with the New Frontier they were only a melting March squall. For while President Roosevelt made 62 requests in that period, President Kennedy made 231 requests for legislation in his first 100 days; and by mid-July of 1962 had mounted 458 legislative requests, according to the Library of Congress and its impartial legislative reference service.

This flood of proposals would literally remake America, establish centralized federal authority over us and our economic system, and end our private enterprise system, which has made us rich, great and the envy of the world.

Again, these collegiate thinkers seem to regard themselves as superior intellects, great thinkers, and prime movers as they act without our permission to run the lives and destinies of the great mass of us who are less well informed, to judge by their statements and actions. They want to take us to new places, even if we think we do not want to go or are determined not to yield. They fail to realize that their juggling of human lives and our national survival is not a game of tin soldiers or Monopoly, but is actual meddling with the lives of each and every American citizen and the very existence of our nation. The game is real.

All of them except Pierre Salinger came from academic backgrounds, although they represent neither the broad stream of American academic thought nor the wide spectrum of American life. Many of them are, or have been, members of ADA, the Americans for Democratic Action. This is the left-wing organization which has put hundreds of its members into the Kennedy and Johnson Administrations, including 42 top spots and two Cabinet positions, as well as into countless other lower jobs. They like to call themselves "Liberals."

Take, for example, Walt Rostow, Chairman of the State Department's Policy Planning Council. Rostow was brought before the Senate Foreign Relations Committee to explain his part in sponsoring and drafting a sweeping master plan for historic changes in our government's attitude toward communism.

This master plan is based on the idea that the Soviets are "mellowing" and that they are abandoning their goal of world conquest. From this basic idea flow our government's current and future disarmament moves, trusting that the "mellowing" Soviets will do the same. This plan—said by those in the press who have read it to cover more than 300 typewritten pages—will also recognize, in effect, as legitimate regimes the Soviet satellites, including East Germany, a move which will put final hopelessness into the hearts of millions behind the Iron Curtain; above all, no encouragement or support must be given to uprisings in Eastern Europe.

The Rostow plan also envisions an eventual "mellowing" of the Chinese Reds and advocates the same conciliatory tactics toward those mass murderers.

Yet when Rostow appeared before the Senate Foreign Relations Committee he refused to discuss a word of this plan, which is of life-or-death importance to every man, woman and child in America and the free world, and to millions behind the Iron and Bamboo Curtains. On the advice of Under Secretary of State George Ball, who accompanied him to the hearing, Rostow invoked "Executive Privilege" and refused to testify about *his* foreign policy.

Then Rostow, together with Ball, hustled to a social event in Washington, where, according to Washington social writers, both men declared that Rostow had cleared himself "brilliantly" before the Senators. The Washington *Post* praised him for having publicly purged himself and decried his nasty detractors. But the fact is that all Rostow had said was "No" when the elected representatives of the American people asked him to outline a master plan which involves the security and survival of every American citizen.

This arrogance is typical of this group of global reformers who apparently regard themselves as especially endowed with knowledge and foresight.

Take Assistant Secretary of State Harlan Cleveland. In digging into the case of Otto Otepka, fired from his job as ranking deputy director of State's Office of Security, the Senate Internal Security Subcommittee rang up the curtain on a backstage maneuver stagemanaged by Cleveland. The Senate investigators uncovered a plan afoot in the State Department to reinstate a number of known security risks, even perhaps Alger Hiss, who was convicted of perjury for lying about his dealings with Soviet agents. Cleveland was masterminding the plan and had already appointed a number of these questionable protégés to State Department personnel advisory posts.

Presidential Assistant Arthur Schlesinger, Jr., is blamed for the fact that the Democratic Administrations' "Alliance for Progress" program means "progress to the Left and opposes progress in any other form," according to Los Angeles *Times* political analyst, Robert T. Hartmann.

Representative Melvin R. Laird, Republican of Wisconsin, analyzing Secretary of State Rusk's role as engineer of the coalition government in Laos, wrote: "The only possible conclusion is that Laos is being surrendered to the Communists as Poland was at Yalta 17 years ago."

Meanwhile, George Ball—whose law firm is registered as a lobbyist for the European Common Market—was busy helping push through Congress a bill to revise and lower U.S. tariffs, which already are the lowest of any major nation in the world except Japan, which has import quotas, and far lower than those of "free-trading" England.

Congress has reacted violently against much of the program of the theoretical thinkers. Congress feels that much of the social and economic program submitted by the Administration is wrong and, moreover, is unpopular with the public. In the Senate, for example, the 16 chairmen of standing committees (all Democrats) voted against the Administration 595 times cumulatively during 1962. This includes liberals as well as Southerners.

Thirteen of the 16 Democratic chairmen voted against the Urban Affairs proposal, which would have placed our cities under Washington bureaucrats. Not a single ·chairman voted for a huge $2 billion stand-by Public Works program or even for the financing of a Congress-reduced works program which would have used the reserves of such organizations as the Federal Deposit Insurance Corporation which protects the bank deposits of millions of Americans. Eleven chairmen, including Majority Leader Mansfield, voted against this measure. Ten of the chairmen voted against Medicare, a poorly drafted and ill-conceived measure which allegedly would have helped the aged, but which actually would have excluded a very large percentage of our neediest elder citizens, while increasing Social Security funds which could be diverted to use for current expenditures.

Yet President Kennedy took the stump in 1962, blaming the Republicans (outnumbered 3-2 in the House and 2-1 in the Senate) for his failures. He went on advocating the extremist policies of his coterie of theorists, and constantly threatened to "take his case to the people" to overcome Congressional resistance. This move was heartily seconded by the New York *Times* correspondent James Reston, a long-time friend and sometimes a house guest of the Schlesingers.

Since these self-appointed world changers form a sort of medicine-ball circle, it is difficult to determine who was most influential with President Kennedy and who most influences President Johnson.

Franklin D. Roosevelt listened to his Brain Trust and then, one by one, dumped them in fairly rapid order, winding up with former social worker Harry Hopkins as his confidant. Wilson had his Colonel House and Eisenhower his Sherman

Adams. But the group President Johnson has inherited is unique. It is fair to say that America has not seen their like before.

It is probably fair to say also, that the one thread uniting this strange group is all-out internationalism, and many of them have publicly asserted that one of their goals is one-world government under the United Nations. Except for a lawyer or two, they have had little practical experience in private enterprise and in the hard realities of making a living in the business world; and in most cases they rely on an "ivory tower" rather than on a practical view of the world around them. Most depend upon materialistic, pragmatic concepts and an economic interpretation of history, and the President voices and gives reality to their ideas.

Let us look at these men and at the dangers facing Americans at their hands.

CHAPTER TWO

DEAN RUSK —
THE GRAY MAN WITH FLAMING IDEAS

"Though fann'd by Conquest's crimson wing,
They mock the air with idle State."
... Thomas Gray—THE BARD

THE MAIN CONDUCT of what foreign policy the United States still has is in the hands of our Secretary of State, Dean Rusk. And what major foreign policy events have Americans witnessed during the Kennedy and Johnson Administrations, with Dean Rusk as Secretary of State? They can be summarized as follows:

The quickening of the tempo of the Soviet drive for world domination to our very shores with the transformation of Cuba into a Soviet nuclear bastion.

Our nation standing by and allowing the Soviets to build and maintain their illegal Berlin Wall.

Planning by our Administration of U. S. "partnership" with the "mellowing" Soviet Union.

Adoption as our official policy the liquidation of our military weapons and turning over, within about ten years, all U. S. armed forces to a UN super-state.

Scrapping the vital U. S. military bases which had ringed the perimeter of the Soviet Union.

Destroying our nuclear "first-strike" capability against the Soviets.

Allowing all Latin America to reach the brink of communism.

Allowing all Southeast Asia to collapse into the arms of communism.

Giving U. S. military and financial aid to the UN "peace" army in Katanga to obliterate in savage and bloody fashion the only anti-Communist government in the heart of Africa.

17

Increasing U. S. aid to pro-Communist emerging African nations, with Ghana and Mali now gone into the Soviet orbit.

Forcing a "coalition" government dominated by Communists on the key Asian nation of Laos.

Sending American soldiers to die in Viet Nam jungle warfare against Communists, while the U. S. helped to smash Viet Nam's anti-Communist government.

Selling out West New Guinea—with a big assist from Robert Kennedy—to the Communist dictator Sukarno, so fanatic an implementer of communism that he was awarded the 1960 Lenin Peace Prize. (Shortly afterwards, President Kennnedy invited Sukarno to the U. S., gave him a 21-gun salute on the White House lawn, and hailed him as "a leader in the world.")

Continuing financial aid to Communist Poland and Communist Yugoslavia, whose own "foreign aid" programs are dispensing millions to Castro's Cuba, and to the Communists in Viet Nam to kill American soldiers.

Continuing military and financial aid to India whose Nehru and Khrishna Menon are outspoken foes of the U. S., a nation which almost always votes against us in the UN, a nation to whom we rushed military aid immediately after India's aggression against Goa, the territory of our anti-Communist NATO ally, Portugal.

Build-up of rapprochement with the Soviet satellites of Hungary, Rumania and Czechoslovakia.

While the fault for some of this may well lie with the Department of Defense, it should be remembered that the main conduct of our foreign policy rests in the hands of Secretary of State Dean Rusk.

Dean Rusk seemed to appear suddenly, out of nowhere, to head the State Department, much as an orchid, without roots, might blossom from the air. But Rusk appeared as a gray, ill-defined figure, and so he has remained.

Dean Rusk has superficially impeccable credentials for his high position. An aura of dignity surrounds him. He maintains an unruffled calm. If he produces no sharp imprint such as John Foster Dulles did, he seems an expert diplomatic technician.

While it is true that Dean Rusk was not nationally known like Adlai Stevenson—twice a Presidential candidate —Averell Harriman, or others who might have been appointed Secretary of State, it was known that Rusk had been named as a compromise when the late Philip Graham publisher of the Washington *Post,* insisted he would cause trouble for the Administration if Kennedy did not appoint as Secretary of State Graham's friend Adlai Stevenson, whom Graham deeply admired. President-elect Kennedy said he would not have Stevenson, who had refused to accept Kennedy as a running mate at Chicago in 1956, as head of the State Department. Rusk was chosen as an acceptable alternative. Stevenson was given, as an assuagement, the top U. S. diplomatic post at the United Nations.

For a man chosen as Secretary of State, Rusk had a plausible background, even though not a publicly known one. He held a degree from Oxford; he had served in various capacities in the State Department, including those of Assistant Secretary and Deputy Under Secretary of State; he had risen to colonel's rank in World War II as a civilian called to military service; and he had served for eight years as head of the Rockefeller Foundation, one of the biggest chunks of private capital extant. These appeared to be passable formal credentials.

It is part of Rusk's modus operandi that few realize that this quiet man runs the State Department with an iron hand and that he is an ideal head man for the whole Administration's foreign affairs show, because—as will be seen—he is in thorough accord with the thinking of the White House clique. The gray cloak hides a man of flaming thoughts.

In truth, Dean Rusk has had a major, and at points perhaps a decisive, influence on U. S. foreign policy since the early 1940's. His air of decorum, in fact, cloaks a startling record:

He was on General "Vinegar Joe" Stilwell's staff in

China when Stilwell sought to arm one million Chinese Communists.

He was State Department aide—as Alger Hiss' successor—to Secretary of State George Marshall, when Marshall's strategy helped to lose China to communism.

He played perhaps the decisive role in the decision to send American troops into the Korean War.

He played the key role in the Korean War decision not to bomb beyond the Yalu River, thus assuring a privileged sanctuary in Communist Manchuria for Soviet air power and for the massing of Red Chinese troops for the "second invasion" of Korea.

He presided over the tragic "Korean stalemate" as Assistant Secretary of State for Far Eastern Affairs.

Having played a considerable role in the loss of China to communism, Rusk has presided over the falling apart of NATO and what has happened in Latin America and in Africa.

Dean Rusk's record is strange, contradictory and, at points, frightening.

Among Dean Rusk's characteristic acts as Secretary of State in the Kennedy Administration has been his engineering of the "coalition government" of Communists and anti-Communists in Laos. He has publicly opposed cutting off U. S. foreign aid to nations which have expropriated American industries abroad.

Rusk has personally supported such questionable diplomatic appointments as that of Foy Kohler as U. S. Ambassador to the Soviet Union. Kohler was once arrested, while intoxicated, carrying secret State Department documents improperly in his car.

Dean Rusk has lobbied, together with his Truman-era friend, John McCloy, for the Inner Circle plan to turn over the United States armed forces to the UN, and to make the UN a super-state.

Parenthetically, John McCloy, whom Kennedy appointed as coordinator of all U. S. disarmament activities, was a protégé of Felix Frankfurter, Assistant Secretary of War during the Roosevelt Administration and U. S. High Commissioner in Germany during Truman's Administration. Mc-Cloy is another member of the LBJ softball team who preach that the Soviet Union is "mellowing" (which sets the stage, of course, for disarmament). For 15 years—from 1925 to 1940—McCloy was a member of the law firm of Cravath, de Gersdorff, Swain and Wood, which helped to engineer U. S. diplomatic recognition of Soviet Russia in 1933.

In 1940, when McCloy was Assistant Secretary of War, he approved an order permitting Communists to be officers in the U. S. Army—a move which, among other delights, opened the gates for infiltration of Communists into the Pentagon, as Major Hamilton Long has so brilliantly summarized in his 1950 pamphlet, *America's Tragedy—Today*. McCloy also vigorously supported J. Robert Oppenheimer after Oppenheimer was denied security clearance.

Other strange doings of Dean Rusk as Secretary of State came to light in a Senate Internal Security Subcommittee report issued in the autumn of 1963, which revealed that up to April 30, 1962—more than one year earlier—Dean Rusk had personally waived security checks for 152 new key State Department officers, most of them over the strenuous objections or flat rejections of State's security office, which regarded them as security risks. Many others were personally given waivers of security checks by Rusk and were actually working in the State Department without the security office's even knowing that they had been hired. One-fourth of all Rusk's waivers were found to be back-dated.

In some cases, the report indicated, the security office regarded these people as being so dangerous that it had recommended they be given a full FBI investigation. Some were such flagrant and obvious risks that the security office had recommended they be rejected outright even without an FBI investigation. Then some of these very men were put on the panel which "reorganized" the security office itself and smashed any effective security against security risks in the Kennedy and Johnson State Department!

It should be emphasized that the figure of 152 new key State Department employees for whom Dean Rusk had personally waived security checks was only until April 30, 1962, when Rusk had been Secretary for only 15 months. In contrast, personal waivers of security checks by the Secretary of State had been exercised only five times during the entire eight years of the Eisenhower Administration.

All of the foregoing personal decisions of Dean Rusk as Secretary of State are merely a handful to illustrate many.

Dean Rusk's acts—and in many cases his failure to act—point to the hard fact that behind this man of sweet reasonableness and diplomatic know-how, this man who learned to dine and deal with our leading financiers in New York City as president of the Rockefeller Foundation, there stands a quite different person.

The question is whether Dean Rusk, in his scramble from nowhere to the top, has been largely an opportunist, or a man with deep convictions which are considerably different from those of the great mass of Americans.

One thing is certain: Rusk's rise began in the academic mill, and his approach to foreign affairs is still academic. Like others of the Inner Circle, he has no "feel" for situations, and instead bases his actions on theory.

David Dean Rusk (he has dropped the David) was born February 9, 1909, on a small cotton farm in Cherokee County, Georgia. His official biography notes that he weighed 11 pounds at birth and was delivered by a veterinarian. His father had been trained for the Presbyterian ministry and his mother had been a schoolteacher. After graduating from Boys' High School in Atlanta in 1925, he worked for two years as a law clerk. He then entered Davidson College in North Carolina, and graduated in 1931 to become a Rhodes scholar.

From then until 1934, Rusk attended St. John's College at Oxford, where he studied international law and during vacations took courses at the University of Berlin.

On returning to the United States, he was invited to teach political science at Mills College in Oakland, California, a left-wing college for women regarded at that time as having "advanced social thinkers" on its faculty, and the names of some of Rusk's co-professors, though not publicly known, support this for the informed.

Rusk taught at Mills from 1934 to 1940, and in 1937 he was "delighted when one of my students, Miss Virginia Foisie of Seattle, consented to become my wife." Rusk studied law at the University of California in his spare time and acquired a commission as a captain in the Army reserve, through his law school ROTC training.

When World War II began, Rusk's big breaks began to come. As a reservist, he was called to active military duty with the rank of captain one year before Pearl Harbor. After that, advancements and opportunities came thick and fast.

According to a story in the December 26, 1960, issue of *Time,* Rusk was saved from combat "by a War Department punch-card machine which snatched him away to noncombatant duty."

The "punch-card machine" (some observers might choose to term it a quite human instrument) seems to have been operating at a high level. Rusk was not only snatched away from combat duty, but with only three years of study at Oxford under his belt he was made chief of the British Empire section of the War Department's military Intelligence.

Rusk was next assigned to the War Department's Far East section of military Intelligence, where, he explains, "I concentrated on South and Southeast Asia and the Southwest Pacific."

In 1943, after a staff course at Fort Leavenworth, Rusk was assigned as a colonel to the staff of that protégé of General George Marshall, the arrogant General "Vinegar Joe" Stilwell, then commander of the entire China-Burma-India Theatre of Operations, and who to this day is idolized by American Communists and in American Communist publications as having played an heroic role for the Communist conspiracy in what Earl Browder, former head of the U. S. Communist Party, has described as the undeviating Communist line of U. S. military and diplomatic policy in China from 1942 to 1946. Also on Stilwell's staff at this time were advisers from the State Department such as John Paton Davies, John Stewart Service, Raymond P. Ludden and John K. Emmerson, all of whom nearly burned out a bearing in successful efforts to sell the Chinese into Communist slavery, which in turn led the United States into the bloody Korean War in 1950. (Emmerson is now the Administration's number two man in the U. S. Embassy in Japan.)

Dean Rusk did well, indeed, on Stilwell's staff. He rose to nothing less than Deputy Chief of Staff of the entire China-Burma-India Theater of Operations—a most extraordinary advance for a non-career officer.

"My duties," Rusk reports, "took me into all parts of India, and on frequent trips to Burma, Ceylon and China . . ."

In China, General Stilwell was then commanding American operations supposedly being carried out in conjunction with the Chinese operations of Generalissimo Chiang Kai-shek. It was while Rusk was on Stilwell's staff that Stilwell pushed his plan to arm one million Chinese Communists, a plan which brought Stilwell into conflict with Chiang Kai-shek.

Rusk was not well known to the press contingent covering Stilwell, and he was not mentioned in the lengthy press dispatches concerning the conflict between Stilwell and Chiang Kai-shek, which were written by usually observant reporters such as Brooks Atkinson of the New York *Times*. Nevertheless, as Deputy Chief of Staff of the entire CBI theater, Rusk held a position of considerable importance. Here, for the first time, he is a gray, shadowy figure, unnoticed in his debut upon the world stage.

In 1945, Rusk returned to Washington and became Assistant Chief in the Operations Division of the War Department General Staff. He was discharged from service in February 1946, with the rank of colonel, and joined the State Department as Assistant Chief of the Division of Internal Security Affairs.

A few months later, in May 1946, Rusk explains that

"Secretary of War [Robert] Patterson asked me to return to the Pentagon as his special assistant, where my duties involved matters of joint foreign policy of military significance and close working arrangements with the Department of State."

In January 1947, General George C. Marshall returned from his disastrous one-year mission in China as President Truman's personal representative there, and immediately became Secretary of State. About six weeks later, in March 1947, Marshall personally asked Dean Rusk, with an "aye" from Dean Acheson, to return to the State Department, giving as his reason that when Army Chief of Staff in China, Marshall had been deeply impressed with Rusk's intellectual attainments. Rusk accepted Marshall's invitation and became Alger Hiss' successor as Director of the State Department's Office of Special Political Affairs.

Marshall was fresh from his China stay, where he had withheld arms and supplies from the anti-Communist army of Chiang Kai-shek in order to force on Chiang a "coalition" government with the Communists. When Marshall did so, he had joyously uttered his classic statement: "As Chief of Staff I armed 39 anti-Communist divisions [of Chiang's]; now with a stroke of the pen I disarm them." Marshall had also forced a series of cease-fire truces between Chiang's army and the Communists—at times when, in fact, the anti-Communists were winning against the Communists.

When he was Secretary of State, Marshall continued to withhold arms, food supplies from Chiang's forces during 1947 and 1948, while Chiang's forces continued to fight valiantly until the Chinese economy disintegrated completely. Marshall did this, even though the 80th Congress had appropriated $125 million in arms and aid for Chiang. Then Marshall was able to force a "coalition" government on Chiang. These machinations sealed the doom of China.

Some Washington insiders believe that Dean Rusk was George Marshall's number one collaborator at State then, and that, more than any other man, Rusk was architect of Marshall's strategy of forcing on China a "coalition" government including Communists in key positions.

Is it mere coincidence that today, a decade and a half after the Chinese tragedy, Dean Rusk, as Secretary of State, has forced on the key Asian country of Laos a "coalition" government which is dominated by Communists in key positions?

When Alger Hiss resigned from the State Department in 1947 to become head of the Carnegie Endowment for International Peace, Secretary of State Marshall asked Rusk to be Hiss' successor, and Dean Rusk succeeeded Hiss both as head of the Office of Special Political Affairs (which included UN Affairs) and as head of the postwar planning division of the State Department. (Hiss, it will be recalled, was publicly exposed in 1948 as a Soviet espionage agent and was convicted for perjury in lying about his Soviet espionage acts. Hiss had been Secretary-General of the San Francisco Conference in 1945 at which the United Nations was formed and the UN Charter drafted.)

In 1952, observers of Senate Internal Security Subcommittee hearings saw Rusk's continuation of at least one of Hiss' policies—allowing identified American Communists to be hired by the UN and to work unhindered there. It should be pointed out that Americans employed by the UN are employed directly by this organization, and therefore are not subject to the usual Civil Service security checks. In fact, the Senate committee learned that the State Department, which heads our UN affairs, never gave to the UN dossiers on the Communist membership and activities of Americans in the UN, even though the FBI had given the State Department a mountain of continuing documentation on American Communists working in the UN. This was during Dean Rusk's tenure.

From October to December 1952, the Senate subcommittee held hearings to investigate Americans employed in the UN Secretariat. On December 17, 1952, the subcommittee heard the following testimony from Carlisle H. Humelsine, then Deputy Under Secretary of State in charge of security:

Question: Is it the gist of your testimony that while Mr.

Dean Rusk was in charge of United Nations Affairs, not only was no position of the [State] Department in opposition to the United Nations but actually there was no such official position so far as you know?

Mr. Humelsine: So far as I know.

However, as the committee counsel continued his questioning, Humelsine revealed that allowing American Communists to be hired and to work in the UN was not a *lack* of policy; it was a *positive* but unofficial policy. Questioned further, Humelsine added some details about how and when this policy was formed:

Mr. Humelsine: I believe that you would say it is the result of a top-level decision made at or about the time the United Nations secretariat was organized.

In response to more questioning, Humelsine said he believed this policy was formulated at a meeting in which Alger Hiss had participated.

The Senate subcommittee report issued at the conclusion of the UN hearings concluded that *specifically during the time Alger Hiss and Dean Rusk headed UN Affairs* ". . . there was no safeguard whatsoever, from the standpoint of the United States against employment by the United Nations of United States citizens who were disloyal to their country, or who were actively engaged in espionage." Moreover, said the subcommittee report, during the period "a number of Americans of doubtful loyalty have secured lodgment and tenure with the United Nations organization."

During these UN hearings, the Senate Internal Security Subcommittee uncovered proof that the UN Secretariat, which is comparable to the top management of a large corporation, was, in the words of the subcommittee's chief counsel, "heavily infiltrated," a situation which was "to say the least, shocking."

Twenty-six high-ranking American employees of the UN Secretariat were subpoenaed by the subcommittee. Many of them were confronted with sworn testimony of witnesses who had known them within the ranks of the Communist Party, and all of them were confronted with evidence of their Communist

Party membership or years-long service for the Communist cause. Some of them had been identified as Soviet espionage agents. But every one of these 26 American employees of the UN Secretariat brazenly invoked the Fifth Amendment, time and time again, on the grounds that their answers might tend to incriminate them.

The evidence against these UN employees presented by the subcommittee, it should be noted, was not obtained by its investigators. It was readily available, and had already been given to the State Department by the FBI. In the short time allotted to it the subcommittee could not launch a full-scale examination, only scratching the surface of infiltration into the UN. Investigations were conducted only into the UN Secretariat—except in the case of Frank Coe—and only of high-ranking Americans working there. It cannot be too strongly emphasized that all of these Americans were employed in the Secretariat, the UN control tower, at high salaries and in positions where they hired and directed the activities of scores of others. Here is just a glimpse of what the Senate subcommittee turned up:

FRANK BANCROFT ... Editor in the Documents Control Division. Committee had explicit and detailed information that he was a member of the Communist Party, and asked if he had held Communist Party card #93158.

DAVID WEINTRAUB ... Director of Economic Stability and Development Division. Identified during hearings as a Communist by Whittaker Chambers. Committee also had explicit information that Weintraub's four assistants were Communists: Irving Kaplan, Sidney Glassman, Marjorie Zap and Herbert Schimmel.

JACK HARRIS ... Senior Research Officer of Trusteeship Division. Hired by UN at special request of Ralph Bunche. Committee had explicit information that he was a Communist and, in addition, an organizer for the Communist Party.

ALFRED VAN TASSELL ... Chief of the Economic Section of the Technical Assistance Administration. Committee had explicit information that he was a member of the Communist Party.

FRANK V. COE . . . Salary of $20,000 per year with UN special agency, International Monetary Fund. Identified during hearings as a Communist by Whittaker Chambers and Elizabeth Bentley. The FBI had compiled 13 different and extensive reports on Frank Coe's Communist activities and membership.

JULIA BAZER . . . Editor in Bureau of Documents. Committee had explicit and detailed information that she was a member of the Communist Party, trained in Moscow from 1934 to 1937, was writer for *Moscow Weekly News* and managing editor of *American Review of the Soviet Union.*

DAVID ZABLODOWSKY . . . Head of UN Secretariat Publications Division. Identified during hearings by Whittaker Chambers as member of the Communist Party and, in addition, a member of the Soviet underground.

This is a mere sampling of the Americans who were working in high positions at the UN Secretariat while Dean Rusk was Assistant Secretary of State in charge of UN affairs. Today, Mr. Rusk is Secretary of State.

As the subcommittee counsel who interrogated these people, Robert Morris had this to say in 1963: "Alger Hiss put his protégés into many of the key posts in the UN—and many of them are there today."

In 1949, according to the *Time* story about Rusk quoted previously, "Secretary Acheson reached over the heads of seasoned career men and tapped Rusk to take over the newly created post of Deputy Under Secretary of State in charge of policy coordination." This was the number three job in the entire State Department.

This choice of Rusk by Dean Acheson is part of the "Tinker-to-Evers-to-Chance" interlocking cooperation among the leaders of government and of the powerful Foundations (which are the lifeblood of so many left-wing causes) which keep the same clique on top, year after year, Administration after Administration. To clarify the team play a bit, here is a glance at it from Freda Utley's *The China Story* (written in 1951), which involves both the Rusk appointment by Dean Acheson and Acheson's previous recommendation of Rusk to succeed Alger Hiss:

It is important here to call attention to the manner in which the members of the "progressive" group in Washington and New York manage to replace each other in important positions inside and outside the Administration. For instance, after Alger Hiss resigned from the State Department to become Director of the Carnegie Endowment for International Peace, Dean Acheson recommended Dean Rusk to take Hiss' place as Director of the Office of Special Political Affairs.

Rusk had previously served under Joseph E. Johnson, who as Chief of the Division of International Security Affairs, under the Special Political Affairs Office, had been chief assistant to Alger Hiss. In 1949, Rusk (chosen by Acheson) stepped higher up the ladder of preferment, becoming First Assistant, and then Deputy Under Secretary of State.

Today, Johnson, who resigned from the State Department in 1947 to return to teaching at Williams College, holds the position with the Carnegie Endowment held by Alger Hiss when he was indicted for perjury.

In March 1950, Rusk became Assistant Secretary of State for Far Eastern Affairs. It was in this position that he played the key role in convincing President Truman that he should send American troops into the Korean War, to fight under the UN flag.

Rusk importuned, said the *Time* story, that this would give "the U.S. a *precious opportunity,* unblocked by a Russian veto, to intervene *through the United Nations.*" Rusk "bent all his gifts of argument" . . . and "his viewpoint prevailed, and the following day, the UN, under U. S. leadership [sic] embarked on a history-making venture in collective security."

Thus, for the first time, American troops fought under the UN flag, in the first and only war the United States has ever lost (because our American soldiers in the field—thanks in great part to Dean Rusk sitting in the State Department— were not allowed to win it), a "UN police action" in which the United States provided about 90 per cent of the troops and suffered about 95 per cent of the casualties.

Americans whose sons and husbands were killed in Korea will not be comforted by the knowledge that Chiang Kai-shek had offered 60,000 combat-ready Nationalist Chinese troops to fight in the Korean War. This was revealed to the nation on April 5, 1951, when Representative Joseph W. Martin read to Congress a letter from General MacArthur dated March 20, heartily assenting to Chiang's offer, and adding his now-historic slogan, "There is no substitute for victory." The Joint Chiefs of Staff, it was learned at the Senate's "MacArthur Hearings" after the general's recall, had also vigorously recommended that Chiang's troops be utilized in Korea. But Chiang's troops were refused—the Senate committee learned—because Dean Rusk had personally ruled against the offer.

It is Dean Rusk—although the American people are not aware of it—who was responsible for the tragic decision to make a privileged sanctuary of Communist Manchuria, out of which almost one million Red Chinese streamed throughout the Korean War in onslaughts on American troops.

The fateful decision was made on November 6, 1950, when word reached the State Department that General Douglas MacArthur was planning to dispatch bombing missions to blow up the Yalu River bridges and the Red Chinese staging areas beyond the bridges in Manchuria. These bridges were the Communists' vital links connecting Korea with Manchuria, and pouring over them then were Red Chinese troops and munitions to reinforce the Korean Communists whom MacArthur had beaten to their knees and driven up to the Manchurian border. Behind the bridges, 200,000 more Red Chinese were massing for an onslaught on the Americans which was to come 20 days later.

But back in the State Department, when word of MacArthur's plan arrived, Dean Rusk was busily persuading President Truman that MacArthur should not touch Red Manchuria or the Yalu bridges—and Rusk's persuasiveness prevailed.

Former President Harry Truman himself places the responsibility for the decision squarely on the shoulders of Dean Rusk. Here is Truman's own account of Rusk's role on that fateful day, as Truman has narrated it in Volume II of his memoirs, *Years of Trial and Hope:*

Assistant Secretary of State Dean Rusk pointed out that
we had a commitment with the British not to take action which
might involve attacks on the Manchurian side of the river without consultation with them.

Rusk pulled out every stop to persuade Truman to make
the decision:

Mr. Rusk also mentioned the danger of involving the Soviets,
especially in the light of the mutual-assistance treaty between
Moscow and Peiping. [Although any American who could read
knew the Soviets had already armed the Red Chinese to the
teeth with Russian guns, Russian tanks, Russian MIG fighters
—everything except men, which the Chinese needed like the
plague. *Author's Note.*]

It was Dean Rusk's advice which prevailed—lock, stock
and barrel. Truman says the Joint Chiefs of Staff were told to
relay to General MacArthur "what *Dean Rusk* had set forth."

This was the message sent to MacArthur, relaying "what
Dean Rusk had set forth":

[MacArthur] was informed that there was *a commitment
not to take action affecting Manchuria without consultation with
the British,* and that until further orders all bombing of targets
within five miles of the Manchurian border should be postponed.

MacArthur's reply from the battlefield was blunt. And
his words are made more blunt in contrast with Dean Rusk's
powder-puff, wrist-slapping substitute for MacArthur's bombers
against the advancing hordes of Red Chinese. Rusk urged instead, says Truman, that "we would try to get a [UN] resolution calling on the Communist Chinese to stop their activities
in Korea." When this resolution did come—three months
later—it did about as much to stop Red Chinese slaughter as
did the UN resolution of 1956 urging the Soviets to stop their
brutality against the valiant Hungarians in the streets of
Budapest.

Truman says Rusk added that waiting for the UN resolution "was necessary in order to maintain UN support for any
further action to be taken." Please note again that the United
States supplied about 90 per cent of the troops and suffered
about 95 per cent of the battlefield casualties in this "UN"

Korean War, for which Mr. Rusk contended that continued "UN support" was necessary.

Here are excerpts of MacArthur's stirring reply, which he sent via the Joint Chiefs of Staff:

> Men and materiel in large force are pouring across all bridges over the Yalu from Manchuria. This movement not only jeopardizes but threatens the ultimate destruction of the forces under my command. . . . The only way to stop this reinforcement of the enemy is the destruction of these bridges and the subjection of all installations in the north area supporting the enemy advance to the maximum of our air destruction. Every hour that this is postponed will be paid for dearly in American and other United Nations blood. . . . Under the gravest protest that I can make, I am suspending this strike and carrying out your instructions. . . . I cannot overemphasize the disastrous effect, both physical and psychological, that will result from the restrictions which you are imposing. . . . I believe your instructions may well result in a calamity of major proportions . . .

But Dean Rusk's persuasions in the State Department prevailed over the pleadings of General Douglas MacArthur from the battlefield. The "Korean stalemate" was launched. And on November 26, 1950, 200,000 Red Chinese troops—later followed by more than half a million more—streamed over the Yalu River from the privileged sanctuary of Manchuria, driving our 105,000 troops southward 70 miles into South Korea in a savage and bloody assault.

And over the "Korean stalemate," paid for dearly with American lives and blood, presided Dean Rusk as Secretary of State for this area, a man who bears heavy and direct responsibility for it all.

On March 20—the same day he had written "There is no substitute for victory"—MacArthur was notified that Truman was preparing to ask a truce of the Red Chinese and the Korean Communists, as "conditions of settlement in Korea." These conditions—based on the assumption that Red China had overwhelming military might—were shaped, for the most part, by the State Department, with Dean Rusk playing a major role as Assistant Secretary of State for the area.

Four days later, on March 24, MacArthur issued a bomb-shell of a statement, exploding the State Department-nurtured thesis that Red China was a mighty nation. Far from wanting to ask a truce of the Communists, MacArthur's "conditions of settlement" for Korea would be an ultimatum to the Reds to vacate South Korea, or else.

General MacArthur's statement disclosed that the great significance of our victories in Korea was the "clear revelation" that Red China, "of such exaggerated and vaunted military power, lacks the industrial capacity to provide adequately many critical items necessary to the conduct of modern war . . . to maintain and operate even moderate air and naval power . . . Red China cannot provide the essentials for successful ground operations, such as tanks, heavy artillery . . ." MacArthur re-vealed that "control of the seas and the air, which in turn means control over supplies, communications and transportation" was in our hands.

"Even under the inhibitions which now restrict the ac-tivity" of his troops and the "corresponding military advantages which accrue to Red China, it has shown *its complete inability to accomplish by force of arms the conquest of Korea.*"

The mask was off. Red China had been proven a weak and impotent opponent on the battlefield, even against military forces whose hands were tied.

MacArthur's ultimatum was a warning to the Red Chinese that "a decision of the United Nations to depart from its tol-erant effort to contain the war to the area of Korea" merely by "an expansion of our military operations to its coastal areas and interior bases, *would doom Red China to the risk of im-minent military collapse.*"

The possibility that the Communist regime in China was doomed if MacArthur was allowed to carry out his threat was, of course, horrifying to the busy little men who had worked for so many years to deliver China to the Reds.

MacArthur's "victory" letter was read to Congress April 5; on April 11 MacArthur was relieved of his command (he learned about it from his wife, who had heard it announced over the radio); and on July 11 we started the ignominious truce negotiations with the Communists, which the North Korean Communists and Chinese Reds immediately hailed on their radio broadcasts as "a glorious victory," and for which Russian Premier Georgi Malenkov dispatched cablegrams to the Communist leaders in North Korea and China calling the Korean armistice negotiations "a great victory for the Communist cause . . . in the Far East and throughout the world."

The U. S. delegation to the Panmunjon truce negotiations was headed by Arthur Dean, a man who has always urged that the U. S. admit Red China "to the family of nations," even though Mao Tse-tung has boasted of killing three million Chinese in order to fasten the Communist regime on China. An experts' report in *Time* magazine of March 3, 1956 revealed that the Red Chinese regime had already murdered *twenty million Chinese.* And that *twenty-three million* more Chinese were in slave labor camps. The Panmunjon negotiations not only assured continuance of the Communist regime over the Chinese and North Korean people; it left the Communists free to subvert and conquer the remainder of Asia, as they are doing today. It abandoned at least 944 American prisoners known to have been captured by the Communists. These American soldiers are still in Communist hands today. Our U. S. Government has never lifted a finger to free them. In fact, when a list of these 944 captured Americans was submitted to the Reds and the Communists arrogantly refused to give any information about them, the U. S. Government, "in an effort to persuade the Communists to be more reasonable," arbitrarily reduced the number from 944 to 540, thus forever abandoning 404 Americans to Red oblivion.

A clear example of the fact that most of the Korean War troops and casualties were American is seen in the figures of "UN prisoners" still held by the Communists in 1959, as submitted by the UN delegates to the Panmunjon meetings: 452 Americans; 20 British; 9 Australians; 8 South Africans; and even smaller numbers from Turkey, Greece, Colombia, Bel-

gium and Luxembourg. The only reply from the arrogant
Communists: "All prisoners of war were returned long ago."

Moreover, the Missing Persons Act has, with the passing
of years, made a "finding of death for missing personnel," and
our soldiers captured in Korea are not only abandoned by our
government, but are systematically written off as "dead" and are
officially deleted from the lists of "missing personnel"—even
though hundreds of U. S. soldiers have been seen in Red
Chinese and North Korean slave labor camps.

General Douglas MacArthur came home from Korea a
triumphant hero in the eyes of the American people, who gave
him the most tumultuous welcome ever accorded any American
and the biggest ticker-tape parade up Broadway in the history
of our country. He was given a tremendous welcome by the
U. S. Congress which invited him to speak before a joint session
of both Houses, where MacArthur gave his "Old Soldiers Never
Die" speech to the cheering representatives of the American
people.

Immediately after General MacArthur's return, the Senate
Committees on the Armed Forces and Foreign Relations held
their "MacArthur Hearings" from May 3 to June 27, 1951,
"to conduct an inquiry into the military situation in the Far
East and the facts surrounding relief of General of the Army
Douglas MacArthur from his assignments in that area."

During the hearings, General MacArthur gave hours of
brilliant testimony to Congress and to the nation, speaking entirely without notes; and MacArthur's analysis of the Korean
stalemate, for which Dean Rusk bears heavy and direct responsibility, stands as one of the most devastating indictments of Rusk
on public record.

It can be seen on page 39 of the testimony that Senator
Leverett Saltonstall asked General MacArthur if he would
comment on an April 15, 1951, television speech of "the Assistant Secretary of State Dean Rusk." Rusk had said in this
April 15 speech, as quoted to MacArthur by Saltonstall during
the hearings:

What we are trying to do is to maintain peace and security without a general war. We are saying to the aggressors: "You will not be allowed to get away with your crime. You must stop it." At the same time, we are trying to prevent a general conflagration which would consume the very things we are now trying to defend.

Senator Saltonstall asked General MacArthur: "I would appreciate it very much, with your knowledge of the Far East, if you will give me your opinion of that statement, and if that is a practical policy."

Under the Senate committee's own title of "Military Appeasement or Victory?" General MacArthur, one of the world's outstanding military experts, with many years of military experience in the Far East, did indeed give his opinion of Dean Rusk's policy—with both barrels:

> That policy as you have read it seems to me to introduce a new concept into military operations—*the concept of appeasement*—the concept that when you use force, you can limit that force.
>
> The concept that I have is that when you go into war, you have exhausted all other potentialities of bringing the disagreements to an end. As I understand what you read, that we would apply to the military situation in Korea certain military appeasements—that is, that we would not use our air forces to their maximum extent, only to the limited area of that Korea; that we would not use our navy, except along the borderlines of Korea.
>
> To me that would mean that you would have a continued and indefinite extension of bloodshed which would be limitless —a limitless end.
>
> You would not have the potentialities of destroying the enemy's military power and bringing the conflict to a decisive close in the minimum time and with a minimum of loss.
>
> It seems to me *the worst possible concept militarily* that we would simply stay there resisting aggression, so-called, although I do not know what you mean by "resisting aggression."
>
> By the very term "resisting aggression," it seems to me that you destroy the potentialities of the aggressor to hit you continually.
>
> If that is the concept of a continued and indefinite campaign in Korea with no definite purpose of stopping until the enemy

gets tired *or you yield to his terms,* I think that *introduces into the military sphere a political control such as I have never known in my life* or have ever studied.

Senator Saltonstall: In other words, you feel that the Korean situation, having gone into an armed conflict, should be brought to an end in the quickest possible way through a military victory.

General MacArthur: I do, Senator, exactly; and I believe if we do not do that, if you hit soft, *if you practice appeasement in the use of force,* you are doomed to disaster.

I believe that *if you continue that way, you are inviting the very thing that you desire to stop.*

Senator Saltonstall: Then, assuming that your four recommendations, as made in your address to Congress, are all adopted, what do you visualize as the result?

General MacArthur: I believe that if you carry that out you stand the best chance that is possible of ending this war in the quickest time and with the least cost in blood.

In fact, I haven't seen any other proposal as to how you can expect to bring it to an end *except by agreeing to the enemy's terms.*

Senator Saltonstall: And you think if your four recommendations were carried into effect it would not necessarily spread the war into Manchuria and China, but by quick and effective action of our power it would be sufficiently limited to Korea as to be brought to an end in that general vicinity?

General MacArthur: I don't think that if you apply the measures that I advocate, which were the measures that the Joint Chiefs of Staff recommended on January 12, that you would necessarily confine the area of conflict to Korea, but I believe it will give you an opportunity *to hit the enemy where he is assembling to hit you.*

General MacArthur's recommendations for ending the Korean conflict in the shortest possible time with the least possible bloodshed were ignored by the State Department, the Defense Department and the White House. They continued to be ignored for two years, while the bloody and senseless fighting continued until July 26, 1953, when we signed the infamous armistice, even though victory was then within our grasp. As General James Van Fleet, who had been commander of the U. S. Eighth Army in Korea, declared in a speech on March 26, 1955: "Victory was denied us back in April and

May of 1953, when we had the enemy on the run. . . . We could have won here and we should have won."

The contentions of General MacArthur and of General Van Fleet were borne out in testimony by the senior military commanders before the Senate Internal Security Subcommittee's investigation into "The Korean War and Related Matters." The subcommittee's report, issued on January 21, 1955, stated in part:

> The senior military commanders [Generals George Strate-meyer, James A. Van Fleet, Edward M. Almond, Mark Clark, and Admiral Charles Turner Joy] in the Korean war theater who appeared before the . . . Subcommittee . . . believe that victory in Korea was possible and desirable . . . that the action required to achieve victory would not have resulted in World War III . . . that political considerations were allowed to overrule military necessities. [They] expressed grave concern over the conduct of this first UN "police action," and hoped that we would never again hazard our troops under similar circumstances . . . believe that *possible subversion,* wishful thinking . . . denied them victory . . . believe that failure to win in Korea has jeopardized our position in the Far East . . . supplied some clues to *possible subversion in Government* departments . . . expressed the hope that the investigation would be continued and would encompass *the source from which their orders were received* . . .

The words of General MacArthur and of the senior military commanders in Korea are blunt words. But words etched on the pages of history with the blood of the 54,000 Americans killed and 104,000 Americans wounded in Korea, and by hundreds of American soldiers still in Communist hands, forever abandoned to the oblivion of Red dungeons—not a few of all these gallant Americans suffering their fates as the direct result of Dean Rusk's policies.

A strange stand for the present stately gray man?

Not so strange, perhaps, if we examine a few of the public speeches which Dean Rusk made—speeches exhibiting his views on Red China. First, on June 14, 1950, Rusk gave a speech to the World Affairs Council Conference of the University of Pennsylvania. This was while he was Assistant Secretary

of State for all of the Far East; it was *one year after all China
had fallen to the Reds,* and after the "agrarian reformers" who
had seized China by violence had been unmasked as full-fledged
Communists; it was exactly ten days before hordes of North
Korean Communists invaded South Korea, armed, abetted and
followed by the Chinese Reds.

Rusk told his startled audience that the "revolution in
China" was comparable to "the American revolt against the
British in 1776"! He even compared Mao Tse-tung with
George Washington.

Rusk declared that the Chinese "revolution . . ." does not
aim at dictatorship."

This is more than even Mao Tse-tung has ever claimed!

Just in case the American people did not know by that
time where Dean Rusk—the Assistant Secretary of State for
Far Eastern Affairs—stood on Red China, he made it quite clear
in a speech on November 15, 1950, as reported in *The China
Story* by Freda Utley. This was nine days after Rusk had
brought on the Korean stalemate and eleven days before 200,-
000 Chinese Reds poured over the Yalu bridges to slaughter
American troops. Mr. Rusk said, writes Miss Utley, that if only
the Chinese Reds "would limit their demands," he and his
State Department Far East policy makers would be happy to
forget how many Americans they had killed. (The official
count, remember, was 54,000 Americans dead.) If the Red
Chinese would only temper their demands a bit, says Miss
Utley, Mr. Rusk et al would gladly give the Chinese Communists the assurance that the United States had no intention
whatsoever of contesting the Communist enslavement of China!

Rusk finished off his shocking speech by dismissing as
not proven the obvious fact—known to any high school student
with two days' study of the Communist conspiracy, let alone to
the State Department's "expert" on the Far East—that the
Chinese Communists are the Far East arm of the world Communist conspiracy. In what should stand as a classic declaration of "ignorance" of communism, the State Department "expert" on the Far East asserted: "We do not know" if the

Chinese Communists' "intervention" in Korea is part of a pattern of "worldwide aggressiveness. We do not know the real explanation."

Let us look at a third speech given by Dean Rusk while he was Assistant Secretary of State for Far Eastern Affairs.

The timing of this speech should be carefully noted: it was delivered on May 18, 1951. This was at the height of the MacArthur Hearings, when public indignation against the State Department's policy in Korea, as guided by Dean Rusk, was at fever pitch; the speech was delivered immediately after General MacArthur had publicly castigated Dean Rusk's Korean stalemate in brilliant and lengthy testimony; and the speech was delivered when the Congressional hearings had revealed Dean Rusk's decisive role in bringing on the Korean stalemate.

The date of this speech is significant for yet another reason. Oliver Edmund Clubb, who was Dean Rusk's right-hand man in the State Department at this time—Rusk's chosen confidant and adviser in forming our entire Far East policy, including the debacle in Korea, the man whom Rusk had put in charge of Chinese Affairs—was about to be publicly dismissed from the State Department as a security risk.

In an effort to clean the skirts of the State Department—and, not incidentally, his own skirts—Dean Rusk delivered this speech to the Chinese Institute meeting at the Waldorf-Astoria, in which at that late date he questioned the legitimacy of the Red Chinese regime.

The American "liberal" press had taken almost no notice of Rusk's two previous speeches—especially not to the June 1950 speech in which he compared the blood-soaked Red Chinese leaders to George Washington and Patrick Henry—but the press excerpted portions of Rusk's Waldorf-Astoria speech and hailed it as a great anti-Communist declaration. It seems to have served the interests of Mr. Rusk and of the State Department that the "liberal" press chose to do this.

The press reports of this speech—which is still dredged up as evidence of Dean Rusk's "hard anti-communism"—would make one believe that Rusk had reversed the praise he had heaped upon the Red Chinese leaders only 11 months previously. However, if one examines the entire speech, it is clear that it hardly differs from his pro-Chinese speech of June 1950.

The fact is that in this Waldorf-Astoria speech Rusk criticized the Red Chinese regime, *not because it was a Communist regime,* but rather *because it was "not Chinese"!*

In fact, Rusk emphasized that he had no objection whatsoever to the Chinese regime's being Communist. He objected to it because, he said, it was entangled with "Russian imperialism."

Rusk even declared in this speech that he would be willing, as Assistant Secretary of State for Far Eastern Affairs, to supply "tremendous support" to the Chinese Communists if only they would disavow Moscow! It is worth noting that this speech was delivered by Assistant Secretary Dean Rusk at the very moment that masses of Red Chinese troops were slaughtering American soldiers in Korea.

Less than two months after Rusk delivered this speech —on June 27, 1951—his right-hand man, Edmund Clubb, was suspended from the State Department as a security risk, by the *unanimous vote* of the State Department's Loyalty and Security Board. Furthermore, Clubb's suspension was upheld by Carlisle Humelsine, then Deputy Under Secretary of State for Security.

Clubb had been a China hand in the State Department since 1928, holding responsible posts in many parts of China before Rusk chose him to head the China desk of the State Department. Clubb had been in the thick of the machinations which ended with China's deliverance into Communist hands, and the public case against him included his intimate and long-standing associations with many identified Communist agents such as Michael Gold, Agnes Smedley, Lawrence Todd, Philip Jaffe, and with a host of Communist sympathizers. Many of Clubb's close associations were with identified Communists in the Institute of Pacific Relations. In his autobiography, *Witness,* Whittaker Chambers recounts an interesting visit of Edmund Clubb to the editorial office of the Communist magazine, *New Masses,* as early as 1932.

The private case against Clubb, gathered by the FBI and by the State Department security agents, has never been made public, but since State's Loyalty and Security Board took the unusual step of dismissing Clubb—by a unanimous vote—the evidence against him certainly must have been conclusive and extremely damaging.

However, when the case faded from the public memory, on February 11, 1952, then-Secretary of State Dean Acheson personally reversed Clubb's dismissal and cleared him, saying that Clubb's case had been reviewed by one Nathaniel Davis. Acheson announced that he had "absolutely cleared [Clubb] on loyalty and security." Clubb was then allowed by Acheson to retire from the State Department on a pension of almost $6,000 per year—paid for by the American taxpayers.

Rusk served as Assistant Secretary of State for Far Eastern Affairs from March 1950 until December 1951, when he resigned to become President of the Rockefeller Foundation. It was during Rusk's tenure as the State Department's architect of our Far East policy that the Senate Internal Security Subcommittee began year-long public hearings to investigate the Institute of Pacific Relations (IPR), and exposed the IPR as the major Communist transmission belt in the United States for propaganda about Communist policies in China and the entire Far East.

Dean Rusk had become a member of the IPR when he was teaching at Mills College. As we shall see, while Assistant Secretary of State for the Far East, he became the top-ranking member of the State Department on whom IPR officials called for support, and in addition procured millions of dollars for IPR from tax-free foundations—all this *after* initial charges of Communist control had been made against the IPR.

Before assessing Dean Rusk's role in the IPR, it is important to see the organization in perspective. IPR was an apparently highly respectable and tremendously influential organization of educators and businessmen interested in the Far East. But behind the window dressing of prominent names on its masthead, IPR's officers, staff members and writers—which included 46 men and women later identified in sworn testimony as Communists—produced a flood of pro-Communist propaganda for nationwide consumption in books, book reviews, newspapers, magazines, radio programs and movies.

Some of the best-known Communists or pro-Communists who were IPR staff members include:

OWEN LATTIMORE . . . of whom more later in this chapter.

ISRAEL EPSTEIN . . . Soviet espionage agent.

AGNES SMEDLEY . . . identified by General MacArthur's Chief of Intelligence, Major General Charles A. Willoughby, as a member of the notorious Soviet spy ring operated by Richard Sorge of Japan.

GUNTHER STEIN . . . Soviet espionage agent.

ANNA LOUISE STRONG . . . identified as a Soviet agent; editor of *Moscow Daily News* and *Soviet Russia Today*.

FREDERICK VANDERBILT FIELD . . . identified as a Communist who was ordered by the Politburo to head the Party's American Peace Mobilization; wrote for Party publications.

PHILIP JAFFE . . . seized by the FBI in 1945 in connection with the theft of 1,800 top-secret government documents. In addition, Jaffe was named as a Soviet agent.

MICHAEL GREENBERG . . . an alien who came to our shores from England to succeed Owen Lattimore as editor of IPR magazine, *Pacific Affairs*. Within about one year, in 1942, Greenberg was working in the White House as aide to Communist Lauchlin Currie, confidential assistant to FDR.

So influential was IPR, that its propaganda became the source of virtually all the information Americans received in the 1940's about China and Russia and their relationships in Asia. Russia and the Far East were so important in the postwar 1940's, that Americans heard constantly about them, mostly through the propaganda of the Institute of Pacific Relations.

To translate their propaganda into effective action, IPR members studiously infiltrated themselves and their propaganda literature into the U. S. State Department, where, according to testimony during the IPR hearings, many personnel depended almost entirely upon IPR studies and publications on the Far East; and it can now be said with assurance that the policies of our State Department with regard to China and all of Asia were molded generally by the agents and allies of the IPR.

Their purpose was nothing less than an ambitious design —which succeeded beyond their fondest expectations—to deliver China and Korea into the hands of the Communist Chinese, as a prelude to turning all of Asia into a Red continent.

The IPR had been under a Red cloud since November 1944, when Alfred Kohlberg, a former member of the American Council of IPR, submitted an 88-page statement to the IPR trustees with chapter and verse excerpts from IPR publications showing the IPR's pro-Communist leanings. Kohlberg also charged that Communist writers dominated the IPR magazine *Far Eastern Survey;* Kohlberg's allegations were later confirmed by the Senate subcommittee.

The Red clouds over the IPR thickened as the 1948 testimonies of former high-ranking Communists Elizabeth Bentley and Whittaker Chambers exposed IPR writers and staff members as members of the Communist Party or as Soviet espionage agents. In 1950, former Communist Louis Budenz added to the list, and both Budenz and Senator Joseph Mc-Carthy charged that the IPR was a pro-Communist organization dominated by a Red cell.

The evidence against the IPR became so weighty that from July 1951 to June 1952 the Senate Internal Security Subcommittee held its year-long hearings on the organization. The subcommittee took testimony from 66 witnesses comprising 14 volumes of almost 6,000 pages, and examined more than 2,000 documents. At the conclusion of its investigations, the subcommittee submitted a unanimous bi-partisan 226-page report to the Senate Committee on the Judiciary, which published it as a Senate report with unanimous bipartisan approval on July 2, 1952. Here are excerpts of the report's conclusions about the IPR:

> The IPR has been considered by the American Communist Party and by Soviet officials as an instrument of Communist policy, propaganda and military Intelligence.
> The IPR disseminated and sought to popularize false infor-

mation including information originating from Soviet and Communist sources.

A small core of officials and staff members carried the main burden of IPR activities and directed its administration and policies.

Members of the small core of officials and staff members who controlled IPR were either Communist or pro-Communist.

There is no evidence that the large majority of its members supported the IPR for any reason except to advance the professed research and scholarly purposes of the organization.

IPR activities were made possible largely through the financial support of American industrialists, corporations, and foundations, the majority of whom were not familiar with the inner workings of the organization.

The effective leadership of the IPR often sought to deceive IPR contributors and supporters as to the true character and activities of the organization.

Neither the IPR nor any substantial body of those associated with it as executive officers, trustees or major financial contributors has ever made any serious and objective investigation of the charges that the IPR was infiltrated by Communists and was used for pro-Communist and pro-Soviet purposes.

The names of eminent individuals were by design used as a respectable and impressive screen for the activities of the IPR inner core, and as a defense when such activities came under scrutiny.

What of Dean Rusk's considerable role in the Institute of Pacific Relations?

When Rusk was selected to be Secretary of State, a U. S. Congressman from Iowa queried the State Department about Rusk's role in the IPR. The State Department downgraded Rusk's IPR role by replying, through Frederick G. Dutton, now Assistant Secretary of State for Congressional Relations, that Dean Rusk had merely subscribed to IPR's magazine "while at a college on the West Coast" before World War II, and that this had automatically carried IPR membership. Dutton added that Rusk had terminated his subscription when he entered military service.

But Dutton's clear implication that Rusk's sole affiliation with IPR was through subscribing to the IPR magazine, and that Rusk had dropped his IPR affiliation more than 20 years earlier, is not borne out by the facts.

In the first place, the membership lists of the IPR show Dean Rusk as a member of the American Council of the IPR while he was teaching at Mills College. The same membership lists define "The American Council of the IPR" as "made up of over one thousand *elected* members, leaders of the country's intellectual and business life." Thus, Dean Rusk had not merely taken a five-dollar subscription to IPR's magazine "while at a college on the West Coast," a subscription which had automatically carried IPR membership. He was, in fact, chosen by the IPR as one of the country's one thousand elected members of the American Council of the Institute of Pacific Relations.

During the hearings of the Senate Internal Security Subcommittee, startling facts about Rusk's influential support and close cooperation with the IPR came to light: Dean Rusk had recommended that U. S. Military Intelligence use IPR publications; as late as 1950—when IPR was under serious attack as a Communist operation and the Senate subcommittee was gearing to investigate it—Dean Rusk asked the Rockefeller Foundation for almost two million dollars to support the IPR; and also in 1950, Dean Rusk asked the Ford Foundation for a large grant for the IPR.

In addition, documents inserted into the hearing records show that Dean Rusk was on intimate terms with the highest echelons of the IPR; that Dean Rusk was *the* State Department official to whom IPR officers went for financial, moral and diplomatic backing; and that Dean Rusk was asked by IPR officials to select American delegates to the IPR worldwide conference held in Lucknow, India, in October 1950.

On page 2870 of the Senate subcommittee hearings on the IPR, the following testimony shows Rusk's considerable role in supporting the Institute of Pacific Relations, as given by Benjamin Mandel, research director of the subcommittee:

> *Question:* Mr. Mandel, was Dean Rusk active in the Institute of Pacific Relations?

Mr. Mandel: Dean Rusk was a member of the American Council of the IPR and actively supported an IPR request from the Rockefeller Foundation as late as 1950. He also suggested the use of IPR publications by the Chief of Military Intelligence, according to a letter in our files.

Mr. Mandel later asserted that Dean Rusk had asked the Rockefeller Foundation to give almost two million dollars to the IPR.

In addition, Rusk also gave his special backing to an IPR request for funds from the Ford Foundation, as seen on page 5023 of the hearing record, inserted as Exhibit No. 853. It is a letter from W. L. Holland, Secretary-General of the IPR, to Mr. Charles Loomis of the office of the American Council of the IPR in Honolulu. The letter, dated April 26, 1950, shows that charges had already been made against IPR as a Communist-dominated organization. It reads in part:

> Needless to say, there are bound to be some adverse effects on the IPR from all the McCarthy and Budenz charges . . .
> For your strictly confidential information, I may tell you that the Rockefeller Foundation officers are going to recommend that a special and very exceptional grant be made to both the American IPR and the Pacific Council at the June meeting of the Foundation. Again for your personal information, I can tell you that there is a good prospect that the Ford Foundation [which officially has not yet begun to operate] will make a preliminary grant to the Pacific Council for research on Southeast Asia. I know that our appeal to the Ford Foundation has had the specific backing of Arthur Dean, Sir George Sansom, Phil Jessup, *Dean Rusk* and Huntington Gilchrist.

The intimate cooperation between Dean Rusk and the IPR officials, Rusk's willingness to use his high position to do extraordinary favors for the IPR, and Rusk's being asked to choose delegates to the IPR international conference are shown as Exhibit No. 858 of the Senate hearings, in the following night letter sent to Dean Rusk at the State Department by W. L. Holland on September 12, 1950:

> URGENT COULD YOU KINDLY CABLE SUPREME COMMANDER URGING HIM FAVORABLY CONSIDER

PERMITTING JAPANESE DELEGATION ATTEND IPR
CONFERENCE LUCKNOW OCTOBER THIRD TO FIF-
TEENTH? I AM ADVISED THAT INFLUENTIAL WASH-
INGTON RECOMMENDATION IS NEEDED TO ASSURE
CLEARANCE. PLEASE PHONE OR WIRE ME COLLECT
IF YOU WISH. IS THERE ANYTHING MORE I CAN DO
REGARDING KAHINS PASSPORT? URGENTLY NEED
HIM AT LUCKNOW. CAN YOU NOW GIVE ME NAMES
OF SPECIAL AMERICAN DELEGATES YOU WOULD LIKE
TO ATTEND LUCKNOW?

Exhibit No. 859 of the Senate hearings, a "Dear Dean"
letter from W. L. Holland to Dean Rusk at the State Department in Washington, etches the intimate cooperation between
Rusk and the IPR even more clearly:

> The Hon. Dean Rusk
> Department of State
> Washington, D. C.
> Dear Dean:
>   I was sorry not to reach you on the phone in New York as
> I wanted to ask you whether you found any well-qualified Ameri-
> cans whom you might especially wish to attend the Lucknow
> conference of the IPR as members of the American delegation.
> I do hope you'll let me know soon if you have any special candi-
> dates. I'm sorry that Senator Graham couldn't accept our invita-
> tion, but I'm hoping that W. W. Waymack will accept the offer
> of a grant from the Carnegie Endowment to enable him to go
> to Lucknow . . .
>   May I make an urgent and probably irregular appeal to you
> to lend your weightiest support to the double IPR financial ap-
> peal which is to be considered by the Rockefeller Foundation on
> September 22. As a Foundation trustee, you know better than I
> that one or two members of the Foundation's Executive Commit-
> tee have been worried about all the McCarthy and Budenz charges
> against the IPR. The officers of the Foundation have given us
> very solid support, but it has been suggested to me that in this
> abnormal situation their hand would be strengthened if an im-
> pressive body of outside testimony and recommendations were
> sent to President Barnard, including letters from former Founda-
> tion officers and trustees . . .
>   *Your own position in this question is peculiarly important*
> and Mr. Swope and I would therefore appreciate it greatly if

you could see your way to indicate your belief in the importance of the IPR *at this time. Your words of support for us to the Ford Foundation were very influential,* even though action on that grant has been postponed pending the forthcoming appointment of a director for the Foundation.

Yours,

Does it not seem strange that Dean Rusk—the State Department's expert on the Far East, the man in charge of our entire Far East policy—should not have been able to recognize the blatant and consistently pro-Communist aims of the Institute of Pacific Relations, which dealt exclusively with the Far East?

Does it not seem strange that Dean Rusk should have been asking for millions of dollars for the IPR—at the very moment when serious charges of Communist domination were being leveled against the IPR, at the very moment when a Senate committee was preparing to investigate those serious charges?

Does it not seem strange that Dean Rusk—far from exercising caution about supporting the IPR in any way until the charges were investigated—was urging the Chief of Military Intelligence to use IPR publications; that Rusk was using his high office as Assistant Secretary of State to do extraordinary favors for the IPR; that he was asked to choose delegates to IPR's international conference; that Dean Rusk continued on the most intimate terms of cooperation with IPR officials to further the aims and purposes of the IPR?

These activities of Dean Rusk do, indeed, seem strange to many observers. And today it seems even more strange to many observers that Dean Rusk has not withdrawn the powerful support of the U. S. State Department—which Dean Rusk now heads—from notorious former high-ranking officials of the IPR who were deeply involved in that organization when it was exposed as a Communist transmission belt.

A case in point is that of Owen Lattimore. When Dean Rusk was one of the one thousand elected members of the American Council of the IPR, Owen Lattimore was on the IPR staff working for the ardent Communist, Frederick Vanderbilt Field. Lattimore—who perhaps more than any other person can be termed "Mr. IPR Himself"—was editor of the IPR magazine *Pacific Affairs*. Lattimore was the author of Red propaganda IPR books, and was found by the Senate subcommittee to be one of about three IPR officials who really shaped IPR policy to push the Communist cause.

Five former Communists, put under oath by a Congressional investigating committee, have identified Owen Lattimore as a Communist agent known to them inside the Communist Party. Although Lattimore denied it, he was also identified as a high-level Soviet Intelligence agent by Alexander Barmine, himself a former Soviet Intelligence agent and Soviet general who defected to the free world.

After months of investigation, the Senate Internal Security Subcommittee named Lattimore as being, since the 1930's, "a conscious, articulate instrument of the Soviet conspiracy."

Lattimore had been not only a writer and policy-shaper for IPR. During the same period he had held high positions in our government.

In 1941, Lattimore was chosen by President Roosevelt to be Roosevelt's personal political "adviser" to Chiang Kai-shek. Actually, Lattimore's years of dedication (and those of most of the U. S. Government clique then assigned to Chiang Kai-shek) to betraying Chiang and all of China into the hands of the Red Chinese was best summed up in Lattimore's words written for the Party-line newspaper, the New York *Compass,* on July 17, 1949:

> The problem was how to allow them [Chiang and his army] to fall without making it look as though the United States had pushed them.

How applicable are these words to today's trouble spots?

Lattimore returned from China in 1942 and was made special adviser to Lauchlin Currie, one of President Roosevelt's six confidential administrative assistants. Currie has been identified under oath as another Communist agent. So close was the personal relationship between Lattimore and Currie, that Lattimore used Currie's own White House office and telephone, and took care of Currie's correspondence while Currie was in China.

Currie skipped the country in 1950 before the Senate investigating committee could finger him, and went to Colombia to set up a government administration there. He was later offered a chance to return to the U. S. to clear himself of charges of being a Communist, but he refused. According to Chicago *Tribune* reports, Currie is now a top economic planner in Colombia, busily spending the Johnson Administration's Alliance for Progress money of American taxpayers to carve a totalitarian government in that South American country.

Merely a few looks such as this one at what the Administration's Alliance for Progress is doing in South America might make American taxpayers gasp, "Progress—toward what?"

In 1944, Lattimore was appointed Chief of Pacific Operations for the Office of War Information (OWI). During this year he also accompanied Vice President Wallace on Wallace's official mission to China and Siberia. In 1945, President Harry Truman named Lattimore a member of the Pauley Reparations Mission to Japan.

On January 30, 1949, John F. Kennedy himself, then a U. S. Congressman, condemned Lattimore as having played a major role in China's being turned over to the Communists.

After the IPR hearings ended in June 1952, Owen Lattimore was unanimously indicted by a 24-man Washington Grand Jury on six specific counts of perjury for having lied about his Communist activities to the Senate Internal Security Subcommittee during the IPR hearings.

(Incidentally, Lattimore's lawyer during these IPR hearings was Lyndon Johnson's long-time friend and close personal adviser, Abe Fortas—one of the seven men Kennedy selected in 1962 for his President's Committee on Equal Opportunity in the Armed Forces. This is the committee which wrote the Civil Rights "Gesell Report," of which we shall see the enormous importance and ramifications later. Fortas is also rumored as a possible nominee by President Johnson to succeed Robert Kennedy as U. S. Attorney General.)

But in 1955 the charges against Lattimore were summarily dismissed by Judge Luther Youngdahl—much to the disgust of the American public—and Lattimore resumed his position as lecturer at Johns Hopkins University. In 1963, Lattimore went to teach at Leeds University in England as head of a Chinese studies department.

Owen Lattimore's hideous pro-Communist record should, it would seem, give pause to our State Department. Not so in the Department presided over by Dean Rusk.

In the summer of 1961, Lattimore was granted a special passport visa by the State Department—a visa which the ordinary American citizen cannot obtain—to travel on a top-secret mission, reportedly for the State Department, to the Soviet state of the Mongolian People's Republic (not so euphemistically known as Outer Mongolia), a deep-freeze barren land at the top of China. According to the Chicago *Tribune's* Washington writer, Walter Trohan, the State Department was then "dickering for the diplomatic recognition of the Russian-sponsored Mongolian People's Republic." These "diplomatic overtures" by Lattimore, said Trohan, "may be a trial balloon for ultimate recognition of Red China, or at least letting Red China into the UN." Trohan, a veteran observer of Washington trial balloons, speculated that "the Kennedy administration might name him [Owen Lattimore] as the first American ambassador to Outer Mongolia."

At least one Senator, Thomas J. Dodd of Connecticut, demanded to know what was going on, saying he did "not think it is an accident" that at the very moment the State Department was dickering for recognition of Outer Mongolia, "Owen Lattimore should arrive there as a visitor."

State Department officials denied that Lattimore had gone to Mongolia on his special passport visa for the purpose of laying the groundwork for an exchange of ambassadors, but they did admit that Lattimore reported to the State Department when he returned to Washington.

In any case, in 1962, the People's Republic of Mongolia was admitted to the UN—a step which Dean Rusk approved—in what many observers saw as a straw in the wind for ultimate U. S. diplomatic recognition of Red China and a UN seat for the Chinese Communists.

As noted previously, Dean Rusk's and the State Department's not withdrawing support from Owen Lattimore is only one case in point. Today, the Administration, the State Department and the American public are benefitting from the dubious services of the following former high-ranking IPR members who are now in top government posts:

EDWIN REISCHAUER . . . Appointed by President Kennedy as U. S. Ambassador to Japan, one of the most sensitive of all Asiatic posts.

On March 23, 1961, Reischauer told the Senate Foreign Relations Committee: "I was never connected with the IPR in any way." The Senate committee, however, could have refreshed Mr. Reischauer's mind by producing a letter written during the IPR hearings by W. L. Holland, then Executive Vice Chairman of IPR, and addressed to the counsel of the Senate Internal Security Subcommittee. The letter, dated September 28, 1951, not only identified Edwin Reischauer as an IPR member from 1944 to 1948, but also stated that he was a contributor to IPR's *Far Eastern Survey* and was co-author of IPR's *Next Step in Asia*. The Senate committee could also have reminded Reischauer that he had written an entire book for IPR, and that he had been a contributor to the IPR magazine, *Pacific Affairs*. Indeed, in 1960, Reischauer co-authored a book, *East Asia: The Great Tradition,* with IPR wheelhorse and OSS China official, John K. Fairbank of Harvard University, who, although he denied it, has been identified under oath as a member of the Communist Party. In fact, as early as 1936, the IPR annual report lists Edwin Reischauer as a sponsor of IPR's Chinese language school for summer 1937 at the University of Michigan. Today, Edwin Reischauer—who arrogantly lied to a Senate committee about his membership and yeoman service in the major Communist transmission belt for Communist propaganda about Asia—is now an American Ambassador to a key Asiatic nation, personally chosen for that exalted post by the late President John F. Kennedy and retained by President Lyndon Johnson.

JOHN K. EMMERSON . . . appointed by the Kennedy Administration as Reischauer's number two man in our Tokyo embassy. Emmerson and Reischauer are old friends from the Stilwell days in China. Stilwell's successor, Lieutenant General Albert E. Wedemeyer, included Emmerson in a report about four State Department men he had inherited who were busting a gusset to sell out Chiang Kai-shek: "Their sympathy for the Chinese Communists is obvious in their reports and recommendations . . ." Emmerson has always specialized in Japan. As early as November 7, 1944, Emmerson wrote a report urging support of the Japanese People's Emancipation League, an outfit run lock, stock and barrel by the Chinese Communists for the sole purpose of indoctrinating Japanese prisoners in communism. In September 1951, a Senate committee learned that in April 1945, Emmerson had recommended that Japanese prisoners of war in American stockades "be turned over to Japanese Communists in the United States for indoctrination."

JOHN STEWART SERVICE . . . Retained by the Kennedy Administration as U. S. Consul in Liverpool, England. He retired in August 1962. Service was another of the four included in General Wedemeyer's report. Service was arrested for espionage on June 7, 1945, by the FBI in connection with the stolen top-secret documents in the *Amerasia* offices. On December 13, 1951, Service was fired as a "loyalty risk" by the Civil Service Review Board. But in 1957—thanks to a decision by the U. S. Supreme Court—Service was put back on the taxpayers' payroll.

ARTHUR H. DEAN . . . Appointed by the late President Kennedy as U. S. Ambassador to the Geneva disarmament conferences. We have had a look at Mr. Dean in Chapter One. But it should be stressed here that Dean was chairman of IPR's Pacific Council and Vice Chairman of the entire IPR; he presided over IPR meetings whenever the chairman was absent; and more than any other man (even more than fellow IPR board member James D. Zellerbach) fought against a clean-up of IPR by the Senate investigating committee.

On January 24, 1962, the late President Kennedy revealed angrily at a press conference, in response to a question by reporter Sarah McClendon, that he had personally cleared for security another former Inner Circle member of IPR—after consultation with Dean Rusk. The former IPR member was J. Clayton Miller, who had written for the IPR mouthpiece,

Amerasia magazine, at the time when 1,800 top-secret documents stolen from Military Intelligence, Naval Intelligence and the State Department were seized by the FBI while the documents were being photostated in *Amerasia's* office.

But Secretary Rusk saw no harm in Miller's handling secret FBI reports at the State Department. Under Dean Rusk's regime, former membership on the infamous staffs of IPR and *Amerasia* are no bar to employment in sensitive positions.

Mr. Kennedy's finger-pointing retort to Mrs. McClendon came with "the most chilling anger" he had displayed to that date at any Presidential press conference, according to the New York *Herald Tribune* report of the incident. "In low tones with icicles clinging to them," said the *Herald Tribune,* Mr. Kennedy stammered that he was "familiar with Mr. Miller's record because I happened to look at it the other day" and that he had personally cleared Miller after the President and Dean Rusk "both looked into the matter."

Mr. Kennedy told the press conference his conclusions about J. Clayton Miller: "In my opinion, the duties which he is now carrying out he is fit for."

Undaunted by what the New York *Times* described as Mr. Kennedy's "icy rebuke," Mrs. McClendon persisted: "Did you both look at Mr. William Wieland, too?"

In her initial question to President Kennedy, Mrs. McClendon had labeled as "well-known security risks" both J. Clayton Miller and Wieland, who had run the State Department's Caribbean desk while Fidel Castro made his way to Havana, and who was a carryover into the Kennedy Administration. Both Wieland and Miller reportedly organized the smashing of security regulations in the State Department at the beginning of the Kennedy Administration. Wieland— one of the two key State Department men who should have known what was common knowledge in Latin American chancellories: that Fidel Castro had been an active Communist revolutionary in Latin America since at least 1947—had buried all Intelligence reports that Castro was a Communist, and had kept assuring all anxious inquirers that Fidel was the savior of the Cuban people and that the bearded hero had absolutely no connection with communism.

Mr. Kennedy responded to the question about Mr. Wieland: "I am familiar with Mr. Wieland and I am familiar with his duties at the present time. In my opinion, Mr. Miller and Mr. Wieland—the duties they have been assigned to they can carry out without detriment to the interests of the United States and I hope without detriment to [their] character by your question."

Curiously enough, the Senate Internal Security Subcommittee later held hearings on the Wieland case, and in a unanimous bipartisan report concluded that there is "substantial evidence" that "State Department records were arranged *after* Wieland had been mentioned at a Presidential press conference, so as to show that he had been cleared several months before."

Thus far, the Senate subcommittee has not found the J. Clayton Miller records tampered with.

To top off the whole thing, the State Department issued a strong defense of Wieland the day after the Senate subcommittee issued its report on him.

The subcommittee's report emphasized the larger significance of the Wieland case, pointing out that Wieland's "record and conduct and the handling of his security case combine to provide a case history which illustrates much of what is wrong with the State Department from a security standpoint." But Wieland is still in the State Department, and so are many more.

The unanimous subcommittee report also revealed that William Wieland had never been given a security check! Furthermore, the report revealed that Wieland worked in the State Department before he ever filled out a job application; that he falsified his job history when he finally did fill out an "application"; and that he falsified his personal history form, declaring that he had never used another name, when in fact he had once used, *in Cuba,* the name Arturo Guillermo Montenegro, the name of his stepfather. The report also revealed that Otto Otepka, the State Department security officer who had conducted a full-scale investigation into Wieland's background and recommended that Wieland be fired, was demoted by the State Department. The Senate report also revealed that Wieland, who had never been given a security check, was "cleared" improperly after Otepka's findings—by a man who had never seen Wieland's security file —in the name of Secretary of State Dean Rusk.

While the IPR investigations were in full swing, Dean Rusk resigned from the State Department in December 1951, to become President of the Rockefeller Foundation. Rusk, a trustee of the Foundation, was recommended for the post by fellow trustees John Foster Dulles and Robert A. Lovett, then Secretary of Defense. (Lovett later recommended Robert McNamara as the Kennedy Administration's Secretary of Defense.)

As president for eight years of the enormously rich Rockefeller Foundation (its current assets are about $600 million, and it has given away almost $1 billion since its establishment in 1913), Rusk presided over the giving away of about $250 million, a great part of it to finance powerful left-wing organizations such as the multi-tentacled subsidiaries and interlocking organizations of the Council on Foreign Relations, whose members—including the late President Kennedy and Dean Rusk—have held, and hold, some of the highest offices in our government. The Council on Foreign Relations was founded in 1919 by Woodrow Wilson's mysterious adviser Edward M. House, and by John Foster Dulles, Allen M. Dulles, Christian A. Herter and Tasker H. Bliss.

A full explanation of the interlocking machinations of the Rockefeller, Ford, Fund for the Republic, and Carnegie Foundations with the Council on Foreign Relations and with left-wing activities in the United States would fill a tome in itself, but readers can find a painstakingly researched and documented, lucid analysis in a 250-page paperback book, *The Invisible Government,* by Dan Smoot, former FBI agent and Harvard Teaching Fellow (The Dan Smoot Report, Inc., Dallas 14, Texas).

On August 1, 1951, Representative E. E. Cox, Democrat of Georgia, introduced a resolution in the House for an investigation into the powerful tax-exempt foundations. Naming the Rockefeller Foundation, Representative Cox charged flatly that Rockefeller Foundation funds "have been used to finance individuals and organizations whose business it has been to get communism into the private and public schools of the country, to talk down America and to play up Russia."

Dean Rusk, when head of the Rockefeller Foundation, was also the organization's chief expert on foreign policy, according to the Washington newsletter *Human Events* of December 11, 1960. The newsletter explains that Rusk "was instrumental in drawing up a [Rockefeller] Foundation report in December 1959, which all but called for Red China's recognition. Rusk's report said the U. S. could not afford to be 'cut-off' from any nation, and it definitely implied that a hard line toward Red China might foment a 'color' war more 'fearful' than a cold war with Russia."

Rusk's Foundation report also recommended that the United States cease giving economic aid directly to other nations, and urged that we give the money to the United Nations, for UN distribution. The report even invited Soviet Russia to join the United States in dispensing largesse. Just for good measure, the report also counseled increased "cultural exchanges" between the Soviets and the free world. Rusk's report urged these last two measures, even though the Soviets have never made any bones about the fact that all Soviet "aid" and "cultural exchanges" are solely political weapons wielded to further the Communist goal of world domination.

While he headed the Rockefeller Foundation, Rusk took the opportunity to lash Congressional investigations into Communists in our government. The McCarthy hearings were then in full swing, and Rusk took to the lecture platform to denounce the hearings as being motivated solely to make political hay. For instance, on March 5, 1953, Rusk de-

clared to a meeting of the National Education Association
(NEA) that the charge of "heresy was being raised in concealed form" by the Senate investigating committee "for political advantage."

Despite the fact that the Senate investigations conducted
by Senator McCarthy touched off the IPR investigations, fer-
reted out identified Communists working in our government,
and forced a host of State Department employees to scuttle
out of employment in Foggy Bottom before Senator Mc-
Carthy's committee could finger them, Rusk has never retracted his charges that the entire investigation was merely
a political flim-flam.

The Baltimore *Sun* reported that on April 5, 1962, in
testifying before the Senate Foreign Relations Committee,
Rusk came out strongly against the withholding of U. S. foreign aid from nations which expropriated American properties.
The newspaper cited the following exchange:

> Senator Capehart (R., Ind.) questioned Rusk about putting
> into the aid legislation a provision to insure that United States
> businessmen who put money into underdeveloped countries will
> not have their property expropriated without compensation. He
> referred to recent seizure by one of the Brazilian states of an
> American telephone company.
>
> Rusk said he hoped the committee would not put into the
> bill a provision which might penalize a whole country for some
> act of a local body not under direct control of the central govern-
> ment.

From the point of view of international law, this attitude was highly questionable. A national government is always responsible internationally for what a state or local government does. In this instance, the attitude was ridiculous, since
Rusk well knew that the "state" Governor involved in Brazil
was a brother-in-law of the Brazilian President. The U. S.
Senate and the House were sufficiently unimpressed, since
they passed and sent to the President a law banning U. S.
foreign aid to nations which expropriated American properties without specific provision for the "prompt and adequate

compensation" provided by international law, and without which expropriation becomes confiscation.

When Congress tried to investigate the burgeoning assortment of scandals in our foreign aid programs, Rusk, in letters to 12 officials of the State Department and of its subsidiary International Cooperation Administration, ordered these officials, who had been called before the House Government Operations Subcommittee, not to tell Congressional investigators anything about scandals in the U. S. foreign aid program. Representative Porter Hardy, Jr., Democrat of Virginia, chairman of the subcommittee, termed Rusk's order "the most arrogant instruction ever given to a government witness."

In November 1963, the State Department under Dean Rusk suffered the latest symptom of what columnists Robert Allen and Paul Scott termed "an incurable case of 'hope springs eternal'," in pushing for disarmament via gentlemen's agreements with the Soviets: "exchanging" our germ warfare and chemical weapons secrets with the Russians, along with our U. S. defenses against germ and chemical warfare. Mr. Rusk was evidently pleased that Soviet Foreign Minister Andrei Gromyko (who, according to the late President himself, lied to Kennedy in October 1962, about Soviet missiles in Cuba) was "deeply interested" in the whole idea, when Rusk and Gromyko discussed it during their private tête-á-têtes at the 1963 opening of the United Nations.

The plan was "fathered by Dean Rusk," who does not plan to ask Congressional approval of the idea, reported Allen and Scott on November 9, who quoted Army chemical warfare experts as greatly alarmed over the proposal. The experts declared it would "open the way for the Soviets' obtaining vital information that could be used with lethal effect against the United States."

It has been said that most Americans ardently want peace, that today they divide into two groups. The first group wants peace with honor; it includes those who believe that no price is too high to pay for continued independence and freedom. The second group is inclined toward peace at almost any price. There are those who think that Dean Rusk tends toward the latter group.

At any rate, Secretary Rusk has a long history in the international peace movement. While a student at Oxford, he won the Cecil Peace Prize—a prize offered by Lord Robert Cecil, drafter of the League of Nations Covenant and a lifetime League supporter.

It is interesting to note that this Oxford peace movement culminated, in the period immediately before World War II, in a shocking declaration of opposition to war for any cause or against any challenge And, as noted, Mr. Rusk's first big official position in State involved trying to reestablish peace in a ravaged and divided world as State's Director of UN Affairs.

Mr. Rusk's type of devotion to peace and to the UN is quite in keeping with the negotiation of a limited atomic test-ban treaty between the U. S. and Soviet Russia in the summer of 1963, at a moment when thousands of Soviet troops were well entrenched in Cuba.

Ignored are the facts that Soviet Russia has broken at least 50 of its 52 major agreements since World War II, and that nonaggression pacts have always been a Soviet tool for lulling prospective victims of Soviet aggression.

Mr. Rusk's background also dovetails with the Administration's program to make a super-state—a World State—of the United Nations.

Today, in his early fifties, Rusk has been described by Mary McGrory of the Washington Evening *Star* as:

"A big man, tall and broad-shouldered. He has a fringe of graying black hair, round cheeks, a cleft chin and lively brown eyes. He speaks with a faint trace of Southern accent. His manner is one of self-possession and reserve."

This "reserve" is not only an analysis of Rusk's manner. Virtually his first act as Secretary of State was an attempt to establish a press censorship. He ordered State tightened up to prevent leaks and issued a statement about this. It has since been made official that this censorship is, among other things, to protect security risks.

Walter Lippmann decided that Rusk's "quiet diplomacy" was acceptable. Lippmann expressed the belief that "a competent government" could "keep the public well-informed without destroying the privacy that is essential to diplomatic negotiation." This, like all of Lippmann's over-simplifications, sounds convincing even though his statement was a non sequitur and Rusk himself was not so concerned about keeping the press informed as he was about tightening leaks.

Almost a year later, Lyle Wilson, vice president of UPI's Washington bureau and a veteran observer of the Washington scene, reported, "The general press policy of the State Dapartment is crumbling into chaos." He charged Rusk with "infatuation" with "electronic public relations," quoting an anonymous observer as stating, "Rusk comes over TV like 'Brand X.' What he needs is less exposure, rather than more."

Murray Marder, writing in the extremely liberal Washington *Post,* sprang to Rusk's defense, asserting that the Secretary of State is "almost as enamored of electronic public relations as he is with grappling with a cobra."

If this is correct, Rusk must have developed a liking for cobras while in India, since the record shows him appearing on television quite a bit. Rusk has been on NBC, CBS, ABC and the BBC—on *Meet the Press, JFK Report, Metrotone Telenews, Reporters' Roundup, Today, Continental Classroom—* and of course on the late Eleanor Roosevelt's program.

Whether speaking to his staff or to the press, Rusk sounds as though he were addressing a class of slightly stupid juniors. He is dull and pedestrian; his humor is forced and larded with attempts to appear scholarly.

Rusk's very first press conference sounded like a trip into "Never-Never Land." He called attention to the fact that we are in "a turbulent world situation" and in any given year, in a situation of this sort, things are likely to be a "little mixed."

Two other such gems are: "One of the prime tasks of for-

eign policy is to try to protect the interests of our country"
and "We are going to have to aim at the future if we expect
to come on target in the present. Otherwise, our problems fly
by and we just knock off a few tail feathers."

Once, when told at his staff meeting that the military was
about to take over a Latin American nation at noon that day,
Rusk asked his shocked assistants, "Can't we get some food
down there fast?"

Rusk's attempts at erudition can be illustrated by his following two statements:

"Bold action has too often been conceived as little more
than putting Russia in a superficially embarrassing, or awk-
ward, position."

"The fateful rivalry of the cold war may persist for a
long time; nevertheless, this is an incident in a far greater
world drama."

The first of these statements, of course, has little basis in
fact and, as one critic remarked, "The Lord knows Rusk has
never embarrassed the Russians—superficially or any other
way."

Since Rusk became Secretary of State, Americans have
witnessed a parade of shocking activities by Rusk's State Department lieutenants. G. Mennen Williams' trail of blunders
across the African continent was so ludicrous that Capitol
Hill wags began to tab Soapy as "the black man's burden."
In fact, the government of Mali was so outraged by Soapy's
disastrous three-day visit to their country that Mali closed
our United States Information Agency office in that country
the day after Williams left. A more serious aftermath of
Soapy's visit was the Mali alliance with Soviet Russia.

Then, Americans witnessed Chester Bowles' magnificent
sweeps around the world; Adlai Stevenson's attacks on our
European allies; young Richard Goodwin's dealings with Soviet
agents at Punta del Este, Uruguay; and, not least, JFK's personal telephone calls directly to Rusk's second-rank as well as
first-rank subordinates. But somehow Rusk has maintained
his ascendency and departmental control.

In the Cuba mess, Rusk has stated that there is no evidence of internal subversion in Latin America directed from Cuba. On December 10, 1962, he implied that we were about to close the books on the Cuban crisis, but three days later he estimated that there were still 10,000 to 12,000 Soviet troops on the island.

On January 11, 1963, he stated that we were convinced all "offensive weapons" had been removed from Cuba. Yet on January 27, in a *Meet the Press* television interview, Rusk admitted that the continued presence of Soviet troops and arms in Cuba was a matter of real concern, that MIG fighters on Cuba are capable of delivering nuclear warheads to the U. S., but that the absence of on-site inspection leaves us unable to prove the presence of nuclear warheads in Cuba.

On February 13, 1963, Rusk spoke at a State Department foreign policy dinner in Los Angeles and admitted it was impossible to determine whether or not all Soviet offensive weapons had been removed from Cuba. Yet he asserted that Cuba "will not become a base for offensive military operations against other countries of the hemisphere." On March 7, in a radio interview, Rusk said that 200,000 Cubans had left Cuba since Castro came to power and that "several hundred thousand" more wanted to leave.

This weaving, vacillating commentary on Cuba reached a climax on April 17 when Dr. Miro Cardona, head of the Cuban Revolutionary Council, declared that the U. S. State Department instead of helping him to assist Cuban exiles, had done nothing but heap abuse on him. Soon after Cardona's accusation, the Democratic-controlled Senate Preparedness Subcommittee, chaired by Democratic Senator John Stennis, released a Senate interim report sharply disputing almost every move and statement Rusk had previously made about the Cuban situation.

Are Rusk's statements on Cuba the words of a "hard anti-Communist," as Rusk was advertised to be when he took over the State Department? Is this honest uncertainty? Perhaps a partial answer might be seen in the words of Senator Strom

Thurmond: "The State Department has made a concerted effort, to the limits of its power, to keep the facts from both the Congress and the people."

In general, just what successes against communism has Dean Rusk obtained for his chief, the President?

The answer must be: virtually none, except those which could easily be obtained through appeasement. That is the only answer—unless one is completely snowed by propaganda that the coalition government dominated by the Communists in Laos is actually a success; or that Ghana and Mali are not really in the Soviet orbit now; or that leaving the Soviets' illegal Berlin wall was in fact a victory; or that the "limited" nuclear test-ban treaty with the Soviets is a meaningful agreement and will really bring security to the free world.

Have Rusk's policies, and the policies he has explicitly or tacitly endorsed, hurt communism?

The answer to that is: If reducing our nuclear retaliatory "first-strike" capability has hurt communism; if the crumbling of our NATO alliance has hurt communism; if the complete loss of our initiative in international affairs has hurt communism—then Dean Rusk's policies have indeed hurt communism. But why do the world's Communist leaders continue to assert that communism can gain a total, worldwide victory without war, if Rusk's policies have hurt communism?

All of history's Communist leaders—including Lenin, Stalin, Khrushchev and Mao Tse-tung—have held that "peace" is possible for the non-Communist world only if it surrenders to communism. Indeed, in Communist Aesopian language, "peace" means the absence of any resistance to communism. It means the final Communist conquest of the world.

Some may regard our very soft U. S. policy toward communism as progress toward *true* peace. To most people, however, ours seems like progress toward submission to communism and many see in the "limited" nuclear test-ban treaty a giant step in that direction. Khrushchev himself termed the test-ban treaty "a victory for communism."

Although a host of nuclear and military experts, including Dr. Edward Teller, "Father of the H-Bomb," and Admiral Arleigh Burke, retired Chief of Naval Operations, gave testimony documenting serious objections against the test-ban treaty, many Senators were persuaded that the treaty, by itself, was meaningless and that a vote against it would be interpreted by their constituents as a vote against "peace." So the Senate approved what is planned to be step-by-step disarmament of the United States.

In voting for the completely unpoliced "gentlemen's agreement" nuclear test-ban treaty, the Senate forgot the late President John F. Kennedy's own statement of March 2, 1962, which he made on a television broadcast to the nation after the Russians had broken the test-ban moratorium: ". . . a new agreement without controls would enable them [the Soviets] once again to prevent the West from testing, while they prepare in secret . . . We now know enough about broken negotiations, secret preparations, and the advantages gained from a long test series never to offer again an uninspected moratorium." How quickly JFK forgot his own words.

There are people in this nation who want to be reassured that everything is all right, those who do not want to look our great danger in the face. To these people, Dean Rusk is a reassuring man. His gravity, dignity and calm add up to a good bedside manner, a tranquilizer against the grevious operations of the Rostows, Schlesingers and Yarmolinskys.

The fact that Rusk's may be a graveside, rather than bedside, manner does not occur to these people.

CHAPTER THREE

Backstage at the Pentagon

"As I was going up the stair,
I met a man who wasn't there.
He wasn't there again today.
I wish, I wish he'd stay away."
 . . . Hughes Means—THE PSYCHOED

SINCE ROBERT STRANGE McNAMARA was appointed Secretary of Defense, a strange breed known as "The Whiz Kids" has been unleashed in the Pentagon, in which the Defense Department is headquartered. They depend upon IBM calculators to overrule the Joint Chiefs of Staff. They call their friends at the State Department before wrecking the careful calculations of military experts who have worked on war games strategy for months and for years. They cancel weapons systems which Soviet Russia blasts as "war-like," without considering our over-all military posture or strategy. And yet, when decisions have to be accounted for, or when the responsibility for a real goof is sought, they disappear into the vacuum from which they seem to have sprung.

Although Secretary McNamara described himself as "a registered Republican from Michigan" when he entered the Kennedy Admniistration, there is, in fact, no such thing in the State of Michigan, and despite the strongest protests from the state, McNamara has never retracted his statement. McNamara could not have been "a registered Republican from Michigan" because there are open primaries in that state and Michigan state law prohibits any Michigan voter from registering in any political party.

Moreover, officials of the Michigan State Republican Party have a record of McNamara's campaign contribution to Michigan's 100-per-cent-ADA Democratic Senator Philip Hart; but they have no record of McNamara's ever having contributed to the campaign of anyone running on the Republican ticket in Michigan, where McNamara lived from 1946 to 1961, when he entered the Kennedy Administration. In fact, Mc-Namara supported John F. Kennedy for the Presidency in 1960, and as far back as 1940, when he was teaching at Harvard, he signed a petition for the re-election of Franklin D. Roosevelt.

Since McNamara entered the Defense Department, he has been built up as a "brilliant mind" and (the Edsel fiasco not being mentioned) as a lofty executive type, who, above all else, embodies that one characteristic necessary for a good executive: the ability to make decisions. Actually, the "executive decision-making ability" build-up of McNamara does strain one's credulity just a bit. For example, one of Mc-Namara's aides told the press that on one occasion, in the space of only one hour, "Secretary McNamara made so many complex decisions" that it would have taken "the greatest military and defense brains of our time hours *each* to weigh adequately the pros and cons necessary for a fair decision."

On the other hand, some have hinted that McNamara's controversial TFX multi*billion*-dollar contract award to General Dynamics was one of McNamara's "fastest and worst" decisions, for what has been described as a "murder plane" for its pilots. Then, of course, there were those in Washington who tabbed the TFX the "LBJ plane" because the fat government contract happened to be awarded to a division of General Dynamics which is in the home state of Lyndon B. Johnson.

In addition, of course, there were nasty rumors (later documented by Congressional probers) that Navy Secretary Fred Korth had been president of the Texas bank which had made hefty loans—still outstanding—to General Dynamics, and that Korth still held stock in the bank. Indeed, McNamara had given the award to General Dynamics because, he stated, that corporation had "the least expensive, time-consuming, [*sic*] research-and-development *before production.*" But at the Senate hearings up popped Boeing official Albert W. Blackburn, who testified that "all of the imaginative aerodynamics fixes devised by Boeing in their third submission [i.e., to the Defense Department of their plane plans for the contract award] somehow found their way into the final General Dynamics design to a degree of similarity that would hardly be a coincidence." That would appear to be one way to reduce expenses "before production," as McNamara terms it.

Nevertheless, the Senate investigation also discovered, contrary to McNamara's claim, that Boeing's bid for the fighter plane contract was about 26 per cent *less* than that of General Dynamics. In any case, Boeing has long had anti-Communist educational programs for its employees, and if the Defense Department under McNamara had stopped anti-Communist educational programs for the American military, it would be hardly fitting for Boeing to receive the multibillion-dollar tactical fighter plane contract.

When the Congressional investigators started breathing down Navy Secretary Korth's neck to probe his conflict of interest in the TFX award, he resigned from the Kennedy Administration, with the "reason" being leaked to the press as his "disagreement" with McNamara over a nuclear aircraft carrier for the Navy. But most newsmen had TFX ideas. And said so.

According to testimony from Pentagon personnel during hearings of the Senate Permanent Investigating Subcommittee, which lasted from February 28 to August 8, 1963, McNamara tried to justify his choice of General Dynamics for the TFX contract by pitting one group of thinkers against another in a sort of "contractors' war game." But when the side opposing McNamara made too much headway, this brought a sudden end to "the war of brains" inside the Pentagon. The TFX contract decision has cost thousands of hours for the American taxpayers in time spent by members of the Senate committee investigating the award, to say nothing of the hours spent by witnesses parading up the Hill and down again from the "fortress across the Potomac."

All this, to the minds of some, in order to justify what has been called a "second-rate aircraft years behind its time." Perhaps Secretary McNamara was running true to form, since as a Ford Motor Company policy-making executive, it was McNamara who with his electronic computers compiled data which persuaded Ford to manufacture the Edsel automobile which was, in the words of a prominent Michigan businessman, "a third-rate motorcar 20 years behind its time."

The Edsel fiasco was the biggest disaster of the automobile industry and one of the major financial flops of U. S. big-corporation history; the blunder cost Ford a cool $350 million. The man who compiled the decision-making data for the Edsel has now moved with his computers to the Pentagon, where today he has in his hands all the military defense of our nation, and where he is making life-or-death decisions for our nation and for the entire free world.

It may be a coincidence that McNamara—after being Ford's financial analyst, controller and vice president—was the first non-Ford named President of the Ford Motor Company, one day *after* John F. Kennedy won the Presidential election in 1960. It was as President of Ford that McNamara was called by Kennedy a few days later to head the Defense Department.

McNamara is another Harvard man in the Administration. Born in San Francisco, June 9, 1916, Mr. McNamara received his A.B. from the University of California in 1937 and went to Harvard Business School, where he received his master's degree in 1939. He taught at Harvard, as an assistant professor of business administration, from 1940 to 1943. At Harvard, during the first two years of World War II, McNamara instructed Army Air Force officers in the use of computers to make decisions, on which McNamara relied so heavily when he went to Ford, and on which he now relies so heavily at the Pentagon.

McNamara joined the Army Air Corps in 1943, and was immediately sent as a lieutenant colonel to the Pentagon to work on statistical control for Air Corps supply. With McNamara in the wartime Pentagon were nine other young officers who, when the war ended, sold themselves in 1946 as a package to the Ford Motor Company—at the time when one Detroit newspaper noted that the Ford management was rated "so low, it could hardly go lower"—where the team became known as the "Whiz Kids." The "Whiz Kid" appellation has stuck and is still applied to McNamara and to the men surrounding him in the Defense Department.

Only a few weeks after he arrived in the Pentagon and surveyed our defense situation, Secretary McNamara startled the nation by declaring that candidate John F. Kennedy's major campaign theme of a "missile gap" was a prefab campaign fabrication. It had been a good idea on the campaign trail at the time, but actually, McNamara explained to thousands of citizens who had been gulled into voting for Kennedy to help "close the missile gap," the whole thing didn't exist . We had enough missiles.

While this was greeted by the liberal press as evidence of ironclad honesty on Mr. McNamara's part, it was actually a neat bit of team play. Since there was no "missile gap," there was no need for the Kennedy Administration or the Defense Department to manufacture more missiles. Now, however, after four years of McNamara and the Kennedy-Johnson Administration, and the deliberate disarming of the United States by destroying our nuclear first-strike capability and by scrapping our big-payload nuclear bombers, there is a genuine and terrifying "missile gap" which is actually inviting Soviet attack upon our nation—as we shall see in the next few pages, wherein are set forth *facts,* not merely rumor, not gloomy opinion, not partisan conjecture, but the stark facts of the perilous situation in which Kennedy and Johnson Administrations have placed the United States of America.

Since coming to the Pentagon, America's first and last line of defense, Robert McNamara has inaugurated a new American "defense" strategy, which can be explained in the following painstakingly researched analysis, under two main headings: Limited Retaliation; and Disarmament.

McNamara's Limited Retaliation policy has been publicized to the nation under three euphemistic subheadings: "controlled response," "counterforce retaliation" and "the doctrine of conventional option."

"Controlled response" means, in simple language, that control of America's nuclear weapons system has been put into the hands of Defense Department civilians by: 1) the "permissive link" system, by which U. S. retaliation against Soviet attack *can be triggered only by civilians in the Defense Department unfastening a mechanical lock to fire our nuclear missiles;* 2) civilian control over the military, at all levels, which is discussed later in this chapter; and 3) a barrier erected between Pentagon military men and Congress, by the channeling of all Pentagon contracts with Congress through the office of Norman Paul, Secretary McNamara's Special Assistant for Legislative Affairs. In addition, many Washington news stories persistently report that McNamara is contemplating unification of our armed services under one head, a move viewed by many experts as fraught with tremendous dangers for our nation.

"Counterforce retaliation" is the assurance which the U. S. has given to the Soviet Union that the United States will never strike the Soviets first. This assurance is coupled with the promise that, in any event, the U. S. will never bomb Soviet cities. (Since the industrial plants which manufacture war weapons are naturally located in heavily populated areas, this promise makes U. S. "retaliation" ridiculous.)

Counterforce retaliation also includes the "balance of terror" theory promulgated by the President's advisers which assures that the U. S. will not outstrip Russia in the production of weapons.

In a 1958 speech, which his aide, ADAer Ted Sorenson, cooperated in writing, then-Senator Kennedy forecast the balance of terror theory, when he declared that during 1960 to 1964 the United States would be in a "position of great peril" if it had then overtaken Soviet superiority in "offensive and defensive missile capability."

The third facet of Secretary McNamara's Limited Retaliation policy is "the doctrine of conventional option." This is the policy which has seen our defense budget under the Kennedy and Johnson Administrations poured into manufacture of old-fashioned conventional weapons, rather than into modern weapons of warfare. These conventional weapons have dragged out bloody wars in Korea, Laos and, now, Viet Nam.

The second major phase of McNamara's "defense" policy is Disarmament. The Defense Department, under Robert McNamara's guidance, is carrying out the Administration's policy of systematically disarming the United States. McNamara is doing this by scrapping our first-strike weapons which are our major deterrent against Soviet attack; by assuring that America's nuclear retaliatory capability is not stronger that that of the Soviet Union; by not developing new weapons vital to our defense; by canceling weapons on the drawing boards; by scrapping our nuclear bases which have ringed the perimeter of the Soviet Union; by recalling U. S. troops from abroad; and by weakening our defenses—all acts destroying our ability to defend the United States, and, not incidentally, acts which are actually inviting the Soviets to attack us.

Some chilling analyses of Mr. McNamara's "defense" policy have been made by retired military officers, who are in a position to do so. One typical analysis came from Rear Admiral Chester Ward, one of the nation's top nuclear war strategists, who declared in a speech in Honolulu on April 8, 1963, that Robert McNamara is carrying out "massive nuclear disarmament of the Unitel States." Admiral Ward said this of Mr. McNamara's policy:

> The so-called "brilliant" McNamara is so confused over the most elementary strategy, that he is attempting to adopt a counterforce strategy with no counterforce weapons. Also, his "sophisticated" targeting is such as to encourage a surprise attack.
>
> We have always assured the enemy of a free first-strike against us; we will never strike first. Now we are saying to the enemy, "You not only may strike first, but when we strike back, we will strike back only at your military installations"—which by that time would be mostly empty missile bases. Thus, we propose to allow a second strike at us—from our enemy's concealed and hardened missile bases—before we strike at all. Now this is certainly inviting surprise attack.
>
> In other words, Mr. McNamara is trying so hard to be sophisticated, he may get us all incinerated.

Mr. McNamara, commenting last week on the general Soviet strategic theories for nuclear war, said, "They're not sophisticated." For once he was right—they're not sophisticated. The Communists have one, simple, unsophisticated idea in a nuclear war—and that is to win it.

Admiral Ward stressed that McNamara is "deliberately cutting back 90 per cent of our nuclear firepower, under the guise of so-called modernization. Consequently, where we used to have at least a two-to-one nuclear lead over the Soviets across the board—across the entire spectrum of nuclear weaponry—the Soviets now have, in the area of strategic warheads, at least a two-to-one lead over us. Khrushchev, by breaking the nuclear test moratorium in 1961, was enabled to develop his strategic nuclear power, which now permits him to threaten the destruction of the United States. We are substantially scrapping our first-strike power," said Admiral Ward. "Our U. S. SAC bombers—our sole sufficiently powerful reliable protection against surprise attack—are being scrapped deliberately and prematurely, in order to assure the Soviets that we will not retain a first-strike capability." Declaring that "the Administration is pursuing the theory that it is safer to be weak than to be strong," Admiral Ward concluded:

There are only two ways we can attempt to assure peace. One is to trust the Russians not to disturb it. The other way is to rely on our own military strength. It has become the fad in certain pacifist, pseudo-intellectual circles to say, "The only alternative to peace is annihilation."

Actually, the only alternative to annihilation is strength.

Another frightening analysis of McNamara's "defense" policy was made by Representative Donald Rumsfeld, Republican of Illinois, who summed it up for the U. S. House of Representatives in mid-September 1963: "The Department of Defense now does not have a single top-priority inner-space weapons program that would assure our security in the face of Soviet threat."

Senator Barry Goldwater—an Air Force reserve Major General—has done a clearsighted analysis of McNamara's disarmament doings, castigating "the great unrealistic push for disarmament at any cost" by the Defense Department civilians "while the Russians . . . an enemy which has sworn to destroy us . . . push ahead with a single-minded purpose of becoming supreme in all military spheres and dimensions." In a speech inserted into the *Congressional Record* of March 14, 1963, Senator Goldwater stated in part:

> Washington in his Farewell Address warned that our form of government could be attacked and destroyed by means other than a direct assault . . . This [disarmament] is an area of great importance to the American people because it directly affects the present and continued security of our Nation in a time of mortal conflict with an enemy which has sworn to destroy us . . . my fear that the course we are presently embarked upon is in the direction of unilateral disarmament . . . we find the United States seemingly hell-bent on accomplishment [of unilateral disarmament] without benefit of Russian reciprocity.
>
> The RS-70 [bomber] has been abandoned, Skybolt has been dropped, manned bombers are being phased out, Nike-Zeus is being delayed, and the Dyna-Soar program is being re-examined for possible junking.
>
> The reluctance of the Pentagon to push for development and production of the RS-70 program—even though all study groups in the Pentagon have recommended it and Congress has voted the necessary funds—has been a contributing factor in my conclusion that we are engaged in unilateral disarmament.
>
> Now, speaking of Skybolt, the air-to-ground missile that the British had been counting on . . . was abandoned at Nassau [Conference] without any consultation, so far as I can determine, with the Air Force, or with our NATO allies other than Great Britain.
>
> The audience might well ask, "Is it important?" Well, I can tell you that the majority of the military people, and I believe that includes a majority of the Joint Chiefs of Staff, think it is as important today as it was in March of 1961. And we might heed what the Russians are saying. An article distributed by the Soviet news agency Tass on February 21 of this year claimed that the Russians have "supersonic rocket-carrying aircraft capable of striking [United States] targets without entering their zone of anti-aircraft defense."
>
> It is important for us to understand that the Skybolt would

have done two things: it would have insured man's place in the air; and it would have given our Air Force and the Royal Air Force of Great Britain a weapon with which the enemy could be attacked from 360 degrees instead of the very few known degrees that ICBMs must travel, thus compounding his defense problem. This, like the RS-70, constituted a vehicle which could carry nuclear weapons. And it was abandoned on the basis of some mysterious computations arrived at by the civilian Pentagon.

We now get into the important area of space . . . Until recently our one official concession to the military possibilities of space was the Dyna-Soar program for manned spacecraft projects. This program called for the development of a piloted spacecraft which could be lifted into orbit by a Titan III rocket and glide back to earth on wings. To my way of thinking, it would add an important new dimension to the defense system, and one that we can rest assured the Russians are at this very moment attempting to master. But the latest reports gleaned from the Defense Secretary's testimony before the House Armed Services Committee, indicate that this important program may become the price of a new missile-armed bomber to follow the B-52. In other words, according to the press reports, if the Pentagon authorizes a new manned bomber it may cancel the Dyna-Soar.

This, of course, is no answer to the heavy criticism the Defense Department has been running into on Capitol Hill. The demand being raised in Congress for adequate defense is not subject to barter, or the trading of one weapons system for another. It is rather a demand for more defense options, for an over-all defense program that will provide us with a maximum of flexibility. This demand is for manned bombers as well as spacecraft. . .

Now if Pentagon cancels Dyna-Soar, as it did Skybolt, and then later changes signals on the development of new manned bombers again, the Air Force will have had it, once and for all. Then *aerospace superiority will pass unquestionably into the hands of the Russians.* [The Johnson Administration has since canceled Dyna-Soar and has not authorized any new manned bomber. *Author's note.*]

If there is one thing we can say for sure about the Pentagon these days with their slide rules, their electronic computers and their blinking lights—it is that they can change their minds faster about more important matters than any other group of planners in the world. They certainly change too fast for our allies to keep up, and I believe that we can find that the reason for much of the disarray in the Atlantic Community today is traceable directly to the Pentagon's inability to make up its mind on what weapons systems are best for the defense of the free world. We began with Skybolt, then switched to Polaris submarines, then switched to Polaris-carrying surface ships. We began with the RS-70, formerly known as the B-70, then switched to an all-missile concept . . . And as I have just pointed out, we began with Dyna-Soar and we are now talking about junking that for a souped-up Gemini. What comes next, I can't tell you. I don't think even the Pentagon's latest model of Univac has the answers as of this minute.

But I can tell you that one of the simplest ways for this Nation to disarm itself is to keep changing our minds every year about military concepts and weapons systems while the Russians push ahead with a single-minded purpose of becoming supreme in all military spheres and dimensions. . .

But I suggest that if the Pentagon thinkers are still holding to the idea of placing our strategic reliance on missiles when today's nuclear strike power finds the men and bombers of SAC responsible for about 90 per cent of our ability, then I suggest *we are traveling down a very dangerous road.*

. . . I can think of no weapon with less commandability and controllability than a missile already launched. On the other hand, the manned aircraft is completely commandable and controllable, *and presents the enemy with the gigantic problem of defending himself from all sectors—not just one.*

Who or what, for example, is going to tell our Commander in Chief what targets were hit and what targets were missed on enemy soil, unless it be the eyes and voice of a man in an aircraft? Certainly, the enemy is not going to cable us that we missed such-and-such a target and hit others. Extend this argument into space. If the enemy has, as they claim they have, a missile-carrying satellite, how can we expect to disarm it by seeing space only as an area to be pursued for peaceful purposes? Man has a place in space and I hope it does not require a Russian man in a weapons-carrying spacecraft to prove it to us in Sputnik fashion.

It is my firm conviction that when we begin concentrating on only what we in the United States can do to lessen the threat of nuclear escalation, we begin to think and act in terms of unilateral disarmament. *Our primary concern in the military field should always be with enemy capabilities and enemy inten-*

tions. It does us absolutely no good at all to think in terms of disarmament unless our yearning and our desire is reciprocated by the forces which have sworn to destroy us. And we have no reason to believe that the Soviets are engaging in anything but a propaganda marathon at Geneva.

So I believe we should stop thinking in terms of disarmament and start concentrating on what the Soviets are doing in the military field. There is no doubt at all that while the talking goes on at Geneva *and we offer one set of concessions after another the Russians are proceeding at top speed and with great determination in all armament areas.*

They are probing the military possibilities of space. They are concentrating on new and wider military options. They are improving their military capabilities in all spheres and placing their main dependence on the manned bomber. They aren't stinting on the development of missiles [as our Defense Department is doing]. They are going ahead with all types. But they are keeping their manned bombers, too, because this increases their flexibility and adds an important option to their military capabilities.

Over-all, the Russians are continuing to apply science and technology to military purposes with huge research and development programs . . . Let me emphasize that there is absolutely no evidence *of any kind* that the Soviets are cutting down the number of their existing weapons systems [as we are].

Let me remind you that for all the decisions and counter-decisions coming out of the Defense Department these days; for all the talk we hear about the efficiency and competence of the Secretary of Defense; for all the money that we are expending for military purposes—*not one new weapons system has been proposed under the present Administration.*

This is not only stagnation; but it is also disarmament. Inertia in defense matters, compounded by indecision and constantly changing concepts, is the same as spotting our enemy an advantage, a running start, if you please, *for the final confrontation.*

. . . as every expert whom I have ever heard speak on the matter has said in one way or another, "He who controls space will control the world." Those who feel that the risk of nuclear war is more real than the risk of not being strong can only see another engagement where triggers are pulled resulting immediately in an all-out nuclear war. These people fail to recognize that *we have been witnessing a world engaged in shooting wars ever since World War II, and there has been no escalation [into nuclear war].* This has been true because, first of all, I am convinced that neither side ever wants to escalate to the ICBM or the MRBM stage; and, second, because our vast superiority in methods of delivery *has driven the hardest facts of war home to the enemy.*

Robert McNamara's thinking on America's defenses was blatantly enunciated by himself on the pages of *The Saturday Evening Post* of December 1, 1962, in an interview with his personal friend and admirer, Stewart Alsop.

In this interview, McNamara, the U. S. Secretary of Defense—the man encharged with keeping America strong in the face of Soviet threat and attack—made the incredible statement that he believes this nation would be better off if the *Soviet Union* would *increase* its nuclear warfare arsenal.

As unbelievable as it seemed to readers, McNamara *lamented* the fact that the United States could wipe out Soviet Russia in one blow. In fact, he asserted that he hoped the Soviet Union would soon achieve "a sure second-strike capability," the sooner the better! This would mean, of course, that Russia could survive atomic attack and still wreak nuclear devastation on the United States.

In case these astonishing statements haven't "taken" at the first reading—what this means is that the United States Secretary of Defense aimed (and this was two years ago) at wiping out America's ability to destroy our enemy's nuclear forces with one blow, the single show of strength which prevents Soviet attack on the U. S.! Instead of the United States remaining stronger than Russia, the American Defense Secretary wants Soviet Russia to become at least as strong as the United States.

This is McNamara's "balance of terror" theory—nuclear stalemate between the United States and the U.S.S.R. Secretary McNamara was evidently not pleased with the fact that the "balance of terror" was balanced in favor of the United States, as it was when he made these statements.

And what has Mr. McNamara done to "unbalance" our

nuclear superiority—make Soviet Russia at *least* as strong as the United States, during the past two years? The answer can be summed up in the single frightening sentence:

Robert McNamara has not developed a single new American weapons system since he took office in January 1961!

Mr. McNamara's dedication to U. S. disarmament did not begin when he entered the Kennedy Administration in January 1961. He had long been an advocate of U. S. disarmament when he was chosen by President-elect Kennedy to head our Defense Department. For example, McNamara is a founding member of the Center for the Study of Democratic Institutions, located in Santa Barbara, California, which—according to its own literature and projects—is dedicated to the unilateral disarmament of the United States. Since the Center was founded, McNamara has contributed $1,000 a year to it.

When Robert McNamara came to the Defense Department he took steps to assure that his right-hand men would implement his disarmament strategy. He chose as his Special Assistant one Adam Yarmolinsky, former National Secretary of the left-wing Fund for the Republic—of which the chief operation is now the Center for the Study of Democratic Institutions. Yarmolinsky makes certain that no dissenting voices are heard in the disarmament of the Defense Department; he does the hiring and firing.

McNamara chose as his Assistant Secretary of Defense for International Security Affairs one Paul Nitze, who has publicly advocated that the United States should disarm *unilaterally*— i.e., whether or not the Russians disarm—because, Nitze says, this will "produce a reciprocal action" by Russia and "will slow down the arms race."

Does George Orwell's *1984* seem so fantastic now?

Under McNamara's regime, the Whiz Kid Defense Department planners have developed a new scheme to by-pass our military experts. The scheme will also transform our enormous defense budget—about one-half of the entire federal budget—into what one Washington newspaper explained as "a political, economic and social weapon," to be used as "a bludgeon in the hands of New Frontier politicos and social engineers."

The scheme is called "Project 60" and it discards the idea of purchasing weapons when they are needed. Instead, military hardware is to be purchased on the advice of "political commissars"—not on the advice of military experts.

Under Project 60, fifteen procurement officers—all political appointees of the New Frontier, none of them military experts, and only a few with any purchasing experience whatsoever—have been named to head 16 military purchasing regions throughout the country. Any area where the New Frontier needs votes, where unemployment is rising, or where anti-New Frontier rumblings are heard, will receive Defense Department orders for missiles, guns, weapons. The nation's defenses may need different weapons from the ones manufactured in the "emergency" area, but the Johnson Administration needs votes first and foremost; so, apparently, the public and our national security be damned.

The fact of Project 60's existence and its then-partial but fast-moving implementation was investigated and confirmed by Representative Earl Wilson of Indiana, after the plan was unearthed in October 1963. Representative Wilson, a member of the House Appropriations Committee and considered an expert on defense management, gave the following description of Project 60:

> If one of these procurement commissars decides his area could use a shot in the arm, he reports to McNamara, who, as you know, reports to the White House . . . If unemployment begins to rise, or if there is a desire to inject much money into a given area, the Pentagon will rush orders for weapons, missiles, etc. . . . Choosing when, where and from whom it will buy, the Pentagon can control raw material sources, manpower pools, and entire segments of the economy with its $53-billion baseball bat.

At this writing, the vast political power which can be wielded under Project 60 remains to be seen—and felt. Some American military men are privately terming the plan "a blueprint for suicide."

Just for good measure, the Defense Department is also using its vast budget to enforce integration and curry favor with Negroes. Representative Wilson noted, in discussing Project 60, that one Wisconsin manufacturing firm was denied a defense contract because the firm employed no Negroes. The defense firm explained that no Negroes lived in the town, or for miles around.

The reply that came back from the Defense Department: "Import some Negroes—if you want defense contracts."

While appearing before the House Defense Appropriations Subcommittee on February 6, 1963, Secretary McNamara consistently dodged questions about the disastrous Bay of Pigs invasion. For example, McNamara said the U. S. had made no plans to use American military forces to strike against Cuban Communists at the Bay of Pigs; but he refused to answer the question of whether or not U. S. forces had been committed to give military *air cover* to the anti-Communist invaders. In refusing to answer this question, McNamara left the clear implication in many minds that U. S. forces had indeed been committed to cover the ill-fated Cuban heroes, and that the promised air cover had been withdrawn, leaving hundreds of gallant men to be slaughtered on the beaches of their homeland which they were attempting to liberate.

Later in the hearings McNamara declared: "There were no *air strikes* by U. S. forces planned or contemplated or considered at any time." But at another point, speaking of the Cuba invasion plans, the U.S. Defense Secretary said: "I do not believe I am the proper authority to gain that information from," and revealed that he was not familiar with all the orders written at the White House with regard to Cuba.

While many U. S. Senators and Congressmen, as well as hordes of Cubans fleeing from the horrors of Castro's Communist regime, were offering evidence and testimony that Cuba was being carved into a nuclear bastion and as a base of operations to export communism to all of Latin America—and beyond, McNamara insisted: "I do not believe that it [Cuba] is being used as a base for the export of communism in any substantial degree today."

Later in his testimony, McNamara declared that the United States is not in a position to use its strength to defeat communism, stating: "We cannot win a nuclear war, a strategic nuclear war, in the normal meaning of the word 'win'."

Despite overwhelming evidence to the contrary, Secretary McNamara insisted that "at no time were the Intelligence reports seriously late, or in error, in reporting on the *offensive* weapons build-up in Cuba . . . nor late, nor substantially in error in reporting on the build-up of *defensive* weapons in Cuba."

Appearing before the subcommittee on the same day, General Maxwell D. Taylor, Chairman of the Joint Chiefs of Staff, refused to testify for or against the subcommittee's analysis of the Cuba invasion.

In fact, General Taylor revealed that his refusal to testify was made under White House aegis. When asked specifically by Representative Gerald Ford (Republican of Michigan) if he was invoking "Executive Privilege" in refusing to testify, General Taylor replied, "Yes, sir."

The tenor of the entire testimony by the Secretary of Defense and his civilian and military advisers was that the United States is moving into an era of mutual deterrence, into coexistence with communism.

Seeing the coexistence hallmark of the testimony after reading the transcript of the hearings, Representative Ford declared to the New Frontier witnesses:

"I refuse to accept that the competence, the quality and technical skill of the American people as a whole is insufficient to prevent from taking place this grim prospect which you describe . . . I am disappointed that we are not willing to gamble on our own competence and come up with some weapons systems both offensive and defensive that would prevent this from taking place."

Secretary McNamara also flip-flopped on his promise to

save more than three-quarters of a billion dollars during fiscal year 1963.

In July 1962, McNamara wrote to members of Congress: "On the basis of *actions initiated to date and reflected in our present budget request* before the Congress, we will save over $750 million *in fiscal year 1963.*"

Yet, when questioned sharply in 1963 by Representative Glenard Lipscomb of the Defense Appropriations Subcommittee about the promised savings which did not materialize in either the 1963 or 1964 budgets, Secretary McNamara replied: "I do not believe I wrote to the Congress making a statement of the kind you outlined. I believe I said that the actions we *hoped to take in fiscal 1963* would, *when completed,* bring annual savings of $750 million."

The Congressional committee was a little confused, since McNamara's letter had explicitly stated that the economy measures had already been initiated by 1962, and that the savings would be realized *in fiscal year 1963.*

Then, Secretary McNamara said that Defense Department economy measures taken through fiscal year 1964 would eventually "yield savings in excess of $2 billion per year," with "between a billion and a billion and a half of the savings . . . reflected in fiscal 1964."

By this time, the committee was thoroughly confused, because McNamara's Defense Department budget *increased* $1.3 billion in fiscal year 1963, and will rise *another* $2.7 billion in fiscal year 1964!

After hearing Secretary McNamara's statements, one Congressman said: "Rescue us from economies. I am glad that McNamara didn't decide to save $5 billion this year. If he had, we would be $10 billion more in debt!"

Another committee member confided to the author after hearing McNamara's testimony: "Each time I heard the Secretary snap out a new saving bigger than ever—when we know that Defense Department spending is actually growing by leaps and bounds—I saw the front of an Edsel gaping at me. I know McNamara was president of Ford Motor Company for only a few days before he was called to Washington; but I also know that McNamara and his Ford research and development people actually led the fight for the Edsel, according to men in the automobile industry."

The loss to Ford of Robert S. McNamara has been a highly questionable gain to the U. S. Department of Defense. Some would say that, through McNamara, both Ford and the American public have lost.

The man who "oversees the operation of all scientifically oriented agencies [of the federal government], such as the Defense Department," according to the New York *Times,* is Jerome B. Wiesner, who was chosen by Kennedy as Special Assistant to the President for Science and Technology.

In his role as the Administration's top scientific planner, Wiesner wields enormous power over the critical government agencies concerned with our nation's defenses—the Pentagon, the Atomic Energy Commission and the National Science Foundation, to name a few. The *Times* article, dated September 3, 1961, explained Wiesner's powers:

> Dr. Jerome Bert Wiesner, a former professor at the Massachusetts Institute of Technology . . . is the top planner, arbitrator and counselor of scientific policy within the Government, and thus, throughout the scientific community at large. . . Wiesner oversees the operations of all scientifically oriented agencies, such as the Defense Department, Atomic Energy Commission and National Science Foundation. . .
>
> [He] operates behind a wall of White House secrecy, somewhat to the dismay of Congress which would like to be privy to his scientific policy advice . . .
>
> Before joining the Administration, Wiesner made no secret of his belief that the United States at times had been almost as much to blame as the Soviet Union for blocking agreement on arms-control measures . . .

A story on Wiesner in the *Saturday Review* of December 10, 1960, before President Kennedy took office, emphasized that Wiesner "looks upon arms control as almost a crusade," and quotes him as asserting that although "any arms agreement with the Soviets may carry calculated risks, science must develop such an overwhelming case in support of the soundness of the calculated risk philosophy, that the fearful politician will have nothing left to hide behind."

Translated, this means that the chief scientific adviser to the President and to the federal government believes we should take a calculated risk by disarming and making an "agreement" on the chance that a nation which is sworn to destroy us will also disarm!

According to the official biography of Detroit-born, University of Michigan-educated Jerome Wiesner, he has "participated in numerous national and international informal conferences on the subject of disarmament." The fact is that Wiesner has also participated in at least one *formal* disarmament conference which has proven vitally important to the American people.

In November 1960, immediately after the Presidential election, President-elect Kennedy sent Wiesner and Walt Rostow to Moscow, to the Sixth Pugwash Disarmament Conference of American and Soviet scientists. On returning to Washington, after attending the conference and meeting in Moscow with a Soviet official, Rostow wrote for Kennedy a blueprint "position paper" on Administration defense policy, directing that the U. S. scrap its first-strike nuclear weapons in order to "relieve tensions" between the United States and Russia. According to the Chicago *Tribune's* crack reporter, Thomas B. Ross, "Rostow's advice reverberated in Kennedy's first defense message" to the nation. Ross adds that the White House meetings, where the defense speech was written, were directed by President Kennedy's Special Counsel, Theodore Sorenson, who, incidentally, was a conscientious objector during the Korean War.

At the Moscow disarmament conference Wiesner delivered a speech on November 29 which might curl the hair of less "sophisticated" Americans who want the United States to remain as strong as possible in order to deter Soviet aggression against us.

Wiesner urged the Soviet Union to *increase* its nuclear arsenal, so that Soviet Russia could defend itself against American nuclear attack! Wiesner urged this increase of Russia's military strength, even though one of the cornerstones of American military philosophy is that we are a peaceful nation and will never strike first.

Moreover, Wiesner gave detailed instructions to the Soviet scientists on how they could protect their own missile sites, in order to protect themselves against American nuclear attack and thus survive for a retaliatory strike *against the United States!* At the same time, he urged the United States to scrap our first-strike intercontinental bombers!

Wiesner also told the Soviet scientists that he is firmly opposed to America's deploying an anti-missile system of defense throughout our nation to protect the American people. Wiesner's reason: it would "unbalance" the nuclear balance of power in favor of the United States!

"What, truly, could be more insane?" asked political analyst Allan H. Ryskind of Washington's *Human Events* in reporting Wiesner's speech. Carried to its logical conclusion, this "balance of terror" theory of Wiesner's (and McNamara, and Yarmolinsky, and Nitze), that America would be better off if the Soviets are at least as strong as the United States, would mean, Ryskind points out, that "we should erect a national monument to Julius and Ethel Rosenberg for stealing our atomic secrets and giving them to the Soviets!"

In any case, the Soviets do not appear concerned about unbalancing the "balance of terror" in their favor: early in 1963 they deployed a fully operational anti-missile installation near Leningrad as a starter in protecting *their* population against nuclear missile attack. On the other hand, Wiesner has succeeded in his promise to keep America from deploying anti-missile defenses for protecting the American people. On June 23, New York *Herald Tribune* reporters Earl Ubell and Stuart H. Loory revealed in *The Saturday Evening Post* that Wiesner had persuaded President Kennedy to shelve deployment of our successfully tested Nike-Zeus missile. The reporters added Wiesner's own words to Kennedy: "Don't deploy Nike-Zeus. . . . Keep it in research and development."

Also under Wiesner's guiding hand, the Kennedy Administration dismantled most of the 68 DEW Line stations which spanned the reaches of the North American continent. The purpose of our DEW Line stations: to alert the United States and Canada to Soviet attack. In addition, we are deferring development of our vital anti-missile missile, which is our key defense against Soviet nuclear missile attack. It might be noted here that, although the word "disarmament" normally connotes an image of ships being scuttled, planes, rockets, tanks and guns being destroyed, and ammunition being dumped into the sea, in today's world the disarmament of a mighty nation can be just as surely achieved by not improving its existing weapons and by its failing to develop new weapons.

Jerome Wiesner's concentration on disarmament is merely one more proof that our Defense Department has taken up the disarmament policy developed by the President's advisers at the State Department and in the White House.

Wiesner also scolds us silly Americans for fancying that those Soviets are big, bad bogeymen. Why, they must be no such thing, since Wiesner chides the West for "always" being "suspicious of Soviet proposals." This silly Western suspicion of the Soviets leads us to do silly things—such as wanting to make sure the Soviets are disarming while we disarm. As Wiesner phrases it, our "suspicion of Soviet proposals" makes us "ultraconservative in the inspection requirements it places upon any system" of disarmament.

Well, anyway, Mr. Wiesner's worry over America's neurotic "suspicions" of those peace-loving Soviets ("mellowing" Russian leaders—in the Administration's official terminology) seems to be ended since Wiesner wrote those words in 1960, because we have now signed the completely unpoliced "limited" nuclear test-ban treaty with the Russians on atmospheric and outer-space testing (the latter cannot be detected at all), which is, as the late President Kennedy asserted, a disarmament treaty. We are further overcoming our "suspicions" of the Soviets by whittling down to zero our on-site inspection demands for the underground nuclear test-ban treaty which the Administration will soon sign with Russia.

And as soon as we have signed the "nonaggression pact with Russia," for which President Johnson is pushing hard at this writing, we will join the honor roll of the East European nations whose "advanced thinkers" spurred them into signing pacts of peace with the peace-loving Soviets. Curiously enough, those same nations were soon smashed by the Soviets' "clenched fist," exactly as Dimitri Manuilsky had joyously predicted in 1931. Or, as Lenin neatly phrased it in instructing his Bolsheviks and in prophesying the master plan for Communist world conquest:

> Promises are like pie crusts—made to be broken . . . We have to use any ruse, dodge, trickery, cunning, unlawful method, concealment and veiling of the truth.
>
> First, we will take Eastern Europe. Then, the masses of Asia. Then we will encircle the United States, which will be the last bastion of Capitalism. We will not have to attack. It will fall like an overripe fruit into our hands.

Since 1917 the Communists have conquered one-third of the world, officially, and vast sectors of the earth are now tobogganing into the Communist orbit. The deadline for final conquest of the entire world, laid down by Lenin and his lieutenants, is 1973.

In case the West should believe that Nikita Khrushchev is a "mellow" successor to Stalin, and that he has abandoned the Communists' primary and unyielding goal of world conquest avidly pursued by every Communist leader from Marx to Lenin to Stalin, Khrushchev—true to the *Communist Manifesto* dictate that "Communists disdain to conceal their aims"—has reminded us:

> If anyone thinks that our smiles mean the abandonment of the teachings of Marx, Engels and Lenin, he is deceiving himself cruelly. Those who expect this to happen might just as well wait for a shrimp to learn how to whistle.

And still the leaders of our Administration pursue their

suicidal program of disarming the United States, because, they tell us, the Soviet leaders are "mellowing."

Yet, the complete story at the Pentagon is even more far-reaching than this. In the summer of 1961, while the Administration focused the national spotlight upon Major General Edwin Walker, lateral civilian control of the military was foisted almost unnoticed upon key field commands and key Pentagon officers. Unnoticed, that is, until the blow of discharge fell upon Admiral George W. Anderson, Chief of Staff of the Navy, and came within a hair's breadth of striking General Curtis LeMay, Chief of Staff of the Air Force, in the same swoop. LeMay, however was given a "brief" extension of duty to keep his views out of the 1964 Presidential campaign.

In the United States, civilian control of the military has traditionally been from the top—from the President and the Service Secretaries. However, while no one was looking, "political advisers" were planted with all major commands such as SAC (Strategic Air Command), responsible for dealing our counterblow if the Soviets should launch an attack, and with the Pacific Fleet.

Edward L. Freers, former State Department Counselor to Moscow, went to SAC, while other hand-picked men were sent to all other vital military commands to complement the work of Freers—an ultracautious type of diplomat. Moreover, the system has been used to punish at least one two-fisted diplomat. Clare Timberlake was exiled to relatively unimportant Maxwell Field as punishment for bucking the Kennedy Administration on Katanga when he was U. S. Ambassador to the Congo. Civilian overseers were also placed with every important admiral, and Air Force and Army general in the Pentagon.

This unprecedented lateral control of the military is remarkably comparable to the commissar system used in Soviet Russia. Under the Soviet system, a political spy is placed with each field commander. Khrushchev, for example, was the commissar assigned to watch Marshal Zhukov. (Incidentally, Zhukov is now head of the Soviets' so-called "cultural exchange" program with the United States, the purpose of which is, in the

words of the U.S.S.R.'s "cultural exchange" commission itself,
to implant Soviet propaganda in the minds of Americans visiting Soviet Russia, and to diffuse Soviet propaganda in the
United States through Soviet groups visiting our shores. These
"cultural" so-called exchanges, made possible by the first Summit Conference in 1955, have certainly succeeded in dispelling
the idea of a Soviet slave state from the minds of many Americans—notwithstanding the fact that Russian ballet dancers,
shot-putters and basketball players defect to the glorious free
world from the not-so-glorious Soviet Union every chance they
get. The American Bar Association did a fine analysis of so-
called "cultural exchanges" in 1958 under their proper heading: "Communist Tactics, Strategy and Objectives.")

In his speech to the Twentieth Congress of the Communist
Party in 1953, Khrushchev showed that the civilian Stalin was
not much of a military strategist, even though he donned a
flashy Soviet uniform, dubbed himself "Marshal Stalin," and
proceeded to make all of Soviet Russia's major military decisions and many minor ones.

Khrushchev actually made an excellent case for a nation's
not allowing civilians to dominate military experts, since he
pointed out that having the civilian Stalin as Soviet Russia's
military overlord unnecessarily cost Russia millions of lives and
much territory (most of which territory they won back at the
conference tables with Roosevelt after the war). The pudgy
little Communist then illustrated his point by saying that Stalin
had turned down one of Nikita's own recommendations from
the field when Khrushchev telephoned him. Apparently Stalin
did not think Nikita (who did not learn to read or write until
he was 26 years old) was a better strategist than himself, because Stalin would not even come to the telephone, Khrushchev
told the Congress with great indignation.

More rigid civilian control over the U. S. military came on
June 21, 1963, when the late President Kennedy sanctioned
the Gesell Report, a set of civilian committee recommendations
which are transforming U. S. military bases in this country into

an instrument of political and social pressure, under the guise of ending racial discrimination in the armed forces.

On that date, President Kennedy wrote to Washington attorney Gerhard Gesell, Chairman of the President's Committee on Equal Opportunity in the Armed Forces: "Your recommendations should have the immediate attention of the Department of Defense and I have asked the Secretary of Defense to report to me on your recommendations within thirty days."

Kennedy urged Secretary McNamara to give the Gesell Report his prompt attention, and Kennedy summarized it as being "in the spirit that I believe should characterize our approach to this matter." McNamara did give the report his "prompt attention" and within about one month began implementing it by issuing to military commanders a series of Defense Department directives based on the Gesell Report.

The 93-page Gesell Report, entitled "Equality of Treatment and Opportunity for Negro Military Personnel Stationed Within the United States," recommended that:

More Negroes should be recruited into the U. S. armed forces. More Negroes should be placed on promotion boards. Negro soldiers should be prohibited from gravitating to one military base service club, and white soldiers to another.

The report stipulates that more Negro hostesses should be hired for service clubs, and adds, "In addition, more Negro girls should be secured for dances."

More significant, however, is the section of the Gesell Report dealing with relations between military base commanders and local communities:

Unintegrated business establishments should be placed off-limits to all military personnel. Homes should be leased in the name of the federal government and Negroes moved into them. Segregated buses should be boycotted. ROTC units in segregated schools should be canceled. Local civic clubs should not be joined if they do not admit Negroes.

Special officers with bi-racial staffs should be appointed on every military base to handle all complaints of Negro servicemen. Base commanders should appoint in their communities joint Negro-white committees to break down local segregation practices.

The traditional function of the military base commander to run his military establishment and to stay out of local controversies should be voided. The base commanders should be encouraged to lead the way to racial homogenization.

And should all these efforts fail, the Gesell Report recommends, the military commander must consider either curtailing activities at his installation *or closing his military base.*

What may prove the most significant facet of the Gesell Report is the report's recommendation to establish "political adviser" liaisons directly between Negro servicemen and the Defense Department. Circumventing the centuries-old chain-of-command discipline, Negro servicemen believing they have been discriminated against should report their complaints directly to "visiting personnel from the Department of Defense" who will make "periodic field checks" under a "monitor" system. Reports of these complaints are to be funneled directly to the Defense Department. This is now being done on military bases throughout the nation.

The Gesell Report stipulates that the identity of the accuser remain anonymous, and that *the accused not be allowed to face his accuser.*

If military base commanders balk at implementing the Gesell Report on their installations and at injecting themselves into local community customs, the report reminds them: "Achievements in dealing with such problems will be considered in rating their performance of duty and in promotion selection." Anyone who has ever served in the armed forces knows that, translated, these words mean that any military man who refuses to carry out the Gesell Report directives will find his military career dead.

What the Gesell Report, with its dizzying ramifications, will do to lower the morale of American troops, to undermine military discipline, and to lower respect for U. S. military officers and superiors can only be surmised at this writing.

A storm of protest was immediately raised in Congress. The real reason for the Gesell Report and its subsequent Defense Department directives, a host of Congressmen pointed out, is political. "Forget segregation, forget integration," said one Congressman. "It is the principle of using the military might and power of this country to enforce a political philosophy of the Administration that is in power at the moment." Representative Melvin R. Laird of Wisconsin added: "All citizens should be granted equal opportunity, but this is abuse of power by the Secretary of Defense and his Department."

Another Congressman pointed out that the Gesell Report and its Defense Department directives make official policy "not equal opportunity, but preference for Negro servicemen, who comprise less than ten per cent of our armed forces." He asked: "Where is there anything in this Gesell Report to protect the rights of white servicemen, who comprise 90 per cent of our armed forces?"

And who wrote the Gesell Report? The report was purportedly written by the seven-man President's Committee on Equal Opportunity in the Armed Forces, of which Washington lawyer Gerhard Gesell is chairman. However, the House of Representatives learned on August 7, 1963, that Gerhard Gesell is merely a protocol chairman for the President's committee.

The report was actually written by a member of the Gesell Report committee, Nathaniel S. Colley of Sacramento, who is a Negro and an official of the NAACP in California.

In addition, the House learned, there are two other Negroes on the Gesell Report committee; and all seven men on the committee are members of either the NAACP or the ADA.

Some other interesting items concerning this Gesell Report committee were brought to light in Congress:

Gerhard Gesell, the protocol chairman, helped to write the whitewash of the 1945 and 1946 Pearl Harbor investigation, when he was a member of the Committee of Investigation on the Pearl Harbor Attack;

Abe Fortas—one of President Johnson's closest personal friends and advisers, the man whom President Johnson may name as the next U. S. Attorney General—is a Washington attorney with a dizzying record of defending in court and at Congressional investigations, men who have been under attack as Communists. One of Abe Fortas' famous clients was Owen Lattimore, who was indicted by a Washington grand jury on six specific counts of perjury for lying about his espionage acts, while testifying under oath to the Senate Internal Security Subcommittee. Lattimore's attorney during these Senate hearings was none other than Abe Fortas. Other luminaries whom Abe Fortas has assisted are Soviet agents Alger Hiss and Harry Dexter White, to name only two. Abe Fortas helped Hiss and White to draft the UN Charter.

The entire Gesell Report is fast being put into action by Defense Department directives, and there are more "Gesell Reports" to come. The committee's letter of transmittal to President Kennedy stipulated that theirs was "an initial report" which covered only "the work of the committee during its first year of existence."

Secretary McNamara started to implement the Gesell Report proposals on July 26, 1963, about one month after President Kennedy had publicly praised it and urged that McNamara give it his prompt attention.

On the date, Secretary McNamara issued his first Defense Department directive based on the Gesell Report, by directing military base commanders to declare "off limits" to all servicemen any business establishments in the base commanders' local communities where racial discrimination is allegedly practiced. (Another directive aims at integrating Southern schools; and still another directive canceled all Pentagon contracts with morticians who would not agree to embalm both white and Negro dead. It appears that the Defense Department is bent on womb-to-tomb integration.)

Since thousands of business establishments near military bases depend almost entirely upon servicemen's business, this means a use of coercion against them, a "conform-or-close-shop" ultimatum. Angry Congressmen protested on behalf of their constituents who run businesses near military bases. Democratic Senator John Stennis protested that a military base commander, using the power of this Defense Department directive, could exert unheard-of economic pressures by prohibiting his servicemen from being customers of particular business establishments in his area. If the power of a military base commander "can be used to influence the social and political life of the people in the area where the base is located," Stennis pointed out, "he can also influence a particular election in the area when it comes. Thus," Stennis emphasized, "a base commander could soon amass social, political and economic power of sufficient strength to be the dominating force in a community or area.

"Such a system operating in a chain of base commanders," Stennis pointed out, "could generate dictatorial power beyond control."

Many observers feel that this summation by Stennis—"dictatorial power beyond control"—is the key to the Gesell Report. It is believed that, under the guises of "racial equality" directives in the military sphere and of "Civil Rights" legislation in the civic sphere, "dictatorial power beyond control" is being foisted on the American people.

On August 15, 1963, Defense Department Directive 5120.27 was issued, implementing the Gesell Report proposal of the "monitor" system for receiving Negroes' complaints at every military installation in the country. Short-circuiting the time-honored military chain-of-command, Defense Department personnel are assigned full-time to make periodic field checks at every military base, to receive Negroes' complaints and channel them directly to the Defense Department's newly established "political adviser" liaison in the person of Alfred B. Fitt, appointed Deputy Assistant Secretary of Defense for Civil Rights. (Mr. Fitt's only previous claim to fame is that he was legal adviser to ex-Governor "Soapy" Williams of Michigan.) The Defense Department directive adds that anyone "who forbids, or in any way attempts to discourage, the presentation of a complaint" is subject to disciplinary action.

Representative George W. Andrews asserted that the designers of this monitor system "have copied experts—a system which has proved its efficiency and effectiveness. The Soviets have had just such a system since the beginning of the Russian Revolution in 1917. It is directed by a man known as the 'political commissar,' whose business it is to watch all military commanders and to report to another agency on their manner of performance of duty."

The effect of this directive on U. S. military life and discipline was summed up by Representative Rivers, ranking Democratic majority member of the House Armed Services Committee: "Never in my 23 years as a member of this body have I seen anything approximating this and its impact upon the future of military commanders."

Who is actually writing this continuing series of Defense Department directives based on the Gesell Report? Although the directives are signed by Secretary McNamara, they are being written by Adam Yarmolinsky, Special Assistant to the Secretary of Defense. The House learned this from Representative F. Edward Hébert of Louisiana during its lengthy and stormy August 7 analysis of the Gesell Report and its subsequent Defense Department directives. Mr. Hébert had done extensive sleuthing into the Defense Department directives and their author:

> I make that statement with no qualifications. Do not let anybody ask me to prove it, if they do not want to have a red face afterward. Mr. Yarmolinsky has one objective in mind—with an almost satanic-like zeal—the forced integration of every facet of the American way of life, using the full power of the Defense Department to bring about this change . . .
>
> I want to tell you something about this Yarmolinsky. I would not repeat this except I repeat it on good authority. He was down in Florida [during the so-called Cuban Crisis, when armed forces were brought into Florida in great numbers], and he ordered the troops integrated in certain hotels that the military had rented. He was informed that the Negroes did not want to be integrated. He said he did not give a damn whether they wanted to be integrated or not, that they would be integrated.

Representative Melvin R. Laird of Wisconsin, who has

served on the advisory boards of West Point, Annapolis and the Air Force Academy, noted that in 1961 Adam Yarmolinsky asked that the military service academies, particularly Annapolis, drop their competitive entrance examinations in favor of "special examinations" which would give "preference" to Negroes. The Congressman added: "This went far beyond 'equal opportunity'."

Who is Adam Yarmolinsky, who bears the title of Special Assistant to the Secretary of Defense—but who is known in Washington inner circles as the "Uncrowned King of the Pentagon"? In the Defense Department Yarmolinsky handles appointments and patronage, and in connection with the hiring and firing of Defense Department personnel, his "yes" is definite and his "no" absolute.

It was shortly after Yarmolinsky arrived in the Pentagon that lateral civilian control was foisted on our leaders, a control which General Douglas MacArthur has described as so inordinate that members of the armed forces have been subjected to the most arbitrary and ruthless treatment for daring to speak the truth in accordance with conviction and conscience.

Yarmolinsky's entrance into the Pentagon also coincided with the start of the muzzling of our military leaders, especially Generals White and LeMay, and later Admirals Burke and Anderson. Then, by clever appointment of conscientious and respected military experts to honorary but meaningless government positions, the New Frontier kept even former members of the Joint Chiefs of Staff from going on record before the public without "prior censorship."

Yarmolinsky appears to have extended his hiring role beyond the confines of the Pentagon. In fact, sources close to both the State Department and the A.I.D. foreign aid agency assert that Yarmolinsky has recommended many employees (most turning out to be woefully inadequate as government workers) in both setups. This is but one of several examples illustrating the close tie-in between policies of State and Defense under the New Frontier.

During the 1960 Presidential campaign, Adam Yarmolinsky became a paid consultant to Candidate Kennedy's brother-in-law, R. Sargent Shriver. Together the two men drew up a list of lawyers, largely left-wingers, now spotted in key decision-making positions throughout the government.

Let us take a close look at Adam Yarmolinsky, the powerful Number Two man in our Defense Department, who is known as the "Uncrowned King of the Pentagon." Today, one of the few available biographical sketches of Adam Yarmolinsky (from the April 1961, issue of *Harper's* magazine) gives only the following information on his background:

> Adam Yarmolinsky, a lawyer and consultant to a number of foundations, last year prepared a report for the Edgar Stern Family Fund called "The Recognition of Excellence." He served in the Air Force in World War II, was formerly secretary to the Fund for the Republic, and is now special assistant to the Secretary of Defense.

Brief words indeed about the man responsible for many of our policies in the State Department as well as Defense Department matters. Yet it is the biography sent by the Library of Congress in response to requests by members of the Senate and House for information about Yarmolinsky.

But a more detailed biography would show that the family circle in which Adam Yarmolinsky was reared in New York City is a most interesting one, since both his parents have a star-studded history of service to Communist causes which can be traced back at least 36 years. Let us take a glance at each of his parents.

Adam Yarmolinsky's mother, who uses her maiden name, Babette Deutsch, was born in New York City in 1895 and graduated from Barnard College. She then taught English at Columbia University, and for years she has been a translator with her husband of books from Russian into English, a co-author with her husband, and an author in her own right.

Adam's father, Avrahm Yarmolinsky, was born in Russia in 1890, attended the University of St. Petersburg (now Leningrad), came to the United States in 1913 after a stopover in Switzerland to graduate from the University of Neuchatel. He attended the city-supported City College of New York and has taught Russian in New York colleges. He returned to Russia for a time during 1923 and 1924. From 1918 to 1955 he was chief of the Slavonic Division of the New York Public Library.

The father maintained close contacts with the early Soviet consuls and other Soviet Government officials in New York, but he has denied being their adviser. He explains that, rather, he had dealings with them in connection with his work at the New York Public Library.

In 1928 Avrahm Yarmolinsky wrote a startlingly pro-Soviet book as one in a nine-part series for Vanguard Publishing Company's *Vanguard Studies of Soviet Russia*. The series was edited by Jerome Davis, one of the best-known Soviet apologists in the history of the United States, who belonged to more than 100 Communist front organizations, and who was named by the Senate Internal Security Subcommittee as a typical sponsor of Communist front organizations. Babette Deutsch wrote the final book, *Art and Culture in Soviet Russia,* in this blatantly pro-Soviet series.

In the opening lines of his book, Avrahm Yarmolinsky wrote: "The French revolution proclaimed the liberty, the equality, the fraternity of all men. The Russian revolution proclaimed the liberty, the equality, the fraternity of all peoples."

Adam Yarmolinsky's mother and father have for years worked jointly as authors, and as translators of Russian books for International Publishers in New York City. This publishing firm was cited by the Special Committee on Un-American Activities of the U. S. House of Representatives as the "official publishing house of the Communist Party" and as "a medium of thought through which extensive Soviet propaganda is subsidized in the United States." The U. S. Attorney General, in his brief in the case against William Schneiderman, cited International Publishers as "the publishing agency of the Communist Party." The parents now direct their joint efforts toward children, Iron Curtain folk tales, published by Harper and Row.

At least as early as 1930, Adam Yarmolinsky's parents

were top-ranking members of the John Reed Clubs of the United States, named after one of the founders of the Communist Party, U.S.A. and the only American buried inside the walls of the Kremlin itself. On page 561 of Volume One of the Dies Committee Report it is stated: "All the John Reed Club leaders are engaged in revolutionary activity."

On May 19, 1930, both parents signed a full-page advertisement in the New York *Times* protesting the then current attacks on Communists and terming the attacks "Red-baiting." The sponsor of this advertisement was the John Reed Club Affiliate of the International Union of Revolutionary Writers, of which both parents were members.

Adam's mother, Babette Deutsch, also has to her credit the following *partial* listing of service for Communist causes, which shows her to be a sponsor or prime mover in many of them:

> 1933 . . . Member of National Committee to Aid the Striking Miners. Working with Babette Deutsch on this committee were Eliot White (champion of the Communist *Daily Worker*) and Robert Dunn, both identified as Communists in Congressional reports.
>
> October 3, 1936 . . . Member, as shown on letterhead, of the Non-Partisan Committee for the Re-election of Congressman Vito Marcantonio, a well known Communist. This was cited as a Communist front operation by the House Special Committee on Un-American Activities.
>
> 1937 . . . Writer for the magazine *Soviet Russia Today,* cited by the Senate Internal Security Subcommittee as "a Communist-controlled publication."
>
> 1937 . . . Sponsor of Writers' and Artists' Committee for Medical Aid to Spain, which aided Communist revolutionaries in that country. Cited as "a Communist front organization" by the House Special Committee on Un-American Activities.
>
> 1937 . . . Sent greetings to Mother Bloor 75th Birthday Celebration of that veteran top-echelon Communist.
>
> 1941 . . . Affiliated with the National Federation for Constitutional Liberties. (This organization was launched in Washington, D. C., June 6 & 7, 1940, at the Conference on Constitutional Liberties in America, cited as a Communist front. One of the sponsors of this organization was Arthur Goldberg, who was

chosen by President Kennedy to be an Associate Justice of the Supreme Court, after first serving as Kennedy's Secretary of Labor.

(It is interesting to note here, also, that Arthur Goldberg was a sponsor of the National Emergency Conference which met in Washington May 13 & 14, 1939, to map strategy against a number of bills then in Congress which would deport all Communist aliens, and enforce registration, fingerprinting and imprisonment of American Communists. Of course, this was cited as a Communist operation. In 1939, Arthur Goldberg was president of the Chicago Chapter of the National Lawyers Guild, which has been cited as the legal arm of the Communist Party. Also in 1939, Goldberg sponsored the Chicago Conference on Race Relations, which has been repeatedly cited as a Communist front operation. In 1957, Goldberg was a member of the executive board of the National Religion and Labor Foundation, cited as a Communist front, which once printed on the cover of its publication a picture of Jesus Christ, with the following: "Wanted for Sedition, Criminal Anarchy, Vagrancy, and Conspiring to Overthrow the Established Government.")

1941 . . . Sponsor of the Citizens Committee for Harry Bridges, formed to oppose the deportation of the veteran Red leader as an alien Communist. This organization was cited by the U. S. Attorney General as a Communist front. Serving on the committee with Babette Deutsch were a number of persons who have been identified as Communists, such as Paul Robeson, John Howard Lawson and Rockwell Kent.

1943 . . . Signer of a message to Congress demanding the abolition of the House Committee on Un-American Activities, which ferrets out Communists. The petition was released under the auspices of the National Federation for Constitutional Liberties which was cited as "subversive and Communist" by the Attorney General of the U.S.

May 17, 1951 . . . Signer of a petition to President Truman opposing any military aid to Spain or alliance with that nation, which had crushed the Communist armed revolution. (*Daily Worker*, May 17, 1951, pages 2 & 9).

May 12, 1961 . . . Sponsor of a meeting of the Conference of Greater New York Peace Groups. This organization was composed of many identified Communists who had been eliminated from the National Committee for a Sane Nuclear Policy, after the revelations of Senator Dodd.

January 29 to February 4, 1962 . . . Sponsor of the "General Strike for Peace," which attempted to organize world-wide "work stoppage" for "peace" during that period. A general strike is a very radical weapon. This is the same organization which flooded Congress with letters urging the ratification of the Moscow Test-Ban Treaty in the autumn of 1963.

February 22, 1962 ... Signer of a full-page advertisement in The New York *Times* which demanded the abolition of the House Committee on Un-American Activities. Co-signers with Babette Deutsch included: Russ Nixon, Elmer Benson, Ernest DeMaio, Rose Russell, Joseph Barnes, Philip Evergood, Rockwell Kent, Claude Williams, Corliss Lamont, Harvey O'Connor, Lee Lorch, Otto Nathan, Dirk Struik, William Spofford and David Rein—all of whom have been identified as Communists.

Adam Yarmolinsky's father, Avrahm, has an equally interesting history, in addition to that already described. In 1937, Avrahm was a *sponsor* and *member of the Board of Directors* of the American Russian Institute for Cultural Relations with the Soviet Union, which has been cited by the Senate Internal Security Subcommittee as "A Communist-controlled organization which was intimately linked with the Institute of Pacific Relations" (IPR). The office of the U. S. Attorney General cited it as "a communist organization," not merely a Communist front.

Yarmolinsky *pére* was an *adviser* and later *Vice Chairman of the Executive Committee* of the American Pushkin Committee, which has been cited as a Communist front operation. Also serving on the Executive Committee with Avrahm Yarmolinsky were identified Communists W.E.B. DuBois, Corliss Lamont, Paul Robeson, Rockwell Kent and others.

Yarmolinsky *fils* says that the views of his parents never influenced him, even as a youth, and that his "public record" is in opposition to communism. This is accepted. Nevertheless, his public record is interesting to many observers.

During his college days at Harvard, Adam Yarmolinsky was head of the Marxist Club. He was a founding member and on the editorial staff of the Marxist magazine *Yardling,* which presented to students the viewpoint of the Young Communist League.

After graduating from Harvard in 1943, Adam found himself in the Army Air Corps until 1946. While he was in the service, the Army held an investigation into his left-wing background and his leftist leanings at college.

After Adam's name was brought up as a former aficionado of the Communist Youth League, at the Senate Armed Services Committee investigations into the muzzling of the U. S. Military in April 1962, Yamolinsky did not ask to appear under oath before the Senate committee to answer the charges against him. Instead, he issued a statement to the press—published in the Washington *Evening Star*—admitting that he had attended meetings of the Communist Youth League, but that he had done so because he was "curious." In 1941, while a Harvard student, Adam attended the American Youth Congress, which was cited in 1947 by the U. S. Attorney General as follows: "It originated in 1934 and has been controlled by Communists and manipulated by them to influence the thought of American youth."

Yarmolinsky also solicited funds for Spanish War Relief, an organization formed by the Young Communist League to aid Spanish Communist revolutionaries in that nation.

Adam graduated from Yale Law School in 1948, and from 1950 to 1951 he was law clerk to Supreme Court Associate Justice Stanley Reed. From 1951 to 1955, he was in law practice with the law firm of George Ball, now Under Secretary of State.

From 1955 to 1957, Yarmolinsky first directed the Washington operations of the multimillion-dollar Fund for the Republic as its Vice President, and became National Secretary of the Fund.

The Fund for the Republic, a branch of the Ford Foundation, has been described thus by news columnist and broadcaster Fulton Lewis, Jr.;

> The Fund for the Republic is the most anti-anti-Communist organization in the country. It is dedicated to the destruction of the House Committee on Un-American Activities, the Senate Internal Security Subcommittee, and all other groups who are

opposed to communism and who want to do something about exposing it.

A few of the expensive studies made and published by the Fund include: "A Community Under Pressure from Right-Wing Pressure Groups," which details the so-called horrors faced by a community in which conservative and anti-Communist groups try to expose the Communist records and backgrounds of certain of its citizens; "Foreign Political Propaganda Restraints," which deplored the government ban on Russian and other Communist propaganda shipped into the United States. (This study appears to have had the desired effect, because on March 17, 1961, only two months after he came into office, President Kennedy personally issued an order lifting the ban on Communist propaganda shipped into this country.) Another Fund for the Republic study is entitled, "Anti-Communism and Employment Practices in Radio and Television." This study deplored denying jobs in radio and television to identified Communists and fellow-travelers—so-called "blacklisting"—where they are in a position to influence the thinking of millions of Americans. This will give readers of this book some small idea of how the vast riches of the big tax-free foundations are being spent—notably those of the Ford, Rockefeller and Carnegie foundations with their many subsidiaries.

One of the Fund for the Republic's biggest studies was done by Adam Yarmolinsky, and it was quite in keeping with the Fund's tradition of warning the nation about the alleged horrors of anti-Communist efforts. In fact, Yarmolinsky's study —which cost a whopping $192,710, and for which Yarmolinsky received a reported $100,000 grant—has been used by leftists as a general policy paper for attacking the federal loyalty and security program. For example, in 1960, the Fund published a pamphlet entitled *Community of Fear,* written by Harrison Brown and James Real, which detailed the horrors of anti-Communist "pressures."

Interestingly enough, this pamphlet received lavish praise from both the Communist *Worker* and the Soviet Army newspaper, *Red Star,* which declared that the "evidence" presented in the Fund pamphlet showed that "the possibility of a coup by the U. S. military is very real." It is interesting, also, to note that it was soon after Adam Yarmolinsky entered the Pentagon that agitation was started for the successful muzzling of our military, and that anti-Communist education programs for our military men were canceled, and that civilian control was clamped onto our U. S. military—all steps to forestall any military attempt to stop a Red takeover of our country.

Yarmolinsky's Fund study, published in August 1955, was entitled *Case Studies in Personnel Security*. These were cases involving government employees charged with Communist activities or otherwise being security or loyalty risks. The cases Yarmolinsky selected had been handled mainly by a small group of lawyers who often represent Communists. He interviewed these lawyers and the accused government employees to form the basis of his study on federal security.

Yarmolinsky then proceeded to write his report. His selection of the 50 cases he described in his study, his method of collecting and evaluating the information, and his subsequent editing of the government hearings produced a highly slanted and highly distorted attack on federal security procedures.

It was perhaps not entirely Yarmolinsky's fault that he did not get the entire government viewpoint on these 50 cases, because under the Eisenhower Administration personnel files were treated as confidential and classified to protect personnel and he was thus not permitted access to any of them.

However, a comparison between the complete published hearings of the accused loyalty and security risks, and Yarmolinsky's version of the hearings in his Fund study, shows that he edited the hearings extensively, deleting words, phrases, sentences and paragraphs in such a way as to give the impression that the accused security risks had not been given fair hearings. In one instance, for example, a question was asked and Yarmolinsky deleted the entire answer, to create not only a false impression, but one which was exactly contrary to the facts.

Two years prior to writing his *Case Studies in Personnel*

Security, Yarmolinsky, in 1953, asserted of the Federal Security Program: "It has serious defects—it lacks common-sense standards." He declared that so-called "current subversion" was merely "popular hysteria"—a statement hardly believable in light of the Alger Hiss case and the cases involving the thefts of our atomic secrets, examples of known subversion and espionage which had already taken place.

An extensive analysis of the Fund for the Republic, written in 1955 by Fulton Lewis, Jr., mentioned that Adam Yarmolinsky had made a call to Senator Hubert Humphrey (Democrat of Minnesota) to inform him that the Fund was issuing a reprint of a favorable statement made by the Senator, to be published by the Fund under the heading "Report on the Security Problem by the Subcommittee of the Committee on Government Operations, U. S. Senate."

Humphrey's statement had been an oral one and his own personal opinion—not a statement by "the Subcommittee of the Committee on Government Operations, U. S. Senate." Despite this, the outright falsification was published by the Fund for the Republic and sent to members of the Federal Judiciary. Later, the Fund officers, including Yarmolinsky, admitted they were wrong. It is this same sort of "carelessness" which one now sees as a pattern within the U. S. Department of Defense —perhaps a hangover from Adam Yarmolinsky's days as Vice President and National Secretary of the Fund for the Republic.

Yarmolinsky left the Fund for the Republic in 1957 to become Public Affairs Director for Doubleday, the publishing campany, until 1959 when he became the lawyer and consultant for several tax-exempt foundations.

In August 1960, Yarmolinsky joined the "Kennedy for President Committee" as assistant on a fee basis to candidate Kennedy's brother-in-law, R. Sargent Shriver. (At this writing Yarmolinsky is temporarily on loan to Shriver, to set up President Johnson's "War on Poverty" and will return to the Defense Department as soon as the assignment is completed.) Yarmolinsky's job was screening personnel and finding prospective high-ranking government employees for the Kennedy

Administration. Yarmolinsky and Shriver jointly picked 75 lawyers, largely left-wingers, who are now spotted in key decision-making jobs throughout the federal government. Perhaps Yarmolinsky was chosen for this job in the Kennedy campaign because he had been in George Ball's law firm. Ball, it will be remembered, was the man who accompanied Walt Rostow to Rostow's hearing before the Senate Foreign Relations Committee.

In reading this chapter, one should bear in mind that Adam Yarmolinsky is one of the advanced thinkers around whom the Administration hopes to shape a new world. Today no one is reportedly hired, assigned or discharged at the Pentagon without Yarmolinsky's O.K. The slanted critic of government security, with his strange background, has become the guardian of security in a most sensitive agency. There have been printed reports that his activities have gone into the policy stage and far beyond. And certainly those of his colleague, Paul Nitze, do.

Paul Nitze was chosen by President Kennedy as Assistant Secretary of Defense for International Security Affairs, a job in which, according to a *Time* magazine profile, he had "the tough job of fulfilling one of Kennedy's major aims: coordinating State [Department] and Defense [Department] policies so that U. S. diplomacy and military power go hand in hand," which might be translated by some as doing yeoman service in muzzling, and clamping civilian control on, the U. S. military. Nitze served as Assistant Secretary of Defense until October 1963, when President Kennedy named him secretary of the Navy.

Nitze also has a highly interesting background.

He was graduated from Harvard in 1928, joined the investment firm of Dillon, Read & Co. (the firm of now-Secretary of the Treasury, C. Douglas Dillon). In 1940, at the age of 33, as World War II loomed on the American horizon, he became a special consultant in the War Department in Washington. Nitze remained in Washington throughout the war and from

1944 to 1946 served as an economist and vice chairman of the Strategic Bombing Survey, along with J. Kenneth Galbraith.

When World War II ended, Nitze moved from the War Department to the State Department, where he was a confidant of then-Secretary of State George C. Marshall, and helped to put many of Marshall's policies into action. In 1950, during the Dean Acheson regime, Nitze became Director of the State Department Policy Planning Staff, and served in this capacity during the Korean War and the Korean stalemate.

During the Eisenhower Administration, Nitze was President of the Foreign Service Educational Foundation, where he constantly assailed the idea of U. S. "massive retaliation" and fed ideas on "limited warfare" and disarmament to top Democrats. During Kennedy's 1960 Presidential campaign, Nitze headed Kennedy's pre-election committee on defense, which shaped the policies of the Kennedy Administration on U. S. national defenses.

Nitze's views on American defense might be roughly termed as not exactly in agreement with those of the majority of Americans. For example, in April 1960, before President Kennedy chose him to shape his Administration's defense policies, Nitze attended the Asilomar National Strategy Seminar held on Monterey Peninsula, California. On April 28, Nitze gave a speech to the 500 people attending, in which he suggested that U. S. nuclear superiority over the Soviets was *not an advantage* to the United States—a position curiously close to that of his future boss, Robert McNamara. To cut down U. S. nuclear superiority, Nitze urged that the United States should undertake ". . . a series of *unilateral* actions designed to produce a reciprocal action on the part of our allies and also *on the part of our enemies,*" to slow down the "arms race." This means that the United States should disarm, whether or not the Russians disarm, and that furthermore, if we do disarm unilaterally, the peace-loving Russians will see that disarmament is so desirable, they will disarm, too!

As a starter in disarming unilaterally, Nitze urged that the United States should "scrap" its "fixed-base" missile bases and bomber bases (one of the main U. S. defenses which keep Khrushchev from raining nuclear holocaust on the American people).

In addition, Nitze proposed that the United States should put our entire Strategic Air Command (SAC—which is our *prime* American defense against Soviet nuclear attack) under a "NATO command"—but that the United States should then inform the UN that "NATO will turn over ultimate power of decision on the use of these systems [i.e., both our "fixed base" missile and bomber bases, and SAC] to the General Assembly of the United Nations." We are now outnumbered more than 110-to-1 in the UN General Assembly, and every year the total votes in favor of the Soviet bloc grows steadily bigger!

In case anyone thinks Mr. Nitze has changed these bizarre views, he reminded the nation at a meeting of the Democratic House Study Group in the summer of 1963 that he is "very proud of this speech."

Two years before Nitze's 1960 Asilomar "Let's-give-away-SAC" speech, he was section chairman of a World Order Study Conference held in Cleveland by the National Council of the Churches of Christ. Nitze's group issued a report which might remind some readers of other platforms, other places:

> International disarmament is a basic goal.
> The United States should suspend nuclear tests "unilaterally if necessary."
> National armies should be made obsolete. Military force should be used only under the control of the United Nations.
> The United States should recognize Red China.
> The United States should push for seating Red China in the UN.
> The United States should "encourage" Chiang Kai-shek to abandon the offshore islands of Quemoy and Matsu.

Is it any wonder that the Chicago *Tribune,* commenting on Nitze's appointment as Secretary of the Navy by President Kennedy, said: "These views are hardly calculated to bring joy to admirals trying to build and preserve a strong naval power. . . . Their new [civilian chief] looks like a McNamara depth charge."

Kennedy named as Nitze's replacement in the Defense Department's number two spot William P. Bundy, brother of Presidential Assistant McGeorge Bundy. President Johnson later named William Bundy to be Assistant Secretary of State for Far Eastern Affairs.

William P. Bundy first made a name for himself by contributing $400 to Alger Hiss to defend himself in court when Hiss was indicted for perjury because he had lied about being a Soviet espionage agent. When the late Senator Joseph R. McCarthy brought this fact to national attention, Bundy's explanation for helping a Soviet espionage agent to defend himself against a prison sentence was: "I believed him worthy of a full defense."

After Bundy's contribution to Alger Hiss and Senator McCarthy's exposure of the fact, CIA Director Allen Dulles hired Bundy as his number two man in the Central Intelligence Agency. William Bundy served as deputy to Dulles for almost ten years, from 1951 until 1961, when Kennedy moved him to the Defense Department, where he served on the U. S. military assistance program.

In September 1963, just before his new appointment as Assistant Secretary of Defense by Kennedy, Bundy accompanied Secretary McNamara and General Maxwell Taylor on their special mission to Viet Nam as a special adviser and top ex-CIA official. A few weeks later the Diem regime, which had been successfully fighting Communist guerrillas for years, fell at the hands of a pro-Communist coup, and most informed observers asserted that it was done with the connivance of the CIA and the White House. Diem and his brother Nhu were brutally murdered after they sought political sanctuary in a church, arranged to surrender to the coup leaders, and were en route to surrender. After the Diem regime fell, with repercussions reverberating throughout the free world and the finger of suspicion pointing at the White House, William Bundy sat side by side with his brother McGeorge at top-level White House emergency meetings, to lay White House strategy for answering the charges and for cementing Administration relations with the new Viet Nam regime.

What Americans will learn about William Bundy in his new role as Assistant Secretary of State for Far Eastern Affairs remains to be seen at this writing.

During early 1963, the results of the McNamara-Nitze-Yarmolinsky combination were noted extensively in the press. Columnist S. L. A. Marshall (a former Army brigadier general) commented, "McNamara has lost the confidence of the armed services." Washington *Evening Star* Reporter Richard Fryklund wrote that "military people believe Mr. McNamara does not understand people, that he is not interested in people . . . A Defense Secretary with no heart is being equated with a Defense Department with no heart."

Top military analyst Hanson Baldwin of the New York *Times* commented in *The Saturday Evening Post* that "the 'unification' of the armed services sponsored by McNamara poses some subtle and insidious dangers . . . that could present . . . almost as great a threat to a secure and free nation as an attempted military coup." Baldwin later saw one of his columns killed by the *Times* News Service which would have said, "Weariness, mistrust, recrimination and mutual suspicion prevail in the Pentagon."

The struggle inside the Pentagon between top military experts and Defense Department civilians who disagree with them and then overrule the military men resulted in the forced resignation in August 1963 of Admiral George W. Anderson, Chief of Naval Operations and a member of the Joint Chiefs of Staff.

On February 20, 1963, Admiral Anderson had testified before the House Appropriations Subcommittee on Defense that he had hoped "to get a nuclear-powered aircraft carrier" for the U. S. Navy for fiscal year 1965. Anderson made it clear to the Congressional subcommittee that he considered the nuclear carrier of critical importance to the continued strength of the Navy and to our American defenses. Secretary McNamara then killed the plans for the nuclear-powered aircraft carrier.

Admiral Anderson had also clashed with the Defense Department civilians over the proposed test-ban treaty, the TFX contract award and—as will be seen in the next chapter—over the Whiz Kids' abandoning the Skybolt missile program and giving our allies Polaris submarines.

In the climax of the struggle, Anderson the military expert was forced to resign as Chief of Naval Operations and was quickly sent to Portugal by President Kennedy as U. S. Ambassador to that country.

Before Admiral Anderson departed for Portugal, he leveled a broadside at the Defense Department Whiz Kid civilians. On September 4, 1963, the retiring Chief of Naval Operations told newsmen in a speech at Washington's National Press Club that "certain aspects of the Department of Defense . . . give me grave concern, a concern shared by many in uniform today."

"I am gravely concerned," said Anderson in his headline-making speech, "that within the Department of Defense there is not the degree of confidence and trust between the civilian and military echelons that the importance of their common objective requires . . . The recommendations of the uniformed chiefs of our services, each backed up by competent military and civilian staffs, are altered or overruled without interim consultation, explanation and discussion . . . " This ignoring of military recommendations "is fraught . . . potentially with grave dangers."

Anderson charged that unfortunately "today in the Pentagon, an unhealthy imbalance has resulted, because at times specialists are used as experts in areas outside their own fields. This has resulted in a tendency to draw conclusions before all the evidence has been examined."

The former Navy Chief of Staff ended his speech with a parting shot at the Defense Department Whiz Kids' electronic gadgetry which today generates much of our vital defense policy: "There is another alarming peril in obscuring the role of the military, found in a modern fallacy that theories, or computers, or economics, or numbers of weapons win wars.

Alone, they do not. Good leadership unfailingly recognizes that man is the key to success or failure."

In a syndicated newspaper column titled "If the Nation Is to Survive," inserted into the *Congressional Record* by Representative Melvin R. Laird, political analyst Ralph de Toledano wrote: " . . . the warning of Admiral Anderson is clear." In the past, "many Americans died because a civilian 'knew better' than those trained in war . . . Today, Secretary McNamara has gagged the uniformed men at the Pentagon in a manner previously unknown to the United States."

de Toledano estimated that "morale in the armed forces is lower today than it has ever been . . . the civilians brought in by Secretary McNamara have shut off debate—like the Napoleon who became intolerant of criticism, stifled his commanders, and ended his great career in utter defeat."

Another retired member of the Joint Chiefs of Staff has also leveled a broadside at what he labeled "the new breed" of defense leaders. Former Air Force Chief of Staff General Thomas D. White declared in *The Saturday Evening Post* of May 4, 1963, after his retirement:

> In common with many other military men, active and retired, I am profoundly apprehensive of the pipe-smoking, tree-full-of-owls type of so-called "defense intellectuals" who have been brought into this nation's capital. I don't believe a lot of these often overconfident, sometimes arrogant young professors, mathematicians and other theorists have sufficient worldliness or motivation to stand up to the kind of enemy we face. War is a brutal, dirty, deadly affair. Our enemy is a coarse, crooked megalomaniac who aims to kill us. Exceptions to the thesis that brute force, not theory, wins war are so rare that every schoolboy must go back 3,000 years to David and Goliath.

Counteracting this criticism, the Inner Circle has benefited by recent fiction bestsellers such as *Fail-Safe* and *Seven Days in May* in which any opposition from the military has been billed as the first stages of military coups, which all leftists fear.

A deadly serious, true-life example of the civilian management of the Defense Department can be seen in the testimony given during hearings held in April 1963 by the House Defense Appropriations Subcommittee. At these hearings it was made public that the maps locating the underseas cables linking our vital Distant Early Warning (DEW) Line stations had been given to the Russians! These DEW Line stations are supposed to sound an early alarm if enemy bombers are en route to attack the United States and/or Canada.

Moreover, the chief union named to handle these DEW Line cables is the American Communications Association. This union has been officially cited as "dominated by Communists" by the House Committee on Un-American Activities, by the Senate Internal Security Subcommittee, and by the Office of the U. S. Attorney General. In fact, in 1950, it was kicked out of the CIO for being dominated by Communists. Moreover, in May 1957 the president of the American Communications Association and five other top-ranking officials and members of this union were asked by a Congressional committee if they were members of the Communist Party—and they all invoked the Fifth Amendment, on the grounds that their answers might tend to incriminate them.

If designating this union to handle our vital DEW Line cables isn't enough "Alice in Wonderland," here is the whole Mad Hatter's tea party: the American Communications Association also handles 75 vital links in the most secret communication of our government, including Pentagon-to-Air Force base communications links at U.S. Air Force bases in England, Canada, Newfoundland, Maine and New York. The members of this one Communist-dominated union have *for at least the past ten years, and right to the present moment* been able to put their hands on all top-secret messages sent over these top-secret channels of our own Pentagon-to-Air Force bases communications system!

But the Defense Department downgraded the horrendous significance of giving our DEW Line underseas cable maps to the Russians, after it was made public. In fact, one Pentagon spokesman brushed off as "undoubtedly accidental" the breaks made in our DEW Line underseas cable by Russian "fishing boats"—after the Soviets had been given the maps.

During the hearings, Representative Daniel J. Flood of Pennsylvania declared it was "utterly fantastic" that these DEW Line maps had been given to the Soviets, since the safety of the American and Canadian peoples so clearly hangs on our DEW Line defenses. Representative Flood strongly recommended that these maps be canceled and that the underseas cables be relaid. But this has never been done.

If the American people could rip off the curtain of secrecy surrounding the hanky-panky in the Defense Department (and throughout the Administration) there might be a "March to Washington" to make all previous "marches" look like Sunday-school picnics. And the man in charge of this secrecy—or "news management"—at the Defense Department is Arthur Sylvester, Assistant Secretary of Defense for Public Affairs, who started his career as a shipping clerk, advanced to stringer of news from the New Jersey suburbs of the Newark *Evening News,* and became Washington correspondent for that paper in 1944. New Frontier leaders were favorably impressed with his consistent journalistic attempts to disparage and belittle anti-Communist activities. Today in the Defense Department, Sylvester has made it an ironclad rule that no one in the Pentagon may talk to a reporter without one of Sylvester's civilian snoopers being present and/or without clearing the talk or contact with one of Sylvester's men. It was Arthur Sylvester who told outraged veteran Washington newsmen on December 6, 1962, that an Administration "has the inherent right to lie" to protect the national interest.

But some Americans believe that the news from the Defense Department is being "managed" for a quite different reason. A sizzling and rather horrifying explanation of the Defense Department's news management came from Admiral Chester Ward, in his speech on April 8, 1963:

> The whole purpose of managed news is to suppress the critical fact of the *growing* Soviet nuclear strength, and the *diminishing* American nuclear strength. The news is being

"managed" to cover Soviet gains in strength. The news is being "managed" to restrain the American people from demanding strong action for U. S. defense.

Under the guise of so-called "modernization" [so termed by McNamara and articulated to the public by Arthur Sylvester] we are cutting back about 90 per cent of our nuclear firepower. Strategists are referring to this in private as *"the clandestine, unilateral, de facto, massive nuclear disarmament of the United States."*

Out of the U. S.-Russia nuclear test-ban moratorium and Khrushchev's subsequent exploding of the agreement with massive atmospheric test blasts of up to the equivalent of 58 million tons, Khrushchev has *completely reversed* the world picture of nuclear strength. Prior to the test-ban moratorium, the United States had a two-to-one lead over the Soviets in nuclear weaponry —across the board, across the entire spectrum of nuclear weaponry. Now, in the area of strategic nuclear warheads, the Soviets have *at least a two-to-one lead over the United States.*

This is one of the things that has been suppressed by this Administration. The managed news techniques by which they have concealed this military disaster from the American people is highly sophisticated. This part of the news management program operates behind three overlapping curtains: the Curtain of Classification; the Curtain of Complexity; and the Curtain of Incredibility. In other words, in the Administration elite circles, they take the position that everything you need to know for the security of your country is either: too secret to trust you with; too complex for you to understand; or too incredible for you to believe.

Consider the removal of our missiles from Turkey and Italy. You'll remember during the Cuban crisis, Khrushchev said, "I'll pull those missiles out of Cuba, if you pull yours out of Turkey and Italy." And the Administration immediately said— for domestic publication—in effect, "No deal. We don't make agreements under pressure." The Administration still denies that we made any such "agreements." Nevertheless, as you know, we are now engaged in pulling those missiles out of Turkey and out of Italy. Actually, this also illustrates another technique of avoiding telling absolute lies, in order to deceive the American people: we don't make "agreements" any more—we engage in unilateral action!

The Administration is pursuing the theory that it is safer to be weak than to be strong. We're abandoning 90 per cent of our massive nuclear strike power—deliberately. We're going to rely on the so-called minimum deterrent of the small-warhead Polaris and Minuteman missiles—and we're not going to have many of those. We are having a thousand less Minuteman missiles than the Air Force asked the Defense Department for.

It is a terrible, terrible gamble that we are taking. We are going to rely on trusting Russian promises, instead of relying on United States strength to insure our security.

Americans *must* try to penetrate the "managed news" curtains and find out what we need to know to make America safe and secure. Cuba was more than a nuclear Pearl Harbor that almost happened. It was much more, and our so-called "strong" reaction was very weak, indeed. It set the stage for a nuclear Pearl Harbor that is *sure to happen this year, or perhaps next year,* if we do not change our national attitude. This we must cure if our nation is to live. The cure can be started very easily by firing some people in Washington.

Americans had just a peek behind the managed news curtain surrounding what's going on in the Defense Department in 1961 when two homosexual code clerks in the supersecret National Security Agency (NSA)—an agency of the Defense Department—defected to the Soviet Union carrying with them, as one newsman put it, "God-only-knows what top military secrets." The NSA deals with super-secret government codes and other electronic-intelligence operations.

When a House investigating committee pried into the case, they found that both men, Bernon Mitchell and William Martin, were well-known, flagrant homosexuals. Moreover, the House probers found that Mitchell had posed naked for obscene photographs and indulged in abnormal sex relations with animals. More than that, William Martin was "friendly" with a raft of identified Communists, and had been for years! The published report of an anonymous co-worker of Martin and Mitchell revealed, "I knew that both of them were flaming homosexuals two minutes after I met them. You couldn't miss it; and yet they were both allowed to work on top-secret codes, cyphers and documents."

All this had been known for years—and yet these two degenerates were allowed to work in our top-secret National

Security Agency until they defected to the Soviet Union with fistfuls of top-secret documents, codes and "God-only-knows what top military secrets."

In the aftermath of the nationwide scandal, the House investigators found that more than half of the NSA's employees had not been given lie detector tests, and by November 1963 —two years after Martin and Mitchell had defected—they had still not been given lie detector tests.

After those two degenerates fled to the Soviet Union, the personnel director of the National Security Agency resigned. The whole scandal was referred by the House committee to the Justice Department for action. But the head of the Justice Department, Attorney General Robert Kennedy, has never done anything about it, up to the very moment of this writing, three years later.

Another scandal in the Defense Department's National Security Agency rocked the nation in the summer of 1963, but Arthur Sylvester tried to gloss over its seriousness in talking to newsmen prying into it, and he brushed it off as being not important. In fact, Sylvester had denied that there was any security leak involved until the story was broken by the Washington *Evening Star.* But two veteran Washington newsmen and columnists, Allen and Scott, described the serious breach of security this way: "Assistant Defense Secretary Arthur ('news management') Sylvester's syrupy glossover of the seriousness of the late Sgt. John Dunlap's espionage is another glaring instance of the Kennedy Administration's attempts to mislead the American public."

Dunlap was a long-time messenger for the National Security Agency, whose job was to deliver a whole range of our most secret government documents to other government agencies and military installations. Only by accident was it discovered that, all the while in his messenger job, Dunlap had been turning over many of these documents to Soviet agents for microfilming. Allen and Scott add: "Unpublishable information is also known about Dunlap's Red contacts."

Dunlap conveniently committed suicide by asphyxiating

himself with carbon monoxide in his automobile before he could be interrogated by the House Committee on Un-American Activities probing the scandal, but it is known that Dunlap probably received more than $100,000 from the Soviets for selling our secrets.

The "accident" which led to Dunlap's exposure was his application for civilian status with the National Security Agency. In the transition, loyal NSA employees scrutinized his record, his high-priced cars, expensive boats, his heavy betting at the race track and around Washington, and then the finger of suspicion pointed at him. Shortly afterwards, Dunlap "committed suicide."

In probing the scandal, the House investigators uncovered the shocking fact that Dunlap had *never* been given a security check. And for years he had access to the most super-secret documents of the top-secret National Security Agency of the Defense Department!

Crackerjack reporters Allen and Scott discovered: "In contradiction of Sylvester's brushoff of this security breach, among the worst in our history, the following is *some* of the highly secret information the spy sold to the Soviets:

> Extensive details of this country's capability to detect nuclear tests and missile launchings. These documents, available only to top officials on a "need to know" basis, contained exhaustive data on Russian nuclear blasts and space shots. The reports gave the Soviets a full picture of the degree to which the United States can detect nuclear and missile operations in the atmosphere and in outer space.

> Central Intelligence Agency documents dealing with Soviet military, nuclear and space capabilities. Also, numerous reports by CIA and National Security Agency agents on Russian naval forces and capabilities, particularly underwater.

Allen and Scott had probed into an even more disastrous angle to Dunlap's espionage: "Very much on the minds of the House probers is whether there is any connection between the information the Russians bought from Dunlap and their agreeing to the atmospheric test-ban treaty."

They quoted one authority, who traced the connection this way:

> "The Soviet definitely knows tests and launchings we detected and those we didn't. That information is invaluable to them for a number of reasons. For one, as a result of this infamous espionage they will be able to cheat on the test-ban agreement with impunity. They know our blind spots."

This official also noted as highly significant that President Kennedy, in his public assurances regarding the treaty, stressed there will be no letdown in continued improvement of detection facilities and methods.

In the President's statement there was no hint of any kind of the vital information Dunlap had peddled to the Communists. But, in the opinion of this important official, there was a direct connection between the two.

More will be heard from this House probe which may prove to be spectacularly explosive.

Senator Barry Goldwater made a scathing indictment of Sylvester's part in the Dunlap scandal and charged that it is part of the Administration's attempt—enunciated by Robert Kennedy—to play down internal subversion by Communists in this country. Senator Goldwater declared:

> The long-delayed and faltering admission by the Pentagon that an Army sergeant had sold vital U. S. secrets to Soviet Russia before he committed suicide last summer points up one of the great security weakness of our time—the obdurate refusal of some key personnel in government to acknowledge the existence of Communist subversion in this country.
>
> As a result of this weakness, countless contacts by federal security workers with suspect persons and activities, which anywhere else in the world would be thoroughly investigated, go unchecked . . .
>
> At the time [of Dunlap's suicide] the Defense Department denied that security matters were involved in the suicide. Early in October, however, Washington *Evening Star* writer Earl Voss reported Dunlap had sold vital U. S. code information, photographs and other secret data to Russian agents for $60,000 . . .
>
> Not until they were confronted with the Voss article did Defense and White House spokesmen admit the security leak had occurred.

Although no reason was given for the blackout of the case, it has been speculated that the pending action on the Moscow test-ban pact was the cause. Realization that the Administration spokesmen were painting a glowing picture of Russia's good intentions at the same time Soviet agents actually were buying our top-most secrets well could have caused the Senate to reject the treaty.

But even more important than the reason for this censorship is the possibility that there may be others in the government who are as dangerous as Dunlap to American security, and that their activities will not be discovered until too late. The far left has consistently fought attempts to question the loyalty and security status of federal employees. As a result, many persons who otherwise would be willing to come forward with material on the backgrounds, associations and activities of security employees hesitate to do so.

Truly, the state of our nation's defenses is alarming. The following excerpts of an analysis made by the Republican Policy Committee of the House of Representatives show graphically how U. S. military posture deteriorated during the first two years of the Kennedy Administration, compared with what it was in 1960, the last year of the Eisenhower Administration:

1. The Administration has refused to build the RS-70 bomber, authorized by Congress, abandoned the Skybolt program, scrapped the B-58 bomber program, withdrawn B-47 bombers from overseas bases, while in 1960 we had 2,000 long-range strategic bombers and 16 wings of tactical aircraft dispersed throughout the world in friendly bases.

2. The Thor missile bases we had in Britain in 1960 have been removed.

3. The Jupiter IRBM missile bases we had in Turkey and Italy have been dismantled.

4. About 40,000 troops have been taken out of Western Europe alone, even while France lags behind in its troop commitments to NATO, whereas in 1960 we had 14 Army divisions, 8 of them abroad or overseas and 6 at home.

5. The Jupiter solid-fuel missile program has been cut to one-half the original projected number.

Taken all together, these decisions point to an abandonment of the "flexibility" concept of military strength advocated by the 1960 Report when it stated that our military forces need flexibility to meet aggression at the time, place and with weapons of our own choosing, with a mix of limited war capabilities.

The *Air Force Magazine* has noted that, in accordance with the Defense Secretary's decision, by 1970 our country will be absolutely dependent on missiles, since manned bombers are already being phased out. One might even go farther with an observation that "flexibility" is being phased out in favor of "rigidity."

The manner in which these and other decisions in defense have been made is worth examining.

The 1960 Report expressed the belief that "a single Chief of Staff for all the services would overconcentrate power and decision-making on the wrong level," and that "such concentration could introduce an imbalance into consideration of our military program . . ."

But since 1960, there has evolved a new concept of organization and authority in the Defense Department. There has been, in effect, a "unification of the armed services" which "poses some subtle and insidious dangers that are political, military and administrative. . . . The unification . . . is dangerous to the nation's political system of checks and balances . . ."

In the Defense Department today, the armed services are "made to speak with one voice," "superagencies" are being established so that there are already a Defense Intelligence Agency (whose miscalculation in the case of Cuba caused the delay of U. S. action thereon) and a Defense Supply Agency procuring so-called common items for all services. There is envisioned a "national Communications Agency" which might well place all government communications under military control.

On top of it all sits the Defense Secretary.

In effect, there has not only been a unification of the armed services; the Defense Secretary himself, a civilian with skimpy military background and experience at best and a political personality to boot, has become the de facto Chief of Staff. "The voice of professional experience has been overridden by a military party line, a single strategic concept. The opinions of the Joint Chiefs of Staff are usually given short shrift."

Our future looks even bleaker when we consider research and development of vital weapons, as the following chart shows. Four full years of Kennedy-Johnson-McNamara have started a total of only seven new research and development programs—all for nonstrategic weapons systems. Also, Mc-

Namara canceled $4.5 billion of weapons already in development, during the first three Kennedy-Johnson years. In contrast, the first Eisenhower term started 29 new aircraft and missile programs, and 18 in the second term. Only $3.1 billion of weapons were canceled in development during the entire eight Eisenhower years:

New guided missile starts and missile types in production, post-Korean period
(Government fiscal years)

Type	1954-57		1958-61		1962-65		Programs remaining in production in 1965
	Starts	Production	Starts	Production	Starts	Production	
ICBM	3	0	1	3	0	4	2
Air to air	0	3	0	3	1	3	1
Air to surface	3	0	3	3	0	4	2
Surface to air	1	2	2	7	1	6	3
Surface to surface	4	7	2	9	2	11	4
ASW	1	0	1	1	0	2	2
Total	12	12	9	26	4	30	14

NOTE.—Does not include canceled programs or research programs (Skybolt, Typhoon), or program definition efforts. Multiple-use weapons are considered 1 program.

New aircraft starts and aircraft types in production, post-Korean period
(Government fiscal years)

	1954-57		1958-61		1962-65		Programs remaining in production in 1965
	Starts	Production	Starts	Production	Starts	Production	
Bomber	0	5	0	4	0	0	....
Attack	2	2	0	4	1	4	2
Fighter	2	12	1	13	1	3	1
Cargo/Transport	3	6	3	7	1	7	5
A S W/surveillance	2	4	2	7	0	4	4
Trainer	3	5	0	5	0	4	3
Utility	5	6	3	12	0	16	6
Total	17	40	9	52	3	38	21

NOTE.—Does not include canceled or research programs (B-70), or program definition efforts. Multiple-use airframes are considered 1 program.

These are but a few examples of how the Department of Defense, under Secretary Robert McNamara, Adam Yarmolinsky, Paul Nitze and Arthur Sylvester and the "Whiz Kids" is, wittingly or unwittingly, destroying the security of the American people. As far as our forces-in-being, command of forces, over-all strategy and defense against first-strike attack from the Soviets are concerned, the Pentagon provides our first and last line of defense.

That is why it is so vital that the American people should understand just who lurks in the shadows directing personnel and policy in that department.

CHAPTER FOUR

The Amateur Strategists vs. the Joint Chiefs

"It is beginning to be hinted that we are a nation of amateurs."
... Earl of Roseberry—RECTORIAL ADDRESS, 1900

TODAY OUR MILITARY establishment is under control of the Administration's civilian Inner Circle. The Joint Chiefs of Staff have been subordinated.

McGeorge Bundy, formerly of Harvard and now President Johnson's Special Assistant for National Security Affairs, informally heads a civilian staff directing not only U. S. military policy, but to a considerable extent, important American military operations as well. To no one's surprise, this is about the same as the White House "Little State Department."

This group—with additions and subtractions depending largely on the matter involved—includes Walt Whitman Rostow, George Ball, Paul Nitze, Adam Yarmolinsky and Adlai Stevenson; occasionally Jerome Wiesner and William Foster. In the JFK years, Bobby Kennedy was a top member.

These men have conducted the two major Cuban operations; they had a large voice in starting and continuing the "secret" jungle war in Viet Nam; they have decided where our latest weapons shall, or shall not, be placed abroad, as well as which weapons shall be used and which scrapped; and they decide how far we shall go with unilateral disarmament and with test-ban and other, still-embryonic, treaties. They thus deal across the board in the defense and survival of the U. S.

From the time of George Washington until John F. Kennedy took office, civilian control of the military always has been exercised in the United States by the President, as Commander in Chief. But he has acted through the Service Secretaries—that is the Secretaries of Army, Navy and now Air Force —who are confirmed by the Senate. Today, however, there is a new, unique, lateral control of the military, exercised through the equivalent of the Soviet political commissars.

126

That classic of everything *not* to do on an amphibious landing—the Bay of Pigs—was arranged by these amateur strategists and tacticians, in conjunction with the CIA. It was the most colossal and ignominious military failure in American history, and it provided a tragic lesson in what happens when politicians and thinkers get their hands on a military operation. This group also masterminded the "eyeball-to-eyeball" so-called showdown between Kennedy and Khrushchev in October 1962.

It is these amateurs who decided to withdraw our "first-strike" weapons from abroad, who threw out weapons which the military wanted (ranging from supersonic planes to ground-air rockets and space platforms), and who engineered the unsecured "limited" test-ban treaty, with Averell Harriman acting as their publicized errand boy.

Military casualties produced by this group include, among others, Major General Edwin A. Walker, removed from command of the crack 24th Division in Germany, and Admiral George W. Anderson, removed as Chief of Naval Operations.

No particular attempt was made to hide the shift of U. S. military direction from our trained, seasoned admirals and generals, to McGeorge Bundy-Robert F. Kennedy & Co. There have been exceptions to this: and Secretary of Defense Robert McNamara—who always gladly fronts for the amateur strategists—misled the public in this regard. He said that no military decision had ever been made during the Kennedy Administration against a unanimous position of the Joint Chiefs of Staff. The truth is that the military chiefs of our Army, Navy, Air Force and Marines are often in unanimous agreement, but they have frequently been overruled by the amateurs because General Maxwell Taylor, the Administration's tame chairman of the Joint Chiefs, has voted against all military service heads.

Because of the magnitude of the April 1961 Bay of Pigs disaster, the role of the civilian "geniuses" and of the political hacks in its planning and operation was dug out and exposed by the press. *Fortune* magazine did the most complete job on how the amateurs had whittled away the original plan for the landings until little remained. Thereupon, the Kennedys had General Maxwell Taylor visit the *Time-Life-Fortune* high command, presumably in hopes of getting the writer, Charles J. V. Murphy, fired, and of at least obtaining some sort of public retraction of *Fortune's* main points. In the discussion with the editors, it developed that General Taylor had no case. There was no retraction.

Somewhat earlier, the White House had inflicted upon Murphy, a colonel in the Air Force Reserve, an irrelevant reprisal. The Air Force was ordered to remove him from a mobilization assignment in the Chief of Staff's office that carried a higher rank.

After the October 1962 Cuban missile "crisis," the New Frontier encouraged the news media, with special emphasis on magazines, to give "the inside story" of the event, because it appeared superficially like a Kennedy victory, and is still officially touted as such.

Since the Bay of Pigs disaster, however, and even to this day, the Administration has apparently done its utmost to protect Castro's Cuba—even to the extent of confiscating ships of anti-Communist Cubans headed for their native land; patrolling waters around Cuba to prevent anti-Castro harassment of the island; and even standing by when anti-Castro Cubans are kidnapped off Caribbean islands in British territorial waters.

The United States has never harassed Castro's Cuba—and now we are preventing anyone else from doing so.

Despite some publicity about the amateur takeover of our military, the American public has assumed that basically matters are just as they always have been in our country. They have taken it for granted that our military has a principal voice in defense policy and that all is well. That they are wrong has not yet seeped through. This is true particularly because the actions, motivations and maneuverings of the Bundys, Rostows and Nitzes have never really been revealed. Where they have been, disclosure has been in such a piecemeal fashion that it is unrecognized as part of a pattern for the amateur takeover of our national defense and retaliatory powers at this decisive moment in the history of our country and of the world.

Military coups long have been especially feared in Europe and Latin America by "liberal" and leftist elements because military coups usually oust leftists from power. It all began in modern times when Napoleon seized dictatorial power and effectively ended the French Revolution. That the United States has never had such a coup has not been dismissed by those in the Administration with recent European backgrounds or by those who follow European thought trends.

The historical fact that we have never had a military coup d'état does not lessen fear of emergence of a "Man on Horseback" in the minds of the Yarmolinskys, Schlesingers and their associates, including those of the ADA.

The first attempt to suppress the American military was coupled with an attempt by the left-wing ADA to call attention away from the fact that its members were in hundreds of key and secondary positions throughout the Kennedy Administration. The diversionary move chosen was an attack on "right-wing extremists," and particularly upon the John Birch Society. The spearhead of this attack was the removal of General Walker and his public smearing which followed. The diversionary attack centered on a general who was an open member of the Birch Society.

It is interesting that this attack followed implementation on January 1, 1961, by Gus Hall, head of the Communist Party, U. S. A., of a Moscow directive of December 5, 1960, ordering an all-out worldwide attack on anti-Communists. The attempt to destroy Walker was doubly convenient because he was executing a National Security policy, ordered but tacitly suspended, of teaching U. S. troops about communism. Whatever one may think of Walker, this was what was behind his removal and disgrace. As Cabell Phillips reported to the New York *Times,* " . . . high officials at the Pentagon" were hopeful that the punishment of General Walker "will have a restraining influence on military men."

Other top military men, from Admiral Arleigh Burke,

Chief of Naval Operations, to General Arthur Trudeau, Director of Army Research and Development and former Chief of G-2, already were having anti-Communist statements removed from their speeches by State Department censors acting under Philip Stern, Deputy Assistant Secretary for Public Affairs, who was Under Secretary George Ball's former partner on the Northern Virginia *Sun*. Stern was allowed to resign quickly from State and was never called upon to testify before the Stennis Preparedness Subcommittee.

But Yarmolinsky, then Special Assistant to Secretary McNamara handling personnel matters, made certain that the admirals and generals would be neutralized. Under the smoke screen of the Walker case, "political advisers," largely, if not entirely, from the State Department, were appointed to every major military command around the world and to every ranking general and admiral in the Pentagon. To SAC, the vital Strategic Air Command, as noted, went Edward Freers, former Counselor of Embassy in Moscow, sometimes referred to by colleagues as "Old Wishy-Washy." Similar appointments were made to Pacific Fleet headquarters and other big operating commands.

Control à la Russe of the U. S. military was well along when the Bay of Pigs landings occurred. The landings began at 2 A.M., April 17, 1961, and collapsed two and a half days later at 2:30 P.M., April 20, when a surviving handful of Cuban patriots were driven back into the sea, the entire landing force having been either killed or captured.

The amateurish blunders were so numerous and the smoke screen around the operation so thick it is doubtful if all that "went wrong" in the Bay of Pigs will ever be known. For example, if any attempt ever has been made to ascertain who was responsible for leaking the facts to Castro before the landing, it has never been disclosed.

The late Ambassador Whiting Willauer, a close associate in China of General Clare Chennault of the Flying Tigers, testified under oath that he was never questioned about the landing plan when Adolph Berle and Arthur Schlesinger, Jr., took over invasion planning from him. Ambassador Willauer had planned to use saboteurs to destroy on the ground, ahead of the landing, Castro's bombers, which eventually decided the adverse fate of the landing party. Why Willauer was never asked about the plans, never de-briefed, remains a mystery still.

All he found out, Willauer himself testified, was that one day the telephone had been removed from his State Department office, and the next day his desk was taken out. Willauer had no difficulty deducing what this meant and went back to Costa Rica, where he had been U. S. envoy, to pick up his belongings. There he eventually received a telephone call from a State Department underling telling him he had been removed. Willauer testified that during the Eisenhower Administration he had been personally commissioned to draft a landing plan.

The Kennedy amateurs whittled down the size of the landing force to only 3,000 men. Air cover over the beachhead was eliminated from the landing plan because, some said at the time, Adlai Stevenson claimed that his standing in the UN would be undermined if U.S.-flown planes participated. Dean Rusk said the decision to cancel the air cover had been made by President Kennedy. Because of Adlai Stevenson's position, the stand was taken that the operation was entirely Cuban and that the U.S. had nothing to do with the landings, although they were U. S. planned, controlled and directed. For a world power that has always been forthright in its actions, this smacked of Balkan diplomacy—moreover, it fooled no one abroad.

At the last moment, the landing place itself was shifted from a relatively remote one, to the Bay of Pigs which was easily accessible to Castro's Russian tanks and bombers. A fast American aircraft carrier only 50 miles away never got planes over the beachhead, although President Kennedy supposedly consulted aides in the White House for seven hours about the advisability of sending in this U. S. air cover when the beachhead began to collapse.

Just four days before the Bay of Pigs landing, President Kennedy told a press conference:

"There will not under any conditions be an intervention in Cuba by American forces."

Not until the spring of 1963 was it disclosed that four U. S. pilots were killed over the beachhead when, very belatedly, they were sent over in B-26 bombers with no top fighter cover to try to save the day. The dead were "contract" National Guard pilots flying U. S. bombers with Castro Cuban Army markings and, therefore, under the twisted thinking of the amateur planners, they were "Cuban" planes.

After Attorney General Robert Kennedy said in a magazine interview that no "top cover" had ever been planned— despite Ambassador Willauer's sworn testimony to the contrary —the widows of some of the participants talked, although they had been threatened by U. S. federal officials and warned to keep quiet.

Attorney General Kennedy had previously added to the ignominy of the American defeat in the Bay of Pigs by masterminding the raising of $62 million blackmail in cash, food and medical supplies demanded from the United States by the seedy little Red dictator of Cuba as his condition for releasing 1,178 men taken prisoners by the Cuban Communists during the Bay of Pigs invasion. Mighty America's bowing to the whim of the cocky Castro drew gasps from free nations around the world— especially from our Latin American neighbors—and it hardly tallied with candidate Kennedy's 1960 Presidential campaign promise to raise U. S. prestige in the eyes of the world. It was certainly a far cry from Theodore Roosevelt's "Big Stick" policy for Latin America.

It was not until the cash and supplies were in Castro's hands that the American public learned that Bobby Kennedy had masterminded the deal, behind a 52-member figurehead Committee to Raise Cuban Ransom. The committee, set up on June 26, 1962, "to accept voluntary contributions," included Eleanor Roosevelt, Walter Reuther, Milton Eisenhower and General Lucius Clay.

After the extortion price was paid to Castro, the press revealed that the "voluntary contributions" had been obtained largely by strong-arm tactics of the Attorney General in telephone conversations with dozens of U. S. corporations. The press also uncovered the fact that Bobby Kennedy had promised the corporations that he would not press antitrust actions against them for cooperating in the "donation" of a total of $50 million in products toward the Castro blackmail demand.

Unlike the Administration's later mere trusting of the Soviets' word that they had removed their nuclear missiles from Cuba, Fidel Castro's henchmen inspected and counted every last banana and packet of medicine which the U. S. sent to Cuba. The recipients of the food and medicines were supposed to be the Cuban people, but refugees from Cuba reported that not a trace of them was ever seen by Cubans. Typical of refugees' reports was this story published under the headline "Cuban Ransom Drugs Disappear" in the New Orleans *States-Item* after the blackmail had been sent to Castro:

> What happened to the more than $60 million in United States drugs and medicine sent to Cuba last month?
>
> Havana doctors still have not seen a trace of the medical supplies nor has the public seen evidence of them in Havana pharmaceutical or drug stores, a newly arrived refugee said in New Orleans today.
>
> The refugee is Robertson Bosch, an X-ray technician who left Havana 15 days ago.
>
> "We can only guess what Castro has done with the medical supplies," he said. "The doctors I know, who are still in Cuba, believe they have either been sent to the Communist countries, or are being hidden or held in reserve for some reason."

And who was "cashiered" for the Bay of Pigs debacle among the amateur strategists? Just one man—Adolph Berle. It seemed the time to call the military back into the picture. Certainly the Inner Circle as military experts did not appear an attractive alternative to the military as pictured in a secret memorandum by Senator Fulbright, chairman of the Senate Foreign Relations Committee, a strategist trained at Oxford University. At the time of the Walker case Fulbright had circulated a secret paper which stated:

> There is little in the education, training or experience of most military officers to equip them with the balance of judgment necessary to put their own ultimate solutions into proper perspective in the President's total strategy of the nuclear age.

The Inner Circle did, however, seem in line with Fullbright's further enlightening assertion:

> In the long run, it is quite possible that the principal problem of the leadership will be, if it is not already, to restrain the desire of the people to hit the Communists with everything we've got.

In the Bay of Pigs landing the Administration's amateur strategists demonstrated that they would not hit the Communists with a powder puff, *even if they so desired.*

Rumblings deliberately circulated by the Inner Circle that the Joint Chiefs of Staff were responsible for a bad Cuban landing plan, and even rumors that the plan had been former President Eisenhower's, took the heat off the amateur directors of our worst military debacle.

President Kennedy privately told a group of the nation's editors gathered at Washington's Statler-Hilton three days after the Bay of Pigs disaster that he had consulted in advance everyone in his Administration whom he had considered the best in the country, about the Cuban landings, "and every one of them was dead wrong!" John F. Kennedy spoke while still suffering from the shock, and his hands trembled. It was the worst indictment ever made by anyone of his amateur high command.

The President made clear to the editors that he would go ahead on Cuba—and then, on counsel from his advisers, did nothing about that island between his April 20, 1961, statement on October 22, 1963. Khrushchev was first incredulous, then he sarcastically told American visitors to Moscow: "At least we finished in Hungary." Finally, Khrushchev started to use Cuba as a military base, beginning his big build-up at least by July 1, 1962, more than a year after the Bay of Pigs failure. The Red leader obviously felt it was now safe to act. As a result, Americans awoke to be told that missiles were pointed at them from 90 miles away.

The role of the Inner Circle during this interim period of one and one-half years consisted of resisting the facts about the Red military build-up in Cuba as laid before them, of establishing a line that sounded feasible, and of attacking those uncouth enough to suggest the Soviets now meant business in Cuba.

Senator Kenneth Keating, Republican of New York, was ridiculed by them in August 1962, when he began making statements that Khrushchev had begun a military build-up in Cuba. The fact that Keating usually takes liberal positions on other issues did not save the gray-haired Senator from the sort of attack, including an attack on his character, usually reserved by the professorial clique for those of solidly conservative persuasion. Only those with full knowledge about Cuba could assay the whole picture, they asserted. Berlin, they claimed, was probably the real Soviet target. The debonair and witty Keating was, it was indicated by anonymous spokesmen, and through leaks to trusted newsmen, a bit on the stupid side. They claimed that Keating was being diverted by Cuba and that this was exactly what the Soviet leaders wanted—to have us pay attention to Cuba while they grabbed Berlin.

This sophistry might have succeeded with a lesser foe. The volume of such abuse had silenced many critics in the past, appalled by the force of invective suddenly hurled against them. But Keating, a seasoned fighter, merely persisted.

When, on August 31, the Republican Senator gave a detailed account of war materials being landed on Cuba, what each ship carried, and the number of Soviet troops already in Cuba, he could no longer be ignored. This was particularly true because Keating described the landing of what he said could well be Soviet medium-range ballistic missiles, describing their arrival at closed sheds on Cuban docks and their being hauled away in covered trucks under maximum security conditions.

The question afterwards was why, if a U.S. Senator could

obtain this information months before the showdown, the Kennedy advisers, with their keen intellects and access to all the agencies of government, could not. On September 4—five days later—the President felt compelled to answer the New York Senator. Kennedy said that only short-range defensive missiles, PT boats carrying rockets with a range of only 15 miles, and Soviet "technicians," not troops had arrived in Cuba. He remarked that there was "no evidence of significant capability in Cuban hands."

President Kennedy voiced his advisers' line that the real danger might be elsewhere, claiming that "the Cuban question must be considered as part of a worldwide challenge posed by Communist threats to peace." This constituted downgrading the Cuban threat. On the positive side, JFK said he would watch Cuban developments.

By mid-September, less than a month before the President was forced to admit that the Russian leaders had lied to him and had been building up an offensive force on Cuba for months, the Administration's amateur strategists had returned to vituperation. This was after Senator John Tower of Texas had warned the Senate on September 11 of possible rocket attack from Cuba. Senator Jack R. Miller of Iowa had called for a "war materiel blockade" on Cuba. Other prominent Republicans had joined in.

By September 18, the President, backing up his aides, himself attacked those whose "loose talk" might serve to give the "thin color of legitimacy to the pretense that a Communist threat exists." The President caustically remarked that "rash talk is cheap."

Then, on information funneled through his advisers, Mr. Kennedy stated: "There is no evidence of any organized combat force in Cuba, of military bases provided to Russia, of the presence of offensive ground-to-ground missiles."

This was the signal. Critics of the inaction on Cuba were at once castigated as "warmongers" by the amateur strategists and their spokesmen. It was declared that "a blockade is an act of war." This ding-dong attack spread from those close to

Kennedy at the White House, in State and at the Pentagon, to Kennedy followers campaigning out on the hustings throughout the nation.

On a campaign trip for Democratic candidates, the President went to New Haven, where he was booed. He went to Illinois, where he found apathetic crowds of a few thousand. The wheels began to turn. He suddenly canceled his campaign swing in the Midwest and returned to Washington. The story was that a break in the weather most fortunately permitted our reconnaissance planes to discover the Soviet medium-range ballistic missiles on pads and almost ready for use.

Senator Barry Goldwater had told his fellow Senators in early September, and had written in his diary: "The political situation is so bad for Kennedy that I predict when he gets around the country a bit and discovers it, he will *in mid-October,* invade Cuba."

It was Monday, October 22, in the late afternoon—after a publicity build-up which involved flying Congressional leaders hastily to Washington in Air Force jet planes for a conference—when Mr. Kennedy, at long last, was ready to act. *It was then two weeks before the Congressional elections.*

The youthful Chief Executive announced to his countrymen and to the world on TV in a calm and forceful manner that "a series of offensive missile sites is now in preparation" on Cuba. He said these constitute "an explicit threat to the peace and security of the Americas."

Instead of a "blockade," the President announced a "quarantine" of "surface missiles, bomber, aircraft, air-to-surface rockets and guided missiles and warheads for any of the above weapons."

In the relief of seeing what they believed was U.S. action at last, many of the American people forgot that this unnecessary threat to the safety of our nation had actually been caused by the Administration's failure to deal with the situation earlier. This segment of the American public stood solidly behind Kennedy, thrilled by the apparently determined President who seemed to be insisting upon only one thing—that Khrushchev get his nuclear rockets and his bombers out of Cuba. When, on the following Sunday, the Red leader apparently agreed, their enthusiasm knew no bounds. They demonstrated it by "standing by the President"—and by voting Democratic in the Congressional elections a few days later.

Not once during the six days of showdown was there any private or public indication that the American people wanted to appease the Soviets, or to have "peace at any price." This was true even though they were led to believe they might be put out of existence any moment by nuclear explosions. The American people themselves were the real heroes of the crisis.

Published reports pictured McGeorge Bundy gathering and analyzing reports dealing with the crisis for the President; the President's brother, Robert F. Kennedy, was credited with making the final decision for a blockade—pardon, a quarantine —and against an invasion on the recommendation of former Ambassador to Moscow Llewellyn Thompson, who argued that this formula gave Khrushchev "a way out." Dean Rusk was cited as being the first to note that Khrushchev's eyelids were flickering in the eyeball-to-eyeball staredown. It was made clear in an inspired syndicated newspaper column by the President's close personal friend, Charles Bartlett, that most of the Inner Circle were involved in the decision-making on the crisis. An "inside" story in *Look* magazine told the same tale.

The only trouble was that, in the moment of apparent victory, the President threw away the whole hand. A story went the rounds in Washington which illustrates how the showdown ended.

An American guide was showing a British visitor our Bunker Hill when the Britisher said: "We won that battle, didn't we?"

"I don't rightly know," said the guide, "but you see who holds Bunker Hill now."

Or as a gleeful Nikita Khrushchev told the meeting of the Congress of the East German Communist Party a few weeks later, in January 1963: "Some say the Soviets suffered a defeat in Cuba. But Cuba exists and it is growing."

The fact is that, despite Administration claims that President Kennedy won the Cuba "showdown," Khrushchev, Castro and the Red Chinese are more firmly in control of Cuba than they were before the so-called "showdown." Fidel Castro has stepped up training of Communist saboteurs and spies and is waging even more intensive political warfare against all of Latin America for the takeover of Central and South America by the international Communist conspiracy. His timetable for the near future includes Panama (where Communist agitators have long been preparing riots preliminary to the takeover of the Panama Canal), and all of Central America.

Overshadowing the whole October-November "showdown'" was the excessive fear by the amateur strategists of what Khrushchev termed "atomic holocaust." Charles Bartlett described how the fear of nuclear destruction led to the Administration's initial decision not to invade Cuba and to the decision not to knock out the emplaced rockets from the air. As is demonstrated by the results of the Cuban missile "showdown," it is this craven fear of atomic war which, in Communist-inspired crisis after crisis, is emasculating America's life-or-death struggle against the Communist march across the earth. As Senator Barry Goldwater has summarized it in *The Conscience of A Conservative,* "If we do that—if we tell ourselves that it is more important to avoid war than to keep our freedom—we are committed to a course that has only one terminal point: surrender . . . If we, and not they [the Soviets] rule out the possibility of using that power, the Kremlin can create crisis after crisis, and force the U.S., because of our greater fear of war, to back down every time. And it cannot be long before a universal Communist empire sits astride the globe."

The history of the cold war demonstrates that the Communists do not want atomic war, and in the few times the U.S. has stood firm against the Communists during Kremlin-inspired crisis, the Communists have backed down on every occasion. During the Cuban "showdown," however, our amateur strategists were guided by an overriding fear of atomic war. The result is that today the Cuban people are still enslaved by communism, and all of Central and South America is being subverted by Communist agents based in Cuba.

During the Cuban crisis, no one in the Inner Circle, apparently, recognized that Khrushchev in effect publicly decided against war during the first day of the blockade, when he gave orders to some of his ships en route to Cuba—ships which were, in fact, carrying additional "offensive" weapons—to turn back. It would seem, also, that no Inner Circle member understands a basic dogma of communism: that the Communists plan to control the world. The Communists do not want to preside over atomic ashes, and therefore they did not want to risk the possible atomic war when the element of surprise was lost. Apparently no one in the Inner Circle realized that, with the atomic weapons superiority we then had, Khrushchev was not about to start an atomic war for continued control of an island 3,500 miles from the U.S.S.R.

The President's relief when Khrushchev announced he would withdraw Soviet rockets and bombers from Cuba was publicly palpable. In that relief from the tension, which his advisers had helped to instill in him, Kennedy was prepared to be overgenerous.

First, Kennedy backed down when Castro said "No" to on-site inspection of Cuba by either the U.S. or the UN to ascertain that the Soviets were carrying out their promise to take their rockets and troops out of Cuba. Then, instead of insisting that the U.S. inspect the Soviet ships leaving Cuba, which the Soviets merely *said* were loaded with missiles taken from the island, Kennedy trusted the Soviets' word. The only "evidence" which the U.S. had that the rockets were removed from Cuba was the sight of tarpaulin-covered forms on the decks of Soviet ships which had left Cuba. Many Americans suspected that the tarpaulin-covered forms were not missiles at all; and refugees from Cuba, as well as reports from the anti-Communist Cuban underground (whose reports, to date, on events in Cuba have never been wrong) declared that the forms underneath the tarpaulins were only wooden dummies. The Soviet missiles, both groups reported, are still in Cuba, hidden in natural caves on the island.

Moreover, revealed the anti-Red Cubans, the Soviet troops who "evacuated Cuba" on Soviet ships did not leave the island at all; they were merely loaded onto transport ships, and then debarked under cover of night in other parts of the island.

An even more serious outcome of the Cuba so-called "showdown" is the probability that the late President Kennedy gave a secret pledge to the Communists that the United States will never invade Cuba, and that we will prevent our allies from invading Cuba—a promise which was given by Kennedy to Khrushchev, it appears, in a series of secret messages exchanged between them during the Cuban crisis. The existence of our "no invasion" pledge was proclaimed as a fact by the Soviet Communist Party in a message to the Chinese Communists, published in the July 15, 1963, New York *Times*. The message read in part:

> Agreement on the removal of missile weapons, in reply to *the United States government's commitment not to invade Cuba, and to keep its allies from doing this*—have made possible the frustration of the plans of the extreme adventuristic circles of American imperialism which were ready to go the whole hog. . . . The United States is keeping its word about not attacking Cuba—there are no interventions in the borders of Cuba.

United Nations Secretary General U Thant revealed, during his secret conferences with Castro in the October missile crisis, that the Administration's plan to make a "no invasion of Cuba" pledge to the Communists was a fact. But, he added, the pledge was to be given only if Castro allowed on-site inspection of the island.

Despite the fact that Castro refused to grant on-site inspections—and even though President Kennedy declared in his first press conference after the Cuba crisis that he had made "no commitment" with Khrushchev of which the American people were unaware—the Soviet Communist Party publicly boasted that the promise had been given and was being kept.

The President and his Inner Circle spokesmen continued to deny the existence of a "no invasion" pledge; but events after the Cuban crisis point to the pledge's being a reality. For example, in an address on the first evening of the San José Conference of the Central American countries, held in the Costa Rican capital from March 18 to 20, 1963, Kennedy made it crystal clear that communism in Cuba is here to stay, that he had no intention of toppling the Cuban Communist bastion, and that he would not enforce the Monroe Doctrine against Cuba. More important, Kennedy also made it clear that he would not wage political warfare against communism in Cuba or anywhere else in the Western Hemisphere.

Mr. Kennedy polished off his attendance at the San José Conference by telling the students of the University of Costa Rica that the United States had made "many mistakes" and had "many failures" in dealing with Latin America. Not once did he mention communism as the enemy in Latin America. On the morning he was leaving the conference, Kennedy received a delegation of laborers, students and teachers who presented him with a scroll signed by 60,000 Costa Ricans beseeching him to "take drastic action against communism" and "to eradicate it in this hemisphere." If the Costa Ricans read Mr. Kennedy's statements to the San José Conference, they knew their pleadings were in vain.

Almost immediately after returning from Costa Rica, Kennedy gave additional striking evidence of the no-invasion pledge. In April—faithful to his advisers' doctrine of "permitting the survival of Communist regimes" as enunciated by Rostow, Bundy, et al—Kennedy ordered the U. S. Coast Guard to intercept and stop anti-Communist Cuban freedom fighters who were trying to carry out hit-and-run raids against Castro's Cuba and against Soviet ships en route to Cuba.

Kennedy's orders to halt anti-Communist refugees from operating went far beyond the Cuban situation. On April 7, 1963, Columnists Allen and Scott reported:

President Kennedy's harsh crackdown on Cuban exile groups is being broadened to include the activities of the anti-Communist eastern European refugee groups in the U. S. This undercover policy shift calls for hamstringing the efforts of the European refugees. . . . The secret crackdown already is compelling Baltic and Russian exile groups to restrict their anti-Communist activities.

The Allen-Scott report noted that the Kennedy crackdown had already closed the Eastern Europeans' center, Baltic House, which had "served as a major exile headquarters for exposing Soviet tyranny, helping defectors escape from the Iron Curtain," etc.

John F. Kennedy's crackdown on anti-Communist Cuban freedom fighters continued unabated, even to the date of his assassination. A report published in *National Review* of November 12, 1963, stated:

Leaders of the Cuban exile militants, it is reported, were called in about a month ago and read a letter. The letter directed that all raids will cease, that anyone participating in, supporting, or connected with these raids will be arrested and prosecuted for violation of the Neutrality Act, and that offenders will be liable to a penalty of 25 years in prison. The letter was signed by John F. Kennedy.

The fact that John F. Kennedy was assassinated by a dedicated Communist and fanatical admirer of Castro is an ironic postscript to Kennedy's painstaking protection of a Communist bastion 90 miles from American shores. After the assassination, there was much speculation that perhaps Kennedy's insistence upon keeping Cuba in Communist hands was more than incidental to his demise.

The polls taken since the Cuban crisis by Mr. Kennedy's crack pulse-taker, Lou Harris, had been showing a rising fever of resentment at Kennedy's do-nothing policy about the Cuban Communist bastion, and for at least six months before the assassination it had been common knowledge in informed circles, both in the U. S. and Latin America, that Kennedy planned to overthrow Castro and replace him with a Tito-type Communist puppet (who would receive American aid, of course), in a ruse to calm the rising fears of the American people—and, not incidentally, to bolster the crumbling image of Kennedy in the Presidential election year. As one example, on July 20, 1963 (four months before the assassination), the anti-Communist Cuban Information Service in Miami published the following report:

> The U. S. and Russia have agreed that Castro must go; he will become the fall guy in a complete reorganization of the regime which will purportedly be free of Soviet influence. The plan calls for "uprisings," "desertions" and "guerilla fronts"— all directed by the Reds in Cuba and their agents in exile.
>
> Castro flees to Moscow; and a new government is set up with such men as David Salvador, Manuel Ray and Hubert Matos as top dogs. . . . Then an election, Soviet style, with the certain winners to be Ray, Salvador and/or Matos.

John Martino, an American citizen of Italian descent who spent three years in the hell of a Castro dungeon, verified plans for the Castro ouster from his home in Miami, where he works closely with Cuban refugees:

> Cuban exiles here understand that plans for this operation were cleared with a Soviet representative in Europe shortly after the missile crisis of last October. The old-line Communists inside the Castro regime were to take part in the operation, together with Castro henchmen who had been paid to switch sides . . .
>
> It was to be staged for February 1964, According to reports from usually reliable exile sources, Khrushchev had agreed to the plan because of the importance to the Soviet Union of re-electing the Democratic Administration.

In the eyes of many observers, Kennedy's planned overthrow of Castro and replacement with another Communist was to be his 1964 Presidential election year companion piece to the Cuban missile so-called "showdown" which he staged two weeks before the Congressional elections in 1962, and which swept so many Democrats to victory at the polls.

But, according to John Martino's informed analysis, Castro's "assassination of Kennedy was a bold way of checkmating this plan." In September, two months before the assassination, Castro himself had hinted broadly that he might kill Kennedy, when Fidel told newsmen at the Cuban embassy in Brazil that CIA agents had been sent to Cuba to assassinate him. If Kennedy was behind this, Castro declared, "the American President should realize that he is not the only politician able to engineer the assassinations of Heads of State."

Considering that Lee Harvey Oswald was a dedicated Communist who was a regional chairman and militant worker for the Castro-operated Fair Play for Cuba Committee, that he traveled to Mexico City with another man and two women for a conference with Castro's consul, Eusabia Azcue, on September 27, 1963, and that almost immediately afterwards he procured a job at the Texas Book Depository for his assassination vantage point—it is hardly outside the realm of possibility that Oswald was a Castro gunman hired to kill Kennedy and thwart his plan to oust Castro.

Although President Kennedy is dead, his policies toward Cuba (and toward everything else) have not missed a beat under President Johnson. America's citizens continue to exist with a Communist fortress 90 miles from our shores, despite the fact that every opinion poll in the nation shows that the American people want action on Cuba. The threat of attack from Cuba is a very real possibility, and as nuclear strategist Admiral Chester Ward has explained:

> What can Cuba-based missiles do that Russia-based missiles can't? Soviet missiles launched from Russia give 30 minutes' warning. U.S. SAC bombers can get into the air in 15 minutes and destroy Russia in retaliation. The Cuban missiles take *only three to six minutes* of travel time, give even less warning than that, and could destroy most of the SAC bombers on the ground in any normal non-alert situation . . .
>
> The Russians can also achieve the same results—that is, of a no-warning spearhead for their surprise attack—by launching missiles from submarines. . . . They do not need nuclear-propelled submarines to launch missiles against the United States. Already, they admittedly have so-called "fishing boat" bases in Cuba . . .
>
> The point is that right now, we have to face the possibility of a surprise attack being launched with the "no-warning" spearhead missiles coming from Cuba, or from Soviet submarines . . .

Remember, Khrushchev doesn't need to have enough missiles outside of Russia to destroy the United States without warning. All he needs is enough missiles to get the no-warning spearhead to destroy SAC.

On September 14, 1960, candidate Kennedy declared: "If communism should obtain a permanent foothold in Latin America . . . then the balance of power would move against us and peace would be even more insecure."

On May 20, 1963, seven months after the Cuban so-called "showdown," the American Security Council answered Mr. Kennedy: "Today, communism does have a permanent foothold in Latin America. The 1960 prophecy of candidate Kennedy has come dismally true. But President Kennedy's advisers, such as Mr. Bundy, are engaged in a massive effort to deny the truth of the President's earlier prophecy."

As a matter of fact, negotiations for a "deal" which went far beyond the Cuba issue were in progress during the Cuban crisis, first through U Thant, and then directly through the Kennedy-Khrushchev messages. One of these messages, a key one, has never been made public.

In those messages which were disclosed, Khrushchev said that if we would withdraw our offensive weapons from Turkey, he would withdraw his in Cuba. Mr. Kennedy replied that he should get his out of Cuba first. Khrushchev properly took this as an agreement and simply *announced* withdrawal of his rockets and bombers. Not too long thereafter we *actually* withdrew our rockets, not only from Turkey but from Italy as well.

Moreover, on October 27, 1962, Kennedy advised Khrushchev: "If your letter signifies that you are prepared to discuss a détente affecting NATO and the Warsaw Pact [Soviet bloc], we are quite prepared to continue to exchange views on this question with you and to find a reasonable solution."

In his statement ending this interchange, President Kennedy remarked:

"It is my earnest hope that the governments of the world can, with a solution of the Cuban crisis, turn their attention to the compelling necessity for ending the arms race and reducing world tensions."

Thus, when the smoke cleared away, Khrushchev held the showdown site, Cuba itself, with something like 38,000 Russian troops and 100,000 satellite personnel, including secret police. Not only were Castro and communism firmly in the Cuban political saddle; not only was a committee of the Organization of American States compelled to state that the solution left "the threat to hemispheric security much more serious"; but Khrushchev now had just the kind of *world* deal with the U. S. he had been looking for. The Joint Chiefs of Staff could feel fortunate that not they, but the Administration's amateur strategists, were responsible for this appeasing "deal."

There are other outgrowths of the Cuban "crisis," and none of them bodes well for the United States: our gentlemen's agreement with the Soviet Union to end nuclear testing everywhere except underground; and the talk of "non-aggression pacts" between the United States and the U.S.S.R., and between the NATO nations and the Warsaw Pact Communist nations— even though such "nonaggression pacts" are traditional Soviet weapons for getting victim nations to let their guards down while the Soviets gear to smash them. The tragic aftermaths of "nonaggression" pacts with the Soviet Union range from the early Soviet reconquest of Georgia, to the Soviet takeover of Czechoslovakia.

Other outgrowths of the Cuba "crisis" have been the previously mentioned stepped-up American unilateral disarmament, and the scrapping of our first-strike weapons and new weapons like the Skybolt missile.

The so-called "hot line" between the Kremlin and the White House now shows the world that our allies have been shoved into the background and that the President of the United States and Khrushchev are dealing directly on matters of life or death for the world, with only the British occasionally allowed to listen in and agree to decisions.

It is ironic that Andrei Gromyko, who Kennedy publicly declared had lied to him about Cuba a few months before, initialed the nuclear test-ban treaty for Red Russia. Although we are pledged to stop vital nuclear tests of our weapons in the atmosphere, the treaty does not prohibit the Soviets from testing their nuclear weapons in the atmosphere in their new Potemkin Village of China, in Cuba, in their East Europe slave satellites—as long as they don't get caught doing the testing themselves.

After initialing of the Test-Ban Treaty, and just before the Senate ratified the pact, President Kennedy spoke before the United Nations and virtually admitted that our $40 billion moonshot, Project Apollo, was another major New Frontier blunder.

In this September 20, 1963, speech the President offered to cancel our moon race. He offered to substitute, instead, a cooperative outer space exploration program "in partnership with the Soviet Union."

When the $40 billion moonshot program was first proposed, we had just suffered ignominious defeat at the Bay of Pigs. Our manned bomber program was on the way to a phase-out. The theory of the New Frontier thinkers was that billions for a moonshot would give a nice shot in the arm to the American economy—not to mention a $130 million lunarnaut training center for Texas, the home state of then-Vice President Lyndon Johnson, plus a $50 million electronics research center for the President's home state of Massachusetts, the state that 30-year-old Senator Ted Kennedy had promised to "do more for."

President Johnson had now taken up international space cooperation in partnership with the Soviets, much as he has taken up internationalism in almost every other area of American endeavor. In the minds of many members of Congress and of informed Americans, this proposal of an outer space U. S.-Soviet "cooperative program" forecasts an end to the Project Apollo moonshot—with billions of U. S. taxpayers' dollars thus poured down the drain.

In an analysis of Kennedy's UN proposal, Clare Booth Luce wrote in the October 1, 1963 New York *Journal-*

American: "What few foresaw, even a month ago, was that the President himself would call off the moon-race concept. Now that he has decided to do so, what is the future of Project Apollo?"

Or, one might add, what is the future of almost every other facet of American national endeavor? Have we embarked on a suicidal program of "cooperation" with the Communists, who have sworn to destroy the United States of America?

After the Kennedy fiasco in Cuba, the amateur strategists took another step in getting control over the military. This came with the removal of none other than the Chief of Naval Operations, Admiral George Anderson. The Navy had performed superbly during the October crisis, forcing Soviet submarines to the surface, for instance, and chasing one almost to Gibraltar to do so. It was not because of naval failure that the admiral was dropped and shunted to Portugal as U. S. Ambassador to that country.

It was because, behind the scenes, Admiral Anderson had stood up the Kennedy politicians and professors in the military realm, as well as on TFX, and it was also because President Kennedy wanted to give away Polaris submarines to our allies, who were dismayed and angry because promised Skybolt missiles would not be delivered. Admiral Anderson took a strong stand against the Inner Circle Whiz Kids cutting in on military communications in the name of the Secretary of Defense. He threatened to make public what was happening unless the authorities, including the Secretary of Defense, halted the practice.

As a result of this and other showdowns, the Chief of Naval Operations ended up with the sole right to communicate with the Polaris submarines, no matter where they were or under whose control. If the submarines were to be given to Britain and others, Admiral Anderson had to go. That is why he, and not Air Force Chief of Staff Curtis LeMay, was bounced. LeMay had publicly indicated his disapproval of the Skybolt abandonment by testing a Skybolt and reporting the test successful, a fact somewhat blurred by quick Salinger and Sylvester statements about what he really meant. LeMay is more blunt than the debonair, usually diplomatic Anderson. But the Polaris submarines simply could not be effectively transferred unless Anderson went.

The Anderson removal, even more than the Walker case, showed who is running our military policies and operations. It showed what happens when one "bucks," even privately, the Inner Circle professors and their associates.

If anyone believes that the Joint Chiefs of Staff willingly approved the nuclear test-ban treaty, he is naive. General LeMay said, in effect, that he did not want to suffer Admiral Anderson's fate, when LeMay testified that he could not judge the "political" merits of the test-ban treaty.

It was a paradox that because Anderson had publicly carried the ball for the President whenever necessary, as an American officer should, members of Congress would not speak out against Anderson's dismissal. The report given here on why Anderson was dismissed has hitherto been known only to a few, and very possibly will be denied by those concerned. It is, nevertheless, accurate.

Slated next to go is General Curtis LeMay right after the 1964 elections.

So today we have an amateur from Harvard, McGeorge Bundy, acting as Chief of Staff of the United States or, if you like, Chairman of the Joint Chiefs. Neither he nor anyone on his civilian staff will ever have to be censored for saying harsh things about communism. Nor do we have to worry about winning the cold war against communism; they have proved in action that they do not want to win. Instead, they favor "accommodation," letting the U. S. become a "peripheral power," and finally reach "an end to nationhood."

Worried about public resentment toward the amateur strategist policies, Dean Rusk once said we do intend to "win" the cold war. He then explained that he meant "not for the United States," but for "mankind." There is only one problem: the Communists believe they represent "mankind."

CHAPTER FIVE

An End To Security — The Otepka Case

"For on his choice depends the safety and the health of the whole state."

Shakespeare—HAMLET, I. iii. 17.

IT WAS A FOREGONE CONCLUSION that with Adam Yarmolinsky—the great critic of federal security against loyalty and security risks—actually in the Kennedy-Johnson Inner Circle, there would take place an effective smashing of security procedures in sensitive federal departments and agencies. The effective smashing of the Security Office of the State Department might well be called Adam Yarmolinsky's "fifty-first case."

The last hurrah for the State Department's security setup came immediately after the advent of the Kennedy Administration, when the State Security Office ruled that now-Assistant Secretary of State Harlan Cleveland should not be given even a temporary security clearance, and this ruling was upheld by the State Department's Acting Administrator of Security.

However, Secretary of State Dean Rusk overrode the evidence against Cleveland and personally waived security requirements for Cleveland. Rusk revealed this in a letter he wrote to a Congressman, and claimed that his personal clearance of Cleveland was "based on FBI reports"; but if this is so, the State Department's professional security officers—who also used the FBI's reports about Cleveland—certainly had drawn quite different conclusions from Rusk's.

Indeed, a Senate Internal Security Subcommittee report issued in the autumn of 1963 revealed that up to mid-1962— more than a year before—Dean Rusk had personally waived security checks for 152 new key State Department employees, most of them over the violent objections of State's security office. In fact, many others had been personally "cleared" by Rusk and were working in the State Department without the security office's even knowing about them.

After the State security office had refused clearance to

151

Cleveland, the security division was "reorganized," reportedly along the lines planned by William Wieland, the "Ex-President of the Fidel Castro Fan Club."

The first "reorganization" move of the Kennedy Administration was to abolish the jobs of 23 of State's professional agents. They were given 30 days to "show cause" why their jobs should not be abolished. Other security men were given minor and meaningless jobs calculated to make them resign. Many key security professionals, who had memorized dozens of security files and who could be "troublesome" if they were accorded too much of "the treatment," were sent abroad to meaningless jobs. Some of these were given foreign assignments on "security," which were so laughable, they could be compared with giving J. Edgar Hoover a job as a traffic cop.

One top security official who received a "show cause" notice was Otto Otepka, chief of all personnel security, whose "security risk" findings at State skyrocketed into headlines across the nation in the summer and autumn of 1963, when Otepka revealed to the Senate Internal Security Subcommittee that Assistant Secretary of State Harlan Cleveland was trying to worm Alger Hiss and a number of other known security and loyalty risks back into the State Department. Otepka told the Senate subcommittee a lot more about the hanky-panky at State, too.

Otepka was no mere cog in the wheel in the State Department's security setup. He was the top man, the ranking Deputy Director of the Security Office, and was in charge of the entire personnel security organization of the U.S. State Department, both in Washington and in American embassies and consulates throughout the world.

Otepka was a hard-nosed security boss and, until the advent of the Kennedy Administration, his security office of the State Department had been one of the most highly professional organizations in the federal government. It was Otepka's security organization, for instance, which had fingered Foreign Service Officer Irving Scarbeck, who was subsequently convicted and imprisoned for giving American secrets to a female Soviet

Polish spy in Warsaw. The Communist Mata Hari revealed in a U.S. court that the Soviet espionage apparatus had forced her to become Scarbeck's mistress in order to wean American secrets from him.

Otepka was absolutely nonpolitical, and had been drafted into the State Department in 1953 from the Civil Service Commission because he was regarded in government circles as one of the finest, most dispassionate and most objective appraisers of personnel records in federal career service. In the federal government since 1936, Otepka has the ability to realize that many people may have at least one skeleton in their family closets, but never to let this by itself disqualify an applicant for service, recognizing that in some cases, one can tell a workman by his chips. In fact, in 1958, Otepka was given the State Department's Meritorious Service Award for his outstanding work.

As chief of personnel security, it was Otepka's duty to investigate State Department "mistakes" about hailing Castro as a Robin Hood and letting Fidel establish a Communist bastion and staging area for communizing all of Latin America, 90 miles from American shores. Of course this involved investigating William Wieland, who had been chief of the State Department's Office of Middle-American Affairs during the Eisenhower Administration and who is a carryover into the Kennedy and Johnson Administrations. Otepka did a thorough investigation of Wieland and wrote a sizzling report on him, which has never been published; but it is known that Otepka said Wieland definitely should be dismissed.

Wieland has not been fired by the Administration; in fact, President Kennedy made it clear that he was pleased with Mr. Wieland. This was brought to national attention at Kennedy's January 24, 1962, press conference when he informed the nation that he had personally cleared Wieland for security (making it plain that he had acted on Dean Rusk's advice) and asserted that Wieland could perform his duties "without detriment to the interests of the United States."

Indeed, far from being dismissed, Wieland was, in fact, the senior officer (with two others, one of whom was J. Clayton

Miller) who reportedly planned the Kennedy Administration's "reorganization" of the State Department's security setup. Naturally, the State Department has denied that Wieland even had a hand in helping to smash State's security organization. Even putting aside Wieland's hideous pro-Communist record, it was a case of a man under investigation as a loyalty and security risk firing his chief investigator, Otto Otepka!

As soon as the State security office had been effectively smashed, the Foreign Service officer in charge, William Boswell, was one of those transferred overseas.

What security against loyalty and security risks now remains in the State Department? Even those few experts still in State's security office are so subjected to pressures from the top that there is no longer any effective security in the State Department. Actually, the New Frontiersmen and the Foreign Service are still policed, except that they now police themselves —politically, but certainly not for security and loyalty, most observers declare.

Self-policing of "security" is now standard procedure throughout much of the federal government under the Johnson Administration. This chapter on State Department security is written only to give the public an idea of the situation throughout Washington and at our government posts overseas.

This self-policing of security procedures extends even to our super-secret government agencies which handle atomic and military secrets, as could be seen in the autumn of 1963, when two traitors were tabbed by the FBI for feeding top-secret Strategic Air Command (SAC) secrets to a ring of Soviet spies. Both men, John Butenko and Jack Conklin (Conklin died mysteriously in an auto crash before arrest), worked for International Electric Corporation on highly secret Air Force contracts and had been cleared by the Air Force Office of Special Investigation, which explained, "It is up to the individual plant to determine what type of clearance is required for an employee. The plant itself can give a lower clearance classification."

When the case broke it was discovered that Butenko,

who held a top-secret security clearance, had Russian parents, a police record, and had been fired from the Navy in the middle of World War II on a medical discharge "because of constitutional traits which rendered him unfit for naval service." Conklin, who had a secret security clearance, had also been strangely discharged from the service in the middle of World War II, had a police record for cruelty to his child, was a habitual drunk, had been married five times, had beaten his fourth wife, and Wife Number Five never knew about Wife Number Four.

The New York *Journal-American's* reporting of the case declared: "Is the nation's internal security being jeopardized by inadequate screening of persons working on 'classified' government defense contracts? The answer is Yes."

What happened to Otto Otepka is an excellent example of what now happens to anyone working for the federal government during the Johnson Administration who raises questions about loyalty or security, or who knows too much.

During Otepka's decade of service as a State Department top security official, he had appraised the file of *every* State Department employee. Otepka was a highly competent professional security agent, as seen by his sleuthing and breaking of the Irving Scarbeck case. In some cases Otepka refused, after careful and impartial investigation, to clear high-ranking State Department employees, among them Assistant Secretary of State Harlan Cleveland.

Otepka obviously was a danger to the Administration, because of his detailed knowledge and prodigious memory of the pro-Communist records and activities of New-Frontier appointees, as well as other appointees' "defects" in character. So Otepka was to be ditched, along with the 23 other State security officers. However, such a howl was raised in Congress, that Otepka was retained, but the New Frontiersmen officially abolished his job and he was demoted to the relatively minor job of evaluating security files. A concerted effort was then made to get rid of Otepka, and finally, when he had adamantly refused to resign, State Department VIPs tried to shunt him off to the

National War College in May 1962. He refused to go, recognizing the move as another step in the plan to get rid of him.

In October 1962, the Senate Internal Security Subcommittee held hearings to investigate William Wieland, and subpoenaed Otto Otepka for testimony; and what Otepka told the Senators blew the whistle on Wieland. Otepka also told the Senators that in the adverse report he had written on Wieland after his investigation, he had specified and documented "serious questions of the man's integrity," and had urged that Wieland's case "should be reviewed and adjudicated under the Foreign Service regulations of the Department of State."

Early in 1963, as part of the Senate subcommittee's continuing interest in Wieland and in other controversial State Department security cases, the subcommittee scheduled hearings to delve into additional State Department cases. Otepka was subpoenaed to testify in secret session.

Otepka testified for six days—and what he told the Senators nearly blew the ceiling out of the hearing room, with what one Senator on the subcommittee termed "political dynamite."

One Senate aide, emerging bug-eyed from the hearing room, grimly told the author: "The number of security risks whom Otepka turned down—only to have them 'cleared' by the top brass of the State Department—is greater than anyone in the nation has realized."

It has been made public that Otepka declared the State Department to be riddled with men of questionable security backgrounds, many of them in the high echelons of the Department.

It is known that Otepka named Walt "The-Soviets-Are-Mellowing" Rostow (who sets all policy for the State Department and has established the whole "Soviets-are-mellowing" policy throughout the Administration); Harlan Cleveland; and William Wieland as being among the men whose backgrounds he considered at least "questionable."

Then the Senators called to these secret hearings several State Department officials to testify about the same cases which

Otepka had discussed. These officials swore that the facts were absolutely opposite to what Otepka had described, and furthermore, they said, Otepka had never even brought these questionable cases to their attention.

The Senators recalled Otepka and ordered him, under oath, to document his previous testimony about the questionable security cases.

Otepka produced State Department memoranda and papers from State Department files, in what one Senator described as "ironclad documentation" of every word Otepka had previously uttered about the security cases involved, and in documented refutation of what the State Department officials had sworn about these same cases.

Furthermore, Otepka also proved that the State officials had lied under oath when they testified that they knew nothing about the cases and that Otepka had never brought the cases to their attention. Otepka produced papers about the cases, initialed and noted in reply to Otepka's bringing the cases to their attention—by the very same State Department officials who had sworn they knew nothing about the cases.

The personal cost to himself of Otepka's testimony can never be fully realized by the American public. When word of Otepka's testimony reached the White House, Otepka was given the full treatment with ruthless efficiency, reportedly at the personal order of Bobby Kennedy.

On June 27, 1963, Otepka was called into the office of John J. Reilly, State's chief security officer, and a personal friend of Bobby Kennedy. Reilly told Otepka that his duties were being taken away from him. His new assignment was to update a handbook on security. As the two men walked back to Otepka's office, six security officers joined them, entered Otepka's office, seized all his records, the contents of 14 safes, and started making arrangements to change the combinations. Otepka went out to keep a luncheon appointment, and when he returned, he found that he was barred from his office and given a cubbyhole in which to update his handbook. His secretary was taken away from him and he was to be allowed secretarial help only with the permission of Reilly.

His cubbyhole was bugged; his telephone was tapped and then taken away from him; the trash from his wastebasket and "burn bag" was collected and searched surreptitiously by Reilly, who had the little burn bag (which is used to destroy classified waste material) marked with a red "X" and brought to the State Department mail room, where he sneaked in into his brief case. Junior G-man Reilly then laboriously pasted together scraps of Otepka's torn papers, peered at reams of Otepka's typewriter ribbons, and devoted hours of the taxpayers' time and money to "git" Otepka. Otepka faced Reilly and asked him for an explanation of the whole thing, but Reilly refused to explain. Finally Bobby Kennedy dispatched FBI investigators to interrogate Otepka for hours on end.

But bravely Otepka struggled on. He refused to resign. He forced the security risks to fire the security officer.

The Senate subcommittee hearings were getting so hot, that Secretary of State Dean Rusk conferred personally and privately with President Kennedy about strategy in the matter of purging the patriot who had struggled to keep security risks out of the State Department. The decision was reached. On August 15, Abba Schwartz, the State Department's Administrator of Security—a political appointee who has had some experience in immigration cases, but who does not have a single day's training in security procedures or regulations—issued an order forbidding State Department employees to appear before the Senate Internal Security Subcommittee, or to have anything to do with the Senate subcommittee personnel. Reilly also gave the same order to his own personnel. The move was lashed in Congress as "an outrageous interference with the right of Congress to investigate, and an interference with the right of free speech."

On September 23, 1963, as soon as the Senate was sewed up to approve the test-ban treaty, the State Department filed charges of "misconduct" against Otepka for allegedly improperly turning over State Department documents to J. G. Sourwine, chief counsel of the Senate Internal Security Subcommittee. Opteka was given ten days to answer the charges, procured a ten-day extension, and was scheduled to be suspended without pay. Since the State Department could not charge Otepka with falsifying testimony before the Senate subcommittee—because he himself had refuted the perjured testimony of State Department officials—they charged him with "misconduct" in giving documents to Sourwine.

The fact is, however, that Otto Otepka had responded to the subpoena of a duly constituted subcommittee of the United States Senate to substantiate charges he had made against alleged security risks in the State Department—in answer to Senators' specific questions—by producing documented evidence carrying notes and initials of the selfsame State Department officials who had sworn they had never laid eyes on the documents! Otepka's act of refuting, chapter and verse, with documented evidence—under subpoena of a Senate subcommittee—the perjury of the New Frontiersmen about security cases was alleged by the New Frontiersmen to be *a violation of security!*

The State Department, caught dead to rights in the act of lying to a Senate subcommittee, based its flimsy charges against Otepka on the basis that he violated a 1948 Executive Order issued by Harry Truman—to bar Congressional probes into the case of convicted Communist William Remington and into the Alger Hiss Case—which says that files on government employees are not to be given to members of Congress, except through the President.

However, that same year, 1948, Congress passed a law (Title V, Section 52 of the United States Code), which reads:

> The rights of persons employed in the civil service of the United States . . . to furnish information to either House of Congress or to any committee or member thereof, shall not be denied or interfered with.

Furthermore, in 1958, a concurrent resolution was passed by both Houses of Congress which reads:

Any person in Government service should put loyalty to
highest moral principles and country above loyalty to persons,
party or Government department.

Otepka cited the U.S. Code statute in his October 14
rebuttal of the charges against him, and furthermore he denied
that he had ever furnished classified documents or other re-
stricted information to any unauthorized person. Moreover,
Otepka cited a Senate report as proof that Dean Rusk himself
had shown classified loyalty documents to a Senator.

In the meantime, the Senate Internal Security Subcommittee, enraged by the total lack of cooperation and the gag
order of the State Department, had been trying since early
July to get Dean Rusk to testify about the case in secret session.
Rusk had first pleaded that he was too busy about negotiations
with Russia; then the Senators forced him into making several
appointments to testify, all of which he broke. Finally on
October 2, the entire bi-partisan Senate Judiciary Committee
took the unprecedented step of dispatching a U.S. Senator to
deliver a document by hand—a ten-page bill of particulars and
statement of charges to Dean Rusk, who was having secret
conferences in New York with Soviet officials. The committee
dispatched Senator Thomas J. Dodd, vice-chairman of its Senate Internal Security Subcommittee, with the document and a
covering letter signed by Senator James O. Eastland, chairman
of the committee.

The sizzling document charged the State Department with
covering up laxity in State Department security operations;
it charged perjury by the State Department officials who had
testified in opposition to Otepka's documented evidence; and
it demanded that Dean Rusk produce witnesses, including himself, to testify about the questionable security procedures and
cases in the State Department.

At a press conference, President Kennedy was questioned
by a reporter about the State Department gag order, about the
whole Otepka scandal in which Otepka had named "William
Arthur Wieland, Walter W. Rostow, and many others." Kennedy completely evaded answering the questions about Rostow

and Wieland "and many others," and simply said that Rusk would appear before the Senators and clear up all those little difficulties.

The Senators finally got Rusk into the testimony chair and grilled him for hours in secret session. Unless Rusk performed some magician's tricks, he must have had some pretty uncomfortable hours trying to answer the Senators' charges. At this writing Rusk's testimony has not been released, but not a few Americans are looking forward with interest to seeing it.

On October 3, the St. Louis *Globe-Democrat* revealed that it was beginning to appear that there was even more behind the effort to oust Otto Otepka "than was first suspected":

> Suspicion is strong in Washington that the plot against him goes even beyond the State Department—that the character moving in on Otepka is a more powerful figure in our Government than the Secretary of State—none other than the President's brother, Attorney General Bobby Kennedy.
>
> What's it all about? . . .
>
> It's more because Mr. Otepka is a career man in Government service of unquestioned loyalty who thinks Congress is entitled to know what's going on, who wants real security measures carried out . . . In other words, Mr. Otepka has been a hard-line, anti-Communist State Department official—just like Miss Frances Knight, Director of the Passport Office, who has been in constant hot water with her superiors for the same reason . . .
>
> With Bobby Kennedy trying to move in *Kennedy people* to run things the Administration way, Mr. Otepka drew the line at *some characters he considered dubious*.
>
> The flimsy charges about what he told the subcommittee are reported incidental to getting rid of the State Department security official *who guarded the door*.

Not incidentally, the three-ring-circus Valachi hearings were stage-managed by Bobby Kennedy at precisely the same time as the Otepka case broke into October's headlines. The Otepka case, of course, is of enormous significance to the future well-being of our national security; whereas, according to FBI Director J. Edgar Hoover (and as corroborated by Hoover's opposite number in the Canadian government), every word

uttered by Valachi has been known for years by law enforce-
ment officers in the United States and other nations. Many
observers asserted flatly that staging the Valachi hearings at
that precise moment was an attempt by the Kennedy Administration to distract public attention from the security risks
scattered throughout the Kennedy Administration—as then
being enunciated by Otto Otepka.

On November 5, Otepka received his dismissal notice
from the State Department. Senators immediately rose to
Otepka's defense. Senator Strom Thurmond declared that
Otepka was "railroaded with methods characteristic of a
police state. Otepka should be reinstated, exonerated, and com-
mended for his courage. The dismissal points to the pressing
need for a full investigation of the State Department."

Thurmond denounced Otepka's dismissal as "a clear-cut
case of retaliation against a Government witness for cooperating
with a Senate committee." He declared that the State Department action is "an offense against the Congress," which may
"constitute contempt of the Senate, which is punishable by imprisonment."

Thurmond declared that the "American public, newspapers and private citizens have joined in demanding that the
State Department, this bureaucratic nightmare, be cleaned out
. . . the State Department is in bad need of a purge."

The Senator concluded, "It now appears that a purge of
personnel is being attempted. Unfortunately, it is the very opposite of what the critics of the State Department have in mind,
for it is, in effect, an attempted purge of patriots . . . The State
Department's attempted purge of patriots must not be tolerated,
and this very attempt is further evidence that a thorough investigation of the State Department is in order."

The Charleston *News and Courier* pointed to the fact
that the possibility of disloyalty in high echelons of the State
Department is hardly to be written off: "In view of the fact
that persons of proven disloyalty have held high posts in the
State Department in years past, the subcommittee has a duty
to dig deeply . . ."

DEAN RUSK

WALT WHITMAN ROSTOW

GEORGE BALL

HARLAN CLEVELAND

ADAM YARMOLINSKY

ROBERT S. MCNAMARA

PAUL H. NITZE

JEROME WIESNER

McGeorge Bundy

Arthur Schlesinger, Jr.

A sample of what one newspaper described as a case "which demonstrates honor as it now exists on the New Frontier" came to light in November. Three of the State Department officials whom the subcommittee had summoned to discuss Otepka's previous testimony and the entire Otepka case were: Elmer Hill, chief of State's technical services division; John Reilly, Otepka's boss, Deputy Assistant Secretary of State for Security, who is a personal friend of Bobby Kennedy, placed over Otepka when the New Frontier made its debut, and the man who set up the bugging of Otepka's cubbyhole, the tapping of Otepka's telephone, and the months-long harassment of Otepka—all reportedly at the personal order of Bobby Kennedy; and David Belisle, Reilly's special assistant.

The Senators asked the three men whether or not they knew anything at all about the bugging and telephone-tapping. All three men swore under oath that they knew nothing about it. But in November, when the subcommittee's investigators informed the Senators that they had ironclad evidence that the bugging and tapping had been done, and that Hill and Reilly had actually set it up, Senator Thomas Dodd charged Hill and Reilly with perjury. Quick as a wink, all three men hastily dispatched letters of "clarification" to the subcommittee. Hill and Reilly admitted that they had not told the whole story under oath, and had, in fact, been the men who bugged and tapped Otepka's cubbyhole.

On November 17, Reilly and Hill resigned from the State Department. Belisle pleaded that he had no "firsthand" knowledge of the shenanigans, but admitted that he knew about them, and that he had been out of the country when they took place. At this writing, Belisle is still ensconced in the State Department, and Bobby Kennedy has not yet given his friend Reilly a new job on the New Frontier.

At this writing, the Otepka affair bodes to be one of the bitterest clashes between the State Department and the Senate in American history, and M. Stanton Evans editor of the Indianapolis *News,* has written an excellent prognosis of the case:

The episode as a whole presents a rather unhappy picture of operating procedure in Foggy Bottom. We have, in order:

1. State Department official William Wieland, covering up the true nature of Fidel Castro's 26 July movement, helping steer the U.S. into diplomatic catastrophe in Cuba.

2. State Department higher-ups covering up for Wieland, overriding sensible security practices to do so.

3. State Department denial of the true facts of the security situation, in order to cover up for their previous cover-up of Wieland.

4. State Department reprisals against a man courageous enough to tell the truth about security procedures, in order to cover up for their general cover-up in the security picture as a whole.

In an interview with Williard Edwards of the Chicago *Tribune*, Otepka commented concerning Cover-up #3: "This put their testimony in conflict with mine and with my official knowledge. Their testimony was untrue. Since they had used the Subcommittee forum to make their statements, I felt entitled to rebut their statements and present the true facts . . . I'm charged with violation of orders when all I did was defend myself."

Considering the Department's over-all record in this field, it seems unlikely its campaign against Otepka is inspired by zeal for security. The Kennedy officials are obviously concerned to prevent Congress from knowing of their misfeasances—merely the latest flowering of Executive arrogance toward the legislature. The Senate Internal Security Subcommittee means to assert the rightful prerogatives of the lawmaking branch, and it is to be hoped the result will puncture the hubris of the foreign policy bureaucracy.

There are yet other ramifications of the Otepka case, embracing Assistant Secretary of State Harlan Cleveland. According to testimony before the Subcommittee, Cleveland has been bringing people of dubious security status into the State Department. Simultaneously, evidence has accumulated suggesting a sustained effort to dismantle the security office of the Department—a move described by former Security Chief John W. Hanes as either "incompetence or a deliberate attempt to render the State Department's security section ineffective." It was Otepka's difference with the New Frontier on these matters that allegedly brought on the vendetta against him. The Subcommittee has also been examining this aspect of the controversy.

The lesson of the Otepka case is plain. The State Department security against penetration by Communists and against other security risks has been smashed and exists effectively no longer.

And the man most knowledgeable on the subject, the man who struggled hardest and the most bravely to keep security in the State Department, is a man hunted, then destroyed, by the security risks themselves.

Why? Because he did a good job, and because he answered the subpoena of a duly constituted committee of the Senate and told what is going on in the State Department, revealing that the men around the President use strange means to get their strange friends into the State Department over the violent objections of men like Otto Otepka.

Another man ditched by the Administration's effective smashing of security in the State Department is Elmer Hipsley, who had been in charge of worldwide physical security in State's Office of Security, as Otepka had been in charge of worldwide personnel security.

Hipsley had been responsible for the safekeeping of such vital items as secret documents, secret codes and safes in U.S. embassies around the world. He was responsible for the personal safety of the Secretary of State wherever the Secretary traveled; and for the protection of all foreign officials visiting the United States.

Hipsley, big, red-haired and a tough ex-policeman, was—like Otepka and others—nonpolitical. In fact, he had entered State from the Secret Service. He is personally a quiet, though a fabulous, man. During the course of his work Hipsley has met the leaders of communism personally, and he understands and detests communism.

Hipsley was the Secret Service agent alone with Franklin D. Roosevelt when he died at Warm Springs, Georgia, in 1945. Hipsley stood behind FDR at Yalta, and knows firsthand what transpired at that disastrous conference. Hipsley was with President Harry Truman at Potsdam, and is believed to have handed Truman the message of the first atomic bomb explosion at Hiroshima.

Hipsley is respected by international security men ranging from Scotland Yard to Moscow and the Sureté. In his work he has known many of the world's Communist leaders, including Stalin—who did a good deal of talking with FDR at both Yalta and Teheran.

Although every patriotic American detests Khrushchev and the Communist slave system, many Americans were genuinely concerned about the possibility of war or similar disaster should harm befall the Butcher of the Ukraine and of Budapest when he was invited by President Eisenhower to visit the United States in September 1959, and covered 6,000 miles from East Coast to West and back. Elmer Hipsley was in complete charge of Khrushchev's safety from the time his plane set down at Andrews Air Force Base until his departure and, as Americans will recall, Nikita arrived, saw Eisenhower, and departed without an incident.

Security arrangements for a trip of this kind take not only highly professional skill but also most detailed planning, involving split-second timing. The problem was complicated by the fact that we have no national police force in the European sense of the world. While Hipsley had the support of the Secret Service, FBI, CIA and other federal agencies, he was largely dependent upon his own arrangements with local police forces, whether Khrushchev was traveling slowly through crowded cities or eating lunch in the middle of an Iowa wheat field.

Khrushchev, receiving hostile treatment from American crowds and protesting pickets, tried to gain sympathy by making a play involving security. Khrushchev complained that he was not being permitted to go to Disneyland, on the outskirts of sprawling Los Angeles, although it was his own security chief, General Zaharov, who had made that decision. After that ploy fizzled, Khrushchev claimed our security was so tight that he was not able to meet Americans freely. As he traveled north toward San Francisco, photographs showed Khrushchev visiting with some children at the Santa Barbara station platform where his train stopped. The Washington *Daily News* printed this picture and captioned it, "Khrushchev after the Relaxation of Security." In the photo, standing with his arms almost circling Khrushchev, was the omnipresent Hipsley. Incidentally, the crowd in San Francisco belied press reports by being as hostile as crowds elsewhere.

Elmer Hipsley's finest protective job, however, was in connection with Khrushchev's odious visit to New York, along with all the satellite stooges from Europe and Cuba, for the opening of the United Nations General Assembly in September, 1960.

Few in Washington thought that so many Communist masters of mass murder and bloody oppression could escape from New York unscathed or without some incident. There was Nasser of Egypt in an area of strong Jewish concentration. There was a racial minority in New York (and a large one throughout the nation) from every satellite nation which has been raped and subjugated. There were, for example, Baltic and Polish peoples whose whole families had been executed or who were still in slave-labor camps. With luck, it was said in Washington, Red leaders might leave the U.S. alive, but without incident? Impossible!

"New York's Finest"—her police force—received well-deserved credit for the fact that nothing happened. (Actually, so many New York policemen had to guard Khrushchev on his first visit to New York that the city later sent a bill to the UN for one million dollars in an attempt to recoup for the taxpayers part of the money they had expended. The UN never paid.) By statute, the State Department—and that meant Elmer Hipsley—was in charge of the safety of all these visitors when they were away from the UN building itself.

In a control room in the Waldorf-Astoria, although it was never revealed, sat Hipsley with a top New York police official. An around-the-clock agent was assigned to every foreign visitor. When one of the visitors prepared to leave his quarters

or office for another location, Hipsley's agent reported. So
close was the coordination that sometimes the New York police
officer and sometimes Hipsley himself cut in on the radio bands
and set up police protection along the route of travel. When
Castro, faking an incident, moved from midtown to a Harlem
hotel, it was Hipsley who accompanied him on his midnight
changeover. When it was all over, and Khrushchev left, one
of his last acts was to give Hipsley grudging thanks for his
protection.

As for Castro, Hipsley had protected him on his first
trip to the United States, too. When Fidel's Cuban security
guards fell asleep, Castro slipped out onto the women-laden
Washington streets to try his luck. It was Hipsley who saw to
it that police cars discreetly trailed him—something unknown
to the Cuban dictator to this day.

To Hipsley flowed police and other security agency reports of all kinds, including those about would-be killers moving in from Miami to "get" Castro, or of a man slipping in
from Mexico to "kill Khrushchev." And Hipsley's orders were
to prevent that man from getting to his target—to take him
"out of play." In addition, so-called "nut" reports run into
thousands during such visits. It has been Hipsley's job to sepa-
rate the nut reports from genuine threats when the cards are
down—a business he has spent a lifetime learning.

Some might ask, "Why stop assassins from killing Castro,
or Khrushchev, or other world Communist leaders?" There
is probably no one who knows and detests communism more
than does Elmer Hipsley. But he is a professional at his job—
and the United States cannot afford to have its official guests
either assassinated or molested.

For a professional job well done, one might expect a
decoration for Hipsley. No. He was given a "pink slip," too,
just like Otepka's. Then, when the fear of investigation and
consequences developed, the group at State headed by J. Clayton Miller, the IPR man whom President Kennedy publicly
"cleared" at Dean Rusk's request (officially minus Wieland,
naturally, since Wieland was not officially involved—even

though he sat in the same office) put through the reorganization plans for the Office of Security. Hipsley was taken from a worldwide anti-Communist operation to a small domestic operation with 20 men under him. Later he was sent to Switzerland, no less, as security officer. This was a long, long way from effective control of anything resembling worldwide physical security for the State Department.

No one in Washington dreamed when Adam Yarmolinsky wrote his 1955 case study on federal security, questioning for the most part accused Communists and their attorneys and doctoring official public records—that the outcome would be the destruction of federal security offices and the smashing of anything but purely political security throughout the federal government.

CHAPTER SIX

Walt Rostow—The Genius from M.I.T.

> *"We have known what is in the mind of the Soviet for thirty years and we do not want to look at it—it is the extension of the Soviet Empire to the entire world."*
>
> ... Salvador de Madariaga

IN THE SPRING of 1962, Walt Whitman Rostow, Chairman of the State Department's Policy Planning Council, stood up in a background press conference and told 700 of the nation's news editors how important he believed was the alleged break between Red China and Red Russia—a thesis becoming one of the keystones upon which the Johnson Administration's foreign policy is based. In fact, those who favor recognition of Red China today argue that we must have representatives on the spot in Peking to observe and "help nurture" this "split."

Other observers think, however, that the Russians and the Red Chinese have deliberately overplayed their differences in order to produce a "let's be friends with the Soviets" policy in Washington.

Rostow based his information on "Intelligence"—the neatest trick of the year. For Rostow, speaking as head of the State Department's Policy Planning Council (the post once held by Alger Hiss) used evidence gathered by an alleged "expert" who discovered the break a decade ago. In the interim, from a seat of academic learning, this "expert" had written at least four papers for the CIA about the alleged break. The name of this expert whose findings were quoted to the editors by Rostow? Walt Rostow himself!

Seldom, if ever, has a secret agent been able to quote himself before as public an audience as one can get as a diplomatic official. It couldn't happen even in Graustark, and it makes the reports of *Our Man in Havana* pale into objectivity.

Now . . . Rostow did not write his reports about the

"break" while sleuthing in the interior of China, or disguised with yellow paint to case a code room in Peking. He wrote most of his discoveries in the halls of M.I.T. where he had been financed by a Carnegie Foundation grant to do a study on "a new American foreign policy." It was his acute intellect, rather than firsthand observation, which led Rostow to deduce from a needle the dimensions of the haystack.

As Rostow, now President Johnson's chief foreign policy adviser, spoke to the editors who had come to Washington to be officially oriented, Red China's third crop failure in three years was what Red bosses Chou En-lai and Mao Tse-tung were publicly worried about. A new wave of refugees was swirling into Hong Kong, and desertions had stripped the Red Chinese army to a strength of less than 20 divisions capable of any substantial operations.

Red Chinese agents were carrying the ball for Communist expansion in Latin America as they had done in Cuba, Southeast Asia and Africa. There had been some ideological friction, partly because the Chinese arm of Moscow's apparatus had been slavishly devoted to Khrushchev's favorite public target—Stalin. But the best judgment of many experts on China was that a real Sino-Soviet break *might* occur in two decades because of territorial competition in the Far East.

Meanwhile, in view of the close Sino-Soviet world-revolution collaboration, it became convenient for the Communist leaders to play up such differences, as they had over Poland or Albania. This struggle between the Stalinists waiting offstage for Khrushchev to trip within Russia itself had little to do with a Soviet-Sino break *per se*. The fact of the matter is that the same experienced Chinese Communist agents who helped to take over China itself were operating actively in Latin America, in the closest collaboration with Soviet agents, according to Ambassador Whiting Willauer—who saw in China the same faces he later saw in Central America, where he was U. S. envoy to two countries.

As veteran foreign correspondent Edgar Ansel Mowrer, in *An End To Make Believe,* stated:

Khrushchev and Mao had not become leaders of their respective domains in order to preside over the liquidation of their common empire. Nor was there the slightest indication that they had abandoned or toned down their basic design of an all-Red world. Nor could anyone be sure that at a favorable moment they would not attempt to break the stalemate of terror by open attack.

Or, in the words of Charles Malik:

> The Communist movement wants to overthrow every existing government regime, system, outlook, religion and philosophy and bring the whole world, all human thought, aspiration, action and organization under its control. This is their declared, unchanged and unchanging objective.

The precise intention of Mr. Khrushchev and Mr. Mao is not something Rostow had to unearth by deep probing into well-kept secrets. It has been set forth by Communist spokesmen as precisely as Adolf Hitler had revealed his purpose in *Mein Kampf*. In fact, today the Russian and Chinese Communists acknowledge that the current argument between them is not "Shall we conquer the United States?" but rather, *"How* shall we conquer the United States?" Indeed, we have this even from the late President John F. Kennedy in a State of the Union Message.

In the eyes of many longtime students of the Communists' Machiavellian strategy and tactics for ultimately conquering the world, this is the strategy of this alleged "split" (nurtured by shadow-boxing between the Chinese and the Russians to give it a veneer of authenticity): engender fear of the dragon of Red China—inflated to hysterical proportions when the Red Chinese choose to announce that they "now have The Bomb" —a Red China feared by Russia and the free world alike . . . and thus ease the free world into the arms of our "ally," Soviet Russia. This view is particularly interesting in view of the propaganda now being spewed in Washington about the "mellowing" Soviets versus the "fearsome" Red Chinese dragon.

It should be remembered that Walt Rostow, the father of this "Soviets-are-mellowing" policy, is one of the high-ranking State Department officials named in 1963 as having "questionable security backgrounds" by veteran State Department chief Otto Otepka. The yet-unpublished documentation by Otepka was termed "political dynamite" by one Senator at the secret subcommittee hearings.

Perhaps the facts unearthed about Rostow by Otepka are what give birth to such alarming statements by Rostow as in a Rostow-McGeorge Bundy policy paper quoted by the Allen-Scott Report syndicated column on April 7, 1963: "Should a national Communist regime be established, we should make a maximum effort short of military action to permit its survival."

Or perhaps one might quote from a speech which Rostow gave at Purdue University on March 15, 1962, shortly before his briefing of the 700 news editors: "We should, therefore, be prepared . . . to find limited areas of overlapping interest with Communist regimes and to work toward a world which increasingly approximates the kind of world we envisaged when the United Nations was set up."

These statements are certainly consistent with Rostow's declaring in a speech at Fort Bragg, North Carolina, on June 28, 1961: "The United States does not want allies, but nations which are neutral," and the U. S. must "protect the independence of the revolutionary process now going forward."

If the average American is bewildered and frightened by our now-official U. S. policy of disarming the United States in the face of the Soviet vow to "bury us," by our signing a completely unpoliced gentlemen's agreement nuclear test-ban with Soviet Union, by our gentlemen's agreement with the U.S.S.R. to slash our production of vital uranium and plutonium, by our bolstering the Soviet empire through trade, by the Administration's seeking "increased understanding between the Soviet Union and ourselves"—he need only know that Walt Rostow, the man who heads the 14-man policy planning council of the U. S. State Department, shapes our policy upon the absurd theory that the Soviet slavemasters are really becoming nice guys at heart, and that they really want peace. From this theory flow all our suicidal policies toward the Communist onslaught.

Rostow, another Rhodes Scholar in the Administration, got off to a flying start in implementing his ideas for the New Frontier. In November 1960, President-elect Kennedy sent Rostow and Jerome Wiesner to Moscow, to attend the Sixth Pugwash Conference on Disarmament and World Security. This conference, perhaps not coincidentally, was held in the Russian capital at the same time as the World Communist Party Meeting of the 81 branches of the Party throughout the world.

The Pugwash Conferences (initiated at the Pugwash estate of the notorious Soviet apologist and Cleveland industrialist Cyrus Eaton, who has been awarded the Lenin "Peace" Prize by the Soviet government) have been investigated by the Senate Internal Security Subcommittee which issued, on May 28, 1961, a staff analysis, concluding in part:

> 1) The Pugwash Conferences were initiated, in part, by individuals having significant records of support of Communist causes.
>
> 2) The Pugwash Conferences were approved by the Soviet government.
>
> 3) The Pugwash Conferences were made possible through the financial support of Cyrus S. Eaton, who has shown strong and unconcealed sympathy for Soviet policies, and hostility to American policies and activities aimed at insuring U.S. national security.
>
> 4) The Soviet delegation to the Pugwash Conferences has always included high-ranking Communist Party officials.
>
> 5) The Pugwash Conferences have served as an organic part of the Soviet cold war design to discredit U.S. nuclear policy within the U.S. and throughout the world.
>
> 6) The proceedings of the conferences have been kept secret from the American public, but not from Khrushchev.
>
> 7) Both the Communist press in the U.S. and the Soviet press have been uniformly sympathetic to the proceedings of the Pugwash Conferences.

In 1955, Bertrand Russell, the British pro-Communist Socialist, and Albert Einstein, who was an organizer and supporter of numerous Communist fronts, held a meeting in London which was attended by internationally known Communists and Socialists, to demand "international cooperation among atomic scientists." Taking a cue from this meeting, Cyrus Eaton held the first Pugwash Conference the following year. The conference was attended—as all the Pugwash Conferences have been—by Communist propagandists and scientists from the Soviet Union, Red China, and the West.

At the second Pugwash Conference, in 1957, plans for Sane Nuclear Policy, Inc., were formulated, and the unilateral disarmament organization was formally launched a few months later, in November 1957, headed by such well-known "Liberals" as Linus Pauling, Norman Thomas and Martin Luther King; and boosted by Eleanor Roosevelt, Walter Reuther and G. Mennen "Soapy" Williams. A May 19, 1960, Madison Square Garden rally, at which the last-mentioned three spoke, was organized by Henry Abrams, a veteran member of the Communist Party. When Abrams' Red record was exposed in the press, the Sane Nuclear Policy officers hastily removed him from the organization's public scene.

When Walt Rostow was sent to Moscow by President-elect Kennedy for the 1960 Pugwash Conference, he held a secret conference with Soviet First Deputy Foreign Minister Vasily V. Kuznetsov, at the Soviet Foreign Office. According to a Chicago *Sun-Times* report of Rostow's tête-à-tête with the Soviet official, Rostow agreed with the Soviet-advanced thesis that the United States should curtail our "first-strike weapons, including the B-70" bomber. Kuznetsov is reported to have told Rostow that America's scrapping of our first-strike weapons "would ease world tensions."

Rostow returned to Washington and served in the White House as Presidential adviser for National Security Affairs, from January to December 1961. Four months after the Soviet official proposed the plan to Rostow, President Kennedy, on March 11, 1961, ordered scrapping of all U. S. first-strike weapons.

Accordingly, our intercontinental bombers (one of our major war deterrents) are no longer being produced; the Skybolt missile has been abandoned; the Dyna-Soar orbital winged flight has been scrapped; and military space programs are not being developed. Our Defense Department's emphasis on nonnuclear armies and on limited deterrents of war also demonstrates that the Kennedy and Johnson Administrations have accepted this "Made-in-Moscow" tactic for "easing world tensions."

By the early 1970's, U. S. nuclear strike-power will rest upon unproven missiles—since with Senate approval of the nuclear Test-Ban Treaty, the U. S. cannot make the space or atmospheric nuclear tests necessary to check the workability of these nuclear missiles. We have pledged ourselves not to make these vital tests, even though U. S. nuclear experts testified during Senate committee Test-Ban Treaty hearings that the Soviets have already made them.

Soon after Rostow's background conference in the spring of 1962, reports began to appear in the press about a drastic U. S. foreign policy shift based upon a supposed "mellowing" of world Communist leadership. These obvious new "leaks" named Rostow as the reported author of the blueprint for this U. S. policy shift. The stories first appeared in pro-Kennedy journals such as *Newsweek* and the New York *Times,* then in a column by Robert Allen and Paul Scott, and finally in other publications throughout the nation.

On June 18, 1962, the Senate minority leader, Senator Everett M. Dirksen of Illinois, discussed in the Senate two articles by Willard Edwards of the Chicago *Tribune* analyzing the Rostow plan:

> Mr. President, over the past weekend there appeared in the Sunday and Monday morning editions of the Chicago *Tribune* two lengthy stories under the byline of Willard Edwards purporting to digest the so-called Rostow draft of a blueprint for future strategy in the struggle against communism.
>
> For many months now we have been told that this document has been in a state of preparation under the guiding hand of

Walt W. Rostow, State Department counselor and chairman of its Policy Planning Board.

On several occasions there have appeared in the press other stories discussing this draft of strategy, but none has presented so much in such detail as Mr. Edwards' story and I am impelled to believe that it is probably accurate.

Many of us who are not unfamiliar with Rostow's thinking have awaited the birth of this new master strategy with considerable trepidation. Mr. Rostow has never been a very devoted disciple of the tough policy line toward Russia. It now develops, on the basis of the Chicago *Tribune* articles, that Mr. Rostow holds some unique ideas about the Soviet Union that are considerably closer to the fuzzy thinking of the late and lamented *Liberal Papers* than even the most liberal members of this body would be willing to accept.

The core of Mr. Rostow's proposal is an assumption that the Soviet Union and its Communist masters are "mellowing"; that Russia is becoming a mature state; that if we are only nice to the Soviets they will drop all their suspicions of the free world and peace will finally bloom.

The most amazing Rostow thesis is this: That both the United States and Russia are losing power and authority in their respective worlds and that an area of "overlapping interests" is developing in which meaningful agreements may be concluded between the Communist and non-Communist worlds.

Mr. Rostow sees no victory by the United States over the Soviet Union. Mr. Rostow sees no victory by capitalism over communism. In fact, Mr. Rostow is a man of little hope and the last person in my opinion who should have been chosen for the all-important task of directing the continuing review of our foreign policy.

The basic philosophy of successful conflict is always to pursue a winning course and always change a losing game. Every high school coach, every big league manager knows this. But apparently our State Department planners do not.

If Mr. Rostow's assumption that the Soviet Union is softening is correct, then what, may I ask, caused it to mellow? To me the answer is obvious. The only times we have ever gotten anywhere with the Soviet Union—the only times the Soviet Union has ever mellowed—have been when the United States was tough.

So logic would say that if Mr. Rostow's basic assumption

were correct and that the Soviet Union is softening, Mr. Rostow is recommending a course exactly diametric to American interests.

But the disconcerting part of the whole picture is this: Our Intelligence agencies say there is little or no evidence to support any such assumption as that made by Mr. Rostow.

How does Mr. Rostow explain the recent Russian course of breaking the moratorium on nuclear testing? How does he explain their recent announcement that they are now going to test a 100-megaton bomb in retaliation for our resumption of testing?

Does the presence of our Armed Forces in Thailand indicate the Communists are mellowing? Does the presence of our Armed Forces in Viet Nam indicate the Communists are mellowing?

I think the Senate is entitled to know—perhaps through questioning by the appropriate committee—what Intelligence information Mr. Rostow possesses to support his basic assumption. Mr. Edwards' articles indicate that Mr. Rostow has held this opinion for at least 10 years. If it is only opinion, I would suggest that it is not proper ground on which to stake the entire future of the American people.

I ask unanimous consent to include as part of my remarks Mr. Edwards' articles, so that the Senate may examine them in detail.

Here is the text of the first Edwards article and pertinent excerpts from the second. (From the Chicago *Tribune*, June 17, 1962.)

DRAFT FOREIGN POLICY REVISION BOWING TO REDS

By Willard Edwards

Washington, June 16—A master plan for historic changes in U.S. foreign policy has been readied for President Kennedy's consideration.

It embraces the theme that the Soviet Union's domestic and foreign policies are mellowing and the way is open for meaningful agreement between the Communist and non-Communist worlds.

This proposed guide for future decisions by the President and the National Security Council, the Nation's highest strategy group, advances these theories:

Russia's leaders are beginning to realize that neither the United States nor the Soviet Union can defeat the other in the world of the future.

Both the United States and Russia are losing power and authority in their respective areas and an area of overlapping interests is developing in which mutually profitable agreements may be negotiated.

Envisioning, as it does, Communist abandonment of the goal of world conquest, this blueprint for future strategy has aroused heated dispute from military leaders and Intelligence agencies who can detect no evidence to support its assumptions.

They quarrel with the contention that conciliation can be as important as a strong defense in future relations with the Kremlin.

Leading sponsor of the plan, which has been more than a year in preparation, is Walt W. Rostow, State Department counselor and Chairman of its Policy Planning Board. He acknowledges that a strong educational campaign will be needed to sell Congress and the public if the proposals are given official sanction.

SHAPED CAMPAIGN SPEECHES

Compiled under Rostow's supervision, the strategy plan represents the work of many officials in the White House, State, Treasury, and Defense Departments. It has been steadily revised and edited down, from an original volume of 285 pages, to a shorter draft.

Despite a host of contributors, the plan bears the Rostow stamp. A former member of the faculty of Massachusetts Institute of Technology, Rostow, 45, is the President's top foreign policy adviser. He played a major role in shaping Kennedy's foreign policy speeches in the Presidential campaign and was deputy special assistant to the President until he took over his present State Department post last December 6.

Rostow's brand of philosophy, not concealed in books, articles, theses, and speeches in recent years, has always envisioned the "evolution" of Soviet Russia into a "mature" state which will come to realize the outdating of the Marxian theory of the class struggle as the moving force in history.

FOR A NEW YOUNG PRESIDENT

As long ago as 1956, he voiced confidence that Communist leaders in the next decade would mend their ways and in 1958 he was depicting Russia as about ready to enter "the age of high mass consumption" reached by the United States a quarter century earlier.

He has now translated this optimistic conviction into a blueprint for basic national security policy, designed to govern future decisions at the highest levels.

It is a conception calculated to stimulate and enthuse a new, young President, who could insure a secure place in history as the American leader who brought peace to the world, ending not only the dread potentialities of nuclear conflict, but the harassments of cold war conflicts which drain the economy.

NOT A SHRED OF PROOF

It is also a theory which has stirred many in the Government's Intelligence agencies to alarm. They report not a scrap of hard data to support the roseate assumptions of the State Department planner.

They note no lessening of Communist intransigence or of grim determination to "bury" the free world. They see in the Rostow recommendations a total misconception of the nature of the Communist conspiracy; a naive brushing off of its treachery as evidenced in a long history of broken treaties and agreements while steadily pursuing the goal of world conquest.

Rostow believes that Premier Nikita Khrushchev of Russia and his associates do not want a major war. He concedes their desire for a total victory for communism but he glimpses changes beneath the surface of old Communist objectives and a willingness among some in Russia to modify old ideological formula in the light of changing reality.

UNITED STATES ON WANE, HE SAYS

Neither Russia nor the United States is going to dominate this century, he contends. To those who speak of a "victory" or "win" policy in the cold war, he retorts that neither of the great leading nations will win over the other. Capitalism will not triumph over socialism. Rather, the victory will be one of "men and nations" voluntarily cooperating under the principles of the United Nations Charter.

"And we deeply believe this victory will come—on both sides of the Iron Curtain," he concludes.

The policy outline pictures the United States and Russia as two aging combatants, both showing signs of waning prestige and power. There is a diffusion of power away from Moscow within the Communist bloc, it asserts, and away from the United States within the free world.

In lesser degree, the "evolution" theory is also applied to Red China and the same conciliatory tactics are advocated. The Chinese Communists can be encouraged to "evolution" into a peaceful state by showing them we have no aggressive intentions.

Possibilities should be explored for expanding contact with Red China, placing it, according to one objector, in the same position as Yugoslavia and Poland.

CAN'T PROMOTE A SPLIT

There is no final bar to entrance of Communist China into more normal relations with the United States if they are prepared to modify present policies, the policy paper asserts. In the meantime, unnecessary revocations should be avoided and informal negotiations pursued.

There is little that the United States can do to promote a Sino-Soviet split, the paper contends.

The proposed foreign policy guidebook does not suggest any weakening of national defense and includes recommendations for a greater build-up of the nation's capacity to wage conventional warfare.

It estimates Soviet policy as designed to avoid any actions which would bring about a nuclear war, ruling out the belief of many military leaders that the Communists will strike whenever they think they can destroy us.

WE WILL WAIT TO BE HIT

Any idea of the United States contemplating a "first strike" is ruled out. Planning in that direction is not relevant since the United States does not plan to initiate a nuclear attack on Communist nations. Military men assail the section as against all sound principles of war for which planning against all contingencies is essential.

Despite all rebuffs to date, strenuous efforts should be continued to get an agreement on limited arms control, the policy paper recommends. It is suggested that the United States might advance a program not requiring formal negotiations.

Again, objectors to this recommendation argued, the proposal totally disregards the nature of the Communist enemy. Any information furnished to Communists will be used against us and any such action will never change their basic aims.

REDS GOING PEACEFUL

Since both arms control planning and research and military planning are directed toward national security, the strategy outline asserts, they should be integrated. General and complete disarmament is a goal which must never be obscured.

There was objection from military men to inclusion of this section. They argued that the nature of communism is disregarded in a process of reasoning which contends that the United States will be secure in a disarmed world.

In seeming answer to these contentions, the proposed policy emphasizes the assumption that the Soviet policy will evolve into a peaceful state.

Even if Communist leaders are unwilling to share the U.S. image of the world's future in the degree necessary to negotiate major arms reduction programs, they may come to realize the dangers of accident, miscalculation, and failure of communications and thus be willing to join the United States in limited measures to reduce those dangers.

(From the Chicago *Tribune* June 18, 1962)

SOFT RED LINE MUST BE "SOLD"—ROSTOW

By Willard Edwards

Washington, June 17—A systematic publicity campaign will be necessary to sell Congress and the American people on the merits of a bold new foreign policy advocating conciliation of Russia, a State Department planner has advised.

The problem of this gap between Government and popular thinking is tackled with candor by Walt W. Rostow, chairman of the State Department's policy planning board in his draft of a master plan which awaits President Kennedy's consideration.

The new policy, the work of a number of experts in Government under Rostow's supervision, is based upon the theory that Russian domestic and foreign policies have mellowed during the post-Stalin period. It holds the way has been opened for cooperation between the Communist and non-Communist worlds.

EDUCATION IS NEEDED

Since the evidence in the form of deeds and words by Soviet leaders runs directly contrary to this assumption, Congress and the people, the Rostow outline confesses, must be educated to acceptance of a fresh approach.

In typical State Department parlance, this can be accomplished by "systematic exposition in forms appropriate for public presentation." The term "indoctrination" is avoided.

One of the appropriate methods of public enlightenment, favored highly by the Kennedy Administration, is the newspaper "leak." This involves funneling of selected information to favored reporters.

In a speech on June 3 at Minneapolis, Rostow said:

"It is sometimes asked if our policy is a no-win policy. Our answer is this—we do not expect this planet to be forever split between a Communist bloc and a free world. We expect this planet to organize itself in time on the principles of voluntary cooperation among independent nation states dedicated to human freedom. We expect the principle that governments derive their just powers from the consent of the governed to triumph on both sides of the Iron Curtain.

"It will not be a victory of the United States over Russia. It will be a victory of men and nations over the forces that wish to entrap and to exploit their revolutionary aspirations."

It is worthy of note that none of the press revelations about the Rostow blueprint was ever denied.

Then came the celebrated hearing before the Senate Foreign Relations Committee in which Walt Rostow did one of his famous magician's tricks by taking the Executive Fifth Amendment and thus "clearing himself," according to reports in liberal newspapers. Committee member Senator Dirksen made clear in subsequent press conference that Rostow had done no such thing—although, true to form, an even later account of the hearings by the New York *Times* declared that Rostow had "won the committee's admiration with his lucid, articulate recital of his views." The fact is that Rostow had simply invoked the Executive Fifth Amendment and refused to talk to what the *Times* described, in one of its own magician's tricks, as "a nervous Senate Foreign Relations Committee" whose members are "politicians" made "uneasy" by "the kind of a [sic] man" Rostow is "in this kind of a [sic] world."

The staid Senate Foreign Relations Committee, together

with most Americans, certainly is made "uneasy" by the kind of man Rostow is; there is no doubt about that. And the fact that Rostow refuses to divulge a word about the Administration's master plan for our position on communism makes them even more uneasy.

Uneasiness about Walt Rostow by informed observers is generated in part by a book by Rostow which, he stated, represented the outgrowth of his years of study at M.I.T. in search of a new American foreign policy. The book, published by Harper's in 1960, is entitled *The United States in the World Arena.*

This astonishing book contains a barefaced summary of the goal of Mr. Rostow and the soft-headed international planners around President Johnson—the liquidation of the United States of America as a sovereign nation. To quote Mr. Rostow:

> It is a legitimate American national objective to see removed from all nations—including the United States— the right to use substantial military force to pursue their own interests. Since this residual right is the right of national sovereignty and the basis for the existence of an international arena of power, *it is therefore, an American interest to see an end of nationhood as it has been historically defined.*

This is indeed a peculiar position for a man who is chairman of the State Department's Policy Planning Council, a top federal official who has taken a solemn oath "to support and defend the Constitution of the United States," which is the very framework of our "nationhood."

On the other hand, perhaps this is exactly what the late President John F. Kennedy had in mind when he chose Walt Rostow as a master shaper of our foreign policy, and then warned in his first State of the Union message to Congress on January 30, 1961:

> Before my term is ended we shall have to test anew whether a nation organized and governed such as ours can endure. The outcome is by no means certain.

Rostow also advocates "a decade of austerity" for the United States—a synonym for a decade of depression. This would limit personal use of automobiles, for example, *in order to raise living standards in other nations, regardless of whether or not they are Communist or pro-Communist nations.* At the end of this period, Rostow declared, U. S. influence in world affairs would be "marginal"—which is likely enough if his policies are followed.

Americans are relatively unfamiliar with the economic views of Rostow, whose foreign aid policies would most certainly bring financial ruin to the United States.

Rostow has served as instructor in economics at Columbia University, professor of history at Oxford and professor of economic history at M.I.T. His published works on economics include *Essays on the British Economy of the Nineteenth Century; Essays, The Process of Economic Growth, The Growth and Fluctuation of the British Economy* and *The Stages of Economic Growth.*

The last-named book, written by Rostow in 1960, (and in which, on page 134, Rostow coined the phrase "new peaceful frontiers" which purportedly was adapted by the Kennedy Administration for its "New Frontier" label—although Henry Wallace used the term "new frontiers" about 30 years ago) expounds these premises for U. S. foreign aid:

Communism is a growing pain of an underdeveloped society which wants to industrialize quickly. As society industrializes, it drops its communism. The less communism, the less aggression. *Therefore, it is in the interest of the United States to strengthen communist countries economically,* thus helping them to pass more quickly through their growing pains. Hence, U. S. aid to Communist Poland and Communist Yugoslavia, for example, are in the interest of the United States.

(It might be noted here that U. S. foreign aid to Communist Poland—paid for by American taxpayers—has enabled Poland to send $13 million in aid to Castro's Cuba, and much to Soviet Russia. Our U. S. foreign aid to Communist Poland has also enabled it to send $15 million in aid to Communist North Viet Nam—aid which reportedly includes arms which are being used to kill American soldiers fighting North Vietnamese soldiers in guerilla warfare in South Viet Nam.)

Commenting on this Rostow theory in his syndicated newspaper column of August 24, 1963, Edgar Ansel Mowrer probably summed up the average American's attitude toward this whole idea by saying: "I think this is rubbish."

Mr. Mowrer said:

"In a survival crisis, we have no money for those who will not help. To avoid nuclear war and overcome communism, the non-communist countries need to stand together, the more the better. They should seek to raise this collective prosperity, the more the better, and reduce that of their enemies.

"Translated into foreign aid, this means no U. S. support for communist countries, neutral countries that take aid from communist or lackadaisical allies. But it means more aid for trustworthy allies."

Rostow's foreign aid beliefs (together with those of his M.I.T. colleague and collaborator on some publications, Dr. Max Millikan), are based mainly on American assistance to help the underdeveloped nations of the world. Nowhere does Rostow include significant provisions for the stimulation and expansion of the private enterprise system. In fact, he is very uncertain that the free enterprise system is the best mechanism for American economic growth, stating only, "We believe that sustained economic growth in a democratic society *probably* requires a pattern of incentives which encourages maximum participation in economic decision-making by all the alert and imaginative elements in our society. A largely private business system such as ours in the United States is *one* way of achieving the participation."

Rostow is explicit on two points: first, we must increase our foreign aid, regardless of the cost to our prestige, to our national beliefs, or to the solvency of our federal treasury. No strings should be attached to our foreign aid, says Rostow. In fact, he suggests, in effect, that we place our dollars in unmarked brown bags and scatter them indiscriminately all over the world, so that no one will be annoyed by the knowledge that this aid comes from the United States. Rostow estimates the cost of his proposed enlarged foreign aid program at a "modest" additional $2.5 to $3.5 billion annually. (Incidentally, there are now only eight free-world nations or principalities which have not received U. S. foreign loans and/or grants. They are: Andorra, Bhutan, Kuwait, Lichtenstein, Monaco, Muscat, Switzerland and Vatican City.)

Second, Rostow writes that we should "face the problem of the next decade by preparing to contemplate an increased degree of austerity." As noted, Rostow would "alter the pattern of our demand for automobiles," perhaps by a horsepower tax, if all other methods fail.

Rostow forgets that the success of our free enterprise system depends on increased, rather than decreased, private consumption, and he urges increased government participation in the economy, both in the United States and abroad. Rostow stands for manipulating human beings with utter disregard for their personal economic choices. He proposes a foreign aid scheme so costly, that it would lead to complete financial ruin of the United States. He takes no account of the effect upon nations into which we would pour these dollars—to say nothing of these nations' need for developing their own sense of personal responsibility and moral fiber.

Rostow's books evoked a special series of speeches by Republican members of the House of Representatives who made a special study of Rostow's policies—speeches which went unchallenged by Rostow.

Representative Robert Stafford, former Governor of Vermont and chairman of the group discussed where the adoption of Rostow's theories would lead:

> Mr. Rostow believes that the United States should adopt a policy of not "rocking the boat." He believes that we should embark on a program of massive foreign aid, without regard to the political complexion of the recipients or their positions on the

issues of the cold war. He admits that such activity would bring about what he terms a decade of austerity that would weaken our ability to resist the onslaught of the Soviet Union.

Thus confronted with a true stalemate, the two main contenders in the cold war would be too weak to prevail. And then those underdeveloped nations, which Mr. Rostow so fervently believes are the seat of all wisdom and justice would constitute the true balance of power that would be able to make both the United States and the U.S.S.R. behave themselves.

What does this all boil down to, Mr. Speaker? It boils down to a world Socialist order, and this is precisely what Marx and Lenin were talking about. We must remember that communism is only a means whereby socialism can be achieved on a worldwide scale. Thus, I think it is fair to say that the Rostow strategy for the cold war is, simply, "If you can't fight them, join them."

Mr. Rostow had better understand one thing clearly right now. The American people are not interested in an end to the cold war which involves our surrender to world socialism. I think that he had better understand that the American people want to win the cold war. I think that he had better understand that there are alternatives to nuclear war that do not encompass an end to nationhood.

Representative Durward Hall of Missouri summarized Rostow's background and concluded:

He is the proponent of a scheme so exorbitant in cost that it would lead to final fiscal ruination of the United States, as well as of the nations upon which we would pour these unneeded dollars, to say naught of their need for emerging sense of obligation and development of moral fiber.

It is high time the American people, who believe that the solution to the problem of the world does not lie in the coffers of the U.S. Treasury, nor in the shamefaced disavowal of the principles in which we believe; realize just how W. W. Rostow is, and in what he believes. When they do, I am sure he will beat a hasty retreat from the "high policy position" in which the President has placed him and others like him, whom he seems unable or unwilling to slough off. I do hope it is soon, lest another flag replaces the Stars and Stripes on the soil of what he calls a "mere island off continental Eurasia."

Representative James Bromwell of Iowa said:

> Perhaps the most dangerous proposal that Professor Rostow has made, and his biggest mistake from the point of view of the current world situation and the threat of world communism, surround his suggestion that the optimum policy still open to the United States is dependent on our ability to perform "an act of persuasion." . . . . Mr. Speaker, "friendly persuasion" through an end to nationhood and an end to our military might is hardly a tactic to use against an enemy still sworn to destroy us "until shrimps learn to whistle." . . . I fear that Professor Rostow does not understand the foundations of America in the same terms as the rest of us. His vision of the United States as a subservient vassal of world government should eliminate him from any top planning position in our hierarchy of military and foreign policy officials.

Representative Alphonzo Bell, former Republican State Chairman of California, tackled the question of Russia's supposed "mellowing" and declared:

> In speech after speech Khrushchev continues to say that he will bury us. Is this a sign of mellowing?
>
> Mr. Speaker, there is no mellowing and there will be none. Only those poor fuzzy-minded wishful thinkers who infest the Administration believe in such nonsense.
>
> They believe in it because they do not understand total dedication. They do not understand it because they are not capable of such total dedication themselves. But the Communist masters of the Soviet Union and Red China understand total dedication. They understand it because they have it themselves. Their fervor for the Communist cause never wavers. It will never waver; it can only be eliminated like the cancer it is by victory for the West. It must be eradicated or, like cancer, it will continue to spread until it engulfs us.

Representative James Battin of Montana concluded the series of speeches by showing the probable military moral and economic effect of Rostow's proposals:

> Not only would our foreign policy, our military and our economic institutions undergo a shattering transformation, but our social and moral principles would undergo a similar examination and change under the Rostow plans. The Soviet suc-

cess, he feels, is the most direct of assaults on the moral foundations of American life. It raises not only the question of whether
the United States may be defeated in war—hot or cold—but
also the question of whether the principles of social organization
which lie at the heart of the American conception of its nationhood are correct; for in one essential dimension, Americanism
as an articulated creed has consisted in the faith that virtue and
success converged, and that this convergence was a model and
guide to humanity at large.

Mr. Speaker, I do not know what proposals Professor Rostow has included in his recommendations on foreign policy
to the National Security Council and to the President. If they
are anything like his previous writings, they would lead to the
destruction, devastation and demoralization of what we today
know as the United States militarily, morally and economically.

The dream of Professor Rostow is truly a nightmare for the
free world, for the American citizen, and for any who aspire
to continued life with meaning in the days ahead.

An amusing parody of *My Gal Sal* was heard about the
halls of Congress at the time, which went like this:

> *They call him wistful Walt.*
> *Hardly worth his salt.*
> *A sad sort of fellow,*
> *He thinks the Reds will mellow.*
> *That's our guy Walt.*

Despite the piecemeal uncovering of some of Mr. Rostow's
fantastic plans for our nation, the public learned very little
about either his detailed views or his background from the
American press, radio or television.

However, on June 20, Senator Barry Goldwater gave a
speech to the Senate exposing Rostow's theories, chapter and
verse, as being opposed to American interests. He also inserted
into the *Congressional Record* an illuminating article on Walt
Rostow and his brother, Eugene, written while Walt Rostow
was at M.I.T., by Alice Widener, a longtime observer of the
Rostow's theories, and published in *U.S.A.* magazine on August
16, 1957. The article said in part:

> Relatively unknown to the American public, but extraordi-
> narily influential in the fields of economic law, and interna-

tional affairs, are the brothers Rostow—Eugene V. and W. W.

Eugene V. Rostow is Dean of the Law School at Yale University.

W. W. (Walt Whitman) Rostow is a professor at the Massachusetts Institute of Technology Center for International Studies.

Each of the Rostow brothers has won high honors and holds a high post in the academic world. Each has occupied positions of heavy responsibility in the U.S. Government and in the United Nations.

Prolific writers, they are busily engaged in telling Americans what they should do and how to do it. Yet close study of the Rostow brothers' views—as expressed in their own writings—has led this writer to form the opinion that W. W. Rostow is bent on persuading Americans to squander a large part of their wealth, and Eugene V. Rostow is bent on hindering their ability to acquire it.

A most significant fact in the Rostow brothers' careers is that each served in Geneva, Switzerland, as Assistant Executive Secretary to Gunnar Myrdal, Executive Secretary of the United Nations Economic Commission for Europe. W. W. Rostow held the post during 1947-49, and was succeeded by his brother, Eugene, who held it during 1949-50.

Gunnar Myrdal (Swedish economist and social scientist who severely hurt the economy of his native land by engineering its disastrous pro-Communist trade agreement with the Soviet Union after World War II) is the author of *An American Dilemma* and the recently published *An International Economy,* books that are among the most radically Leftist documents of the twentieth century . . .

It is not surprising that Myrdal picked the brothers Rostow as his special executive assistants; the three men are intellectually compatible, strong supporters of concepts originally embodied in the proposed U.N. Havana Charter of 1948. Wholly rejected by the U.S. Congress, *this Charter called for socialization of the world, including the United States . . .*

Today the dauntless brothers Rostow continually seek to implement the Havana Charter's aim of creating *a single world Socialist economy,* and each strives unceasingly for adoption of a measure essential to success . . .

Dean Eugene V. Rostow advocates adoption of the U.N. Restrictive Business Practices Proposal which will set up U.N. control over all American business . . .

In sponsoring the SUNFED [Special UN Fund for Economic Development] philosophy (as expressed in the Millikan-Rostow Report submitted to the U.S. National Security Council in 1956, a report which has greatly influenced the U.S. International Development Loan Fund proposed now before Congress), Prof. W. W. Rostow wants the United States to make a lump-sum appropriation of $10 billion to $12 billion to be spent "without any sort of military or political strings attached" during a five-year period on grants-in-aid and on long-term, low-cost, unprofitable loans to "underdeveloped" nations. Professor Rostow doesn't expect this squandering of U.S. taxpayers' money "to win friends" for the United States or to "foster free enterprise."

To insure the "success" of the SUNFED plan under its alias "The Millikan-Rostow Report," Prof. W. W. Rostow envisages adoption of all the international economic controls that are standard operating procedure for Socialist schemes: international price stabilization, food and fiber banks, currency control, elimination of U.S. tariffs, control over production, consumption and distribution of agricultural products and manufactured goods.

Like all Socialist five-year plans, Professor Rostow's is just a starter. On page 59 of the Millikan-Rostow Report, he and co-author Max Millikan of MIT declare: "Although an initial 5-year allocation is recommended, the plan would look ahead for a longer period, at least a decade."

Also according to Socialist dogma, the profit motive is banned from such U. S.-financed, Rostow-devised dealings with foreign lands. On page 79 of the Millikan-Rostow Report there is the flat assertion: "The narrow criterion of whether a [development] project can repay from its own revenues is at best irrelevant and at worst may be seriously misleading."

Thus it is perfectly clear that W. W. Rostow wants the United States to put up at least $20 to $24 billion for a scheme in which profits are at best "irrelevant" and at worst "misleading."

. . . If W. W. Rostow's views should prevail in our country, then the U. S. Government will subsidize the economic "development" of more than a billion underdeveloped peoples with the result that many American stockholders of corporations making private investments abroad will be financially wiped out and American taxpayers would be pauperized.

As further evidence of this, the New York *Daily News* stated in an editorial that "the 'Declaration of International

Interdependence' portion of President Kennedy's July 4 speech sounded as if it had been rewritten from Rostow's book."

Mr. Rostow may well be intelligent, diligent and dedicated to implementing his policies. This hardly matters!

Even if Walt Whitman Rostow had been George Washington's aide, his ideas are completely at odds with the basic beliefs of the American people. He is on record as strongly advocating policies which are diametrically opposed to the very foundations of our Constitution. Nevertheless, he is one of the chief directors of our foreign policy under President Johnson, in perhaps the last stages of our death struggle against communism, atheism, regimentation and the obliteration of the dignity and rights of the individual.

Walt Whitman Rostow may be seeking solutions as he sees them. But that does not make him one whit less dangerous.

CHAPTER SEVEN

Harlan Cleveland —
The Maxwell Mythologist

"For human bodies are sic fools, for a' their colleges and schools."
. . . Robert Burns—THE TWA DOGS

A NUMBER OF PROMINENT New Deal, Fair Deal and New Frontier decision-makers have been products of the Maxwell Graduate School of Citizenship and Public Affairs at Syracuse University, New York. Included in this number are two of the first three deans of the school, which specializes in a left-wing treatment of government and public affairs.

One of these was Paul Appleby, former Assistant Secretary of Agriculture and Director of the Bureau of the Budget under F.D.R., and later a coordinator of the ill-fated Harriman Administration in New York State. Some of Appleby's detractors referred to him as "the Red Dean of Maxwell," and it is easy to see why, in view of his celebrated statements, such as: "A man in the employ of the government has just as much right to be a member of the Communist Party as he has to be a member of the Democratic or Republican Party."

However, Appleby's views on government (if not his judgment about the Maxwell students he recommended to Washington bureaucrats) are relatively mild in comparison with those of Harlan Cleveland—his successor as dean at Maxwell from 1957 to 1960, when President-elect Kennedy chose Cleveland to be his Assistant Secretary of State for International Organization Affairs—including our UN affairs.

It is important to remember that when Kennedy chose Harlan Cleveland as one of his Assistant Secretaries of State, the State Department security office investigated Cleveland's background and activities—and ruled that Cleveland should not be granted even a temporary security clearance. However, Secretary of State Dean Rusk overrode the security office's findings; personally waived the security clearance for Cleveland, and Harlan Cleveland was installed February 23, 1961.

Who is Harlan Cleveland, to whom State's security office refused even a *temporary* security clearance?

James Harlan Cleveland was born in New York City in 1918, grew up in Madison, Wisconsin, and Europe, and was graduated in 1934 from Phillips Academy at Andover, and in 1938 from Princeton. At Princeton he majored in international relations and, as an undergraduate, was president of the campus Anti-War Society for three years. In his Princeton yearbook, the *Nassau Herald,* he boldly listed himself as "a Socialist." Cleveland spent a year at Oxford as a Rhodes scholar, from 1938 to 1939.

In the 25 years since Cleveland finished his schooling he has spent 17 years on the government payroll, 11 of them giving away taxpayers' money to foreign countries, many of which are now officially Communist, or are fast getting there.

His career as a government employee has been broken only by four years at Maxwell and three years as editor and pulisher of *The Reporter* magazine. He first went to Washington to spend a year as an "intern" at the National Institute of Public Affairs.

The National Institute of Public Affairs, where Harlan Cleveland spent a year after finishing as a Rhodes scholar, was financed by the State Department and other government agencies for the dissemination of bulletins and reports on various New Deal socialistic enterprises, such as the National Resources Board. For this agency, for example, the Institute wrote blueprints and sent up trial balloons for the nationalization of all American natural resources, power and transportation.

Cleveland presumably received adequate training as an intern at the Institute, since in 1940 he graduated to the Farm Security Administration as a writer in the information division. This was the government agency considered so important as an incubator for Communist infiltration into other government agencies that Soviet spymaster Nathan Silvermaster had ensconced himself there as Director of the Labor Division. Silver-

master planted in the Farm Security Administration a covey
of members of his famed Silvermaster Cell, as explained in
detail in sworn testimony before Congressional committees by
Elizabeth Bentley, who had acted as courier, paymaster and
contact for both the Silvermaster Cell and its fellow govern-
ment-infiltrator, the Perlo Cell. Both cells, along with the
Ware cell (which was exposed by Whittaker Chambers),
placed scores of Soviet agents, in the thirties and forties, in
government agencies, especially Agriculture and the Treasury.
In a sort of musical-chairs spiral, they gave each other straight
A's on personnel ratings and salary increases, promoted and
hired each other and many more in a trail which finally fanned
out through the entire federal government. Some of these infiltrators have been exposed by Congressional committees, but
how many hundreds are still there, concealed in the government woodwork and in the high echelons, and for years hiring
scores of others?

In 1942, after two years in the Farm Security Adminis-
tration, during which time he married Lois Burton, a librarian,
Harlan Cleveland became an official of the Board of Economic
Warfare and of its successor, the Foreign Economic Adminis-
tration. Both agencies were set up by F.D.R. to intertwine
America's economy and financial resources with those of Europe.

The Board of Economic Warfare was, in the words of
Louis Budenz, ex-editor of the Communist *Daily Worker,* a
special nesting-place for "large-scale Communist colonization
into governmental posts," along with "the Office of War Information (OWI), the publicity services of the armed forces,
and the Office of Strategic Services (OSS)."

Cleveland's career then took him to Rome for three years
beginning in 1944, when, at the age of 26 and out of college
barely five years, he was made executive director of the entire
economic section of the Allied Control Commission, a fore-
runner of our massive giveaway programs which rebuilt Europe
from its postwar ruins. The following year Cleveland was
promoted to acting vice-president of the economic section,

which decided where and how and through whom the rebuilding of Europe was to be done.

In 1945, Harlan Cleveland was a member of the American delegation to the third council session of the UNRRA council in London, and in 1946 and 1947 he served as deputy chief of the UNRRA mission in Italy.

Operating UNRRA in Italy during this period was Harold Glasser.

Glasser was a Soviet espionage agent, a Harvard graduate, who entered the government through the Perlo Soviet espionage Cell (surprisingly enough, since the Ware Cell specialized almost exclusively in Harvard Law School graduates and professors, while the Perlo Cell specialized in Columbia and City College of New York graduates). After a stint at the Brookings Institution, Glasser worked for the WPA, the Department of Agriculture, then was taken into the Treasury Department by fellow Soviet agent Harry Dexter White, and became the official American financial expert on the UNRRA council under both the late Herbert H. Lehman, former New York Governor and Senator, and Fiorello La Guardia, former Mayor of New York City, UNRRA's successive general directors. Needless to say, with Harold Glasser as UNRRA's chief financial expert, the Communists of Europe and Asia had little reason to be dissatisfied with the whole program.

UNRRA (United Nations Relief and Rehabilitation Administration) deserves special mention among American-financed organizations which helped to put the Soviet and Red Chinese economies on their feet after World War II, by helping to finance the establishment of Communist regimes throughout Eastern Europe and in China. Once the Communists were in control these organizations fastened the Communist deathlock on their captive people by shoveling out American money, food, clothing, tools, farm equipment—in short, everything needed for survival and rebuilding—to the Communist slavemasters, for distribution (or for sale at extravagant prices) to members of the Communist Party, and not to anti-Communists who resisted Communist terrors.

UNRRA was supposed to be a UN operation, but like all UN operations, Uncle Sam footed the bill. The whole UNRRA giveaway cost the American taxpayers almost $3 billion, and after UNRRA was disbanded, the UN made Uncle Sam cough up an additional one-third of a billion to wind up the operation.

From its very inception, "UNRRA was widely infiltrated by Communists and fellow travelers," to quote just one competent source, ex-Communist Eugene Lyons, now an editor of the *Reader's Digest*. Just a few of the infiltrators into UNRRA would include the following:

Harold Glasser, who after his stint as UNRRA financial expert, returned to the Treasury Department and made several more trips to Europe to check on UNRRA's progress—at taxpayers' expense—was then made George Marshall's private adviser on the general's final Moscow mission in 1947. He left the Treasury Department in 1947 with a personal letter of recommendation from Dean Acheson.

David Weintraub of the Perlo complex, who went to the budding UNRRA as deputy director in charge of all supplies, after stints in the WPA, War Production Board, as special assistant to Harry Hopkins and the State Department's office of foreign relief. In UNRRA he was, in other words, at the top, and left in 1946, getting a job in a jiffy at $14,000 per year at the UN, where he became director of the Economic Stability Division of the UN Secretariat. Of course, in the UN Secretariat he did not forget his friends, and hired a host of them at high salaries, many of whom turned up along with Weintraub himself in the Senate Internal Security Subcommittee's investigations into the UN Secretariat. (After the investigations, to soothe the ruffled feelings of 11 of these Fifth Amendment cases, the UN awarded them a total of $179,120.)

Henry Julian Wadleigh, whom Whittaker Chambers identified as a Soviet agent along with Alger Hiss and Harry Dexter White, who went into the State Department with Hiss, and into UNRRA with Weintraub.

Solomon Leshinsky, a member of the Perlo Cell.

George Perazich, a member of an espionage cell who

entered through the Social Security Administration, went to the NRA, then to UNRRA and wound up in the UN Secretariat.

Ruth Rifkin, member of the Perlo Cell, identified by Elizabeth Bentley as a source of material for a Soviet espionage apparatus in the government, who went into UNRRA, and also wound up in the UN Secretariat.

Eda Glaser, identified as a member of an espionage cell within the government, who worked in China as an UNRRA interpreter.

A single glance like the foregoing at the people who staffed UNRRA makes it not at all surprising that from its very beginning, a vast portion of UNRRA funds and vital supplies was given outright to the Communists, and another vast portion was indirectly channeled to the Communists. In fact, so successful was UNRRA from the Communists' viewpoint, that of the 15 countries UNRRA aided, half are now Communist and others are well on their way.

One good example of how UNRRA worked was seen on May 14, 1953, in testimony before the House Committee on Un-American Activities by Colonel Jan Bukar, a Czechoslovakian officer who escaped to the United States. Colonel Bukar testified: "In the distribution of goods through UNRRA, the people who got any portion of the goods had to be enrolled as members of the Communist Party . . . I want again to state that through UNRRA the Communist Party gained many members."

UNRRA money was shoveled out unreservedly to Communists in the now-Iron Curtain countries; UNRRA food fed the discontented masses of Eastern Europe, quelling rebellion against their new Red regimes, finally locking the grip of the Communists upon them.

A good illustration of how UNRRA actually operated can be seen in the electrifying book *I Saw Poland Betrayed,* by the late Arthur Bliss Lane, former U. S. Ambassador to that postwar nation, who gave up his 30-year diplomatic career, his friends and literally his life in a heroic effort to awaken the

American people to the massive Communist penetration of our government.

In his book, Lane explains: "Over my personal protest, Director General Herbert H. Lehman had appointed as director of the first UNRRA mission to Poland the Soviet member of the UNRRA council, Mr. Menshikov [later the smiling, gray-flannel Soviet Ambassador to the United States], whose first duty would be the negotiation of an agreement with the Polish [Communist] Government for the reception and distribution of UNRRA supplies."

The result, says Lane, is that "the Polish Government, and not UNRRA, [had] complete jurisdiction over UNRRA supplies in Poland." All UNRRA clothes, food and supplies went only to members of the Polish Communist Party, while Polish patriots—men, women and children—literally starved and froze to death in the streets. Although about 95 per cent of the Polish people are Roman Catholics, Lane says that the Communist Party officials openly boasted: "No UNRRA supplies are to be given to 'reactionary' organizations such as the Roman Catholic Church," and that included almost all Poland's hospitals, schools and orphanages, which were run by Catholic nuns and priests.

Furthermore, says Lane, UNRRA food supplies, paid for by American taxpayers, were brazenly exhibited in Warsaw shop windows and some were even peddled on street corners; all, of course, at fantastic prices which could be paid only by the privileged Communist Party members, who are the only people in any Communist "people's republic" able to purchase anything beyond the shabbiest of bare necessities.

While Harlan Cleveland was a high official in the European operations of UNRRA, that organization took part in the merciless cruelities of "Operation Keelhaul," officially named that by our Pentagon military because keelhauling—or hauling a man under the keel of a ship—was the cruelest punishment known to the European navies of the past, which had devised a full repertoire of cruelties to punish insubordination.

Operation Keelhaul was initiated by Josef Stalin, who

ordered the millions of Russians, Ukranians, Slavs and East Europeans, people who since 1939 had escaped from the bloody horrors of the Soviet regime to Western European countries, sent back to their "countries of origin," where they faced liquidation, torture or slave-labor camps. This was agreed to by Franklin Delano Roosevelt at the infamous Yalta Conference on February 11, 1945, but according to the New York *Times,* massive forced repatriations of these anti-Communist patriots had already been operating for long months prior to the Yalta agreement, at the personal, private, unilateral, decision and order of our Supreme Commander in Europe, much to his everlasting discredit.

The horrors of Operation Keelhaul cannot be recounted on these pages. Over their terror, their tears, their pleadings and their total desperation, between two million and five million human beings were shipped back into Soviet bondage. The number of mass suicides—even among hundreds of gallant Polish officers who had fought as volunteers side by side with our American troops in bloody fighting throughout the war— have never been counted. So sickened were our own battle-hardened officers and enlisted men at having to ship back their own comrades along with those thousands of men, women and children, that they entered an official protest to our Supreme Commander, but in vain. Operation Keelhaul is not a proud moment in American history, or a well-publicized one.

Eugene Lyons said of UNRRA's role in Operation Keelhaul, in the *American Legion Magazine* of December 1954:

> The role of UNRRA in riding herd on Stalin's enemies, both under Herbert Lehman and Fiorello La Guardia, was hardly one to make Americans proud of their statesmen . . . Hundreds of thousands of refugees from the Soviets who evaded "repatriation" by our military monitors ended up in displaced persons' camps under UNRRA control. Again force was used—not outright violence, but propaganda, threats, lies, pressures—to make them go home.
>
> . . . hordes of DPs in American hands [i.e., in UNRRA camps] were cajoled and frightened into going behind the Iron Curtain. Under Lehman's successor, La Guardia, came the notori-

ous "Secret Order No. 199," which not only instructed [UNRRA]
DP camp officials to effect speedy return of "Soviet nationals"
[*sic*] to their homeland in accordance with the Yalta agreement,
but outlined pressures and hinted at punishments toward that end.

One might look at it from the Communists' viewpoint
and see that every Communist publication in the world had
nothing but praise for UNRRA and its operation—just as today
the Communist press lavishes praise upon our U. S. foreign aid
giveaway programs, both government-operated and through
the UN, of which UNRRA was one of the forerunners. An
examination of the UNRRA personnel of the 1940's and a
comparison of it with our U. S. and UN giveaway programs
today will clarify this—and much more—for the informed.

Harlan Cleveland was transferred in 1947 from UNRRA's
European operations to its China operations, where at the age
of 29 he became director of the entire $650-million China pro-
gram, with headquarters in Shanghai.

The massive UNRRA program in China, like its counter-
part in Europe, joyously handed over millions directly to the
Chinese Reds, and millions to Madame Sun Yat-sen, wife of the
Chinese Red leader, to finance the Red takeover of that country.
UNRRA's director general, Herbert Lehman, again arranged
this little operation, and the UNRRA China headquarters in
Shanghai did the handing over, and much more.

Freda Utley in *The China Story,* written in 1951 after
many years in China, gives us just a glimpse into the UNRRA
operations there:

> Communist guerrillas [in China] quickly destroyed the
> Yellow River flood rehabilitation work of UNRRA engineers,
> constructed at a cost of millions of dollars. They similarly de-
> stroyed roads and railways repaired with UNRRA funds. While
> engaged in this deliberate destruction, they were receiving
> UNRRA relief supplies. For we insisted that a due portion of
> UNRRA aid be furnished to the Communist areas.

The 80th Congress, which had voted millions for the
Marshall Plan for Europe's economic recovery, decided to save
China with additional millions. Secretary of State George Mar-

shall, whose work in the fall of China to the Reds has been discussed elsewhere, authored a bill sent to Congress which asked for $570 million for China, specifying that half of the money should go to the Chinese Reds headquartered in Yenan. The $125 million which Congress voted to Chiang exclusively in the spring of 1948, was sabotaged by Marshall and the State Department with the help of the Commerce Department.

In 1948 and 1949, Harlan Cleveland became director of the China program of the Economic Cooperation Administration (ECA), which dispensed U.S. government money in China as well as the massive Marshall Plan aid in Europe. This was the period when first North China, and then all China south of the Yangtze River, fell to the Reds. The Chinese Reds established the "People's Republic of China" in September 1949.

Harlan Cleveland, who in 1949 had been made deputy administrator of the China ECA operations, assumed in 1950 the additional job of acting head of the entire Far East program of ECA, and until 1951 he supervised the ECA program to five Southeast Asian countries; this was financed in part by about $100 million in unspent funds from the original ECA China aid program.

For this post Cleveland was personally recommended by Paul G. Hoffman, a most interesting move, in view of Hoffman's lifetime devotion to the cause of one-world government under the UN, and to a host of left-wing activities which happen to further the Communist cause.

Hoffman is now the Director of the Special United Nations Fund for Economic Development (SUNFED), which persists in sending American taxpayers' money to Fidel Castro. He was formerly president of the Studebaker-Packard Corporation.

Paul Hoffman is a former president of the Ford Foundation and is honorary chairman of its Fund for the Republic. Hoffman has held many powerful positions in government since the days of FDR, and recently married Anna Rosenberg, FDR-Sidney Hillman-Nelson Rockefeller stalwart, which appears to be a perfect match from almost any angle. Hoffman now devotes much of his spare time to being an officer of the Institute for International Order, financed 75 per cent by powerful foundations and devoted to disarming the United States and to establishing one-world government by the UN.

Paul Hoffman also devotes his spare time to being a prominent member of the American Association for the United Nations, which specializes in UN pamphlets, press releases, lecture series and meetings in schools and clubs, and in stories and programs in the news media, radio and television throughout the country, propagandizing the UN as "the world's sole hope for peace."

In 1950, at Hoffman's instigation, World Brotherhood was founded at UNESCO House in Paris by the National Conference of Christians and Jews.

The Party-line edicts of the World Brotherhood conference in 1958 at Geneva, referred to in the pages on John McCloy, are astounding enough, but we shall see presently the 1960 edicts of the World Brotherhood conference which Harlan Cleveland attended as an official of World Brotherhood.

Another of Mr. Hoffman's prize projects is the National Committee for an Effective Congress, which is far left of even the ADA, and to which Mr. Hoffman donated a thousand dollars when he helped organize it. The Committe for an Effective Congress masterminded the "censure" of Senator Joseph McCarthy, and actually wrote every word of the censure motion against him which was introduced on the floor of the Senate (with a big assist from Edward R. Murrow and a claque of leftist newsmen), by that self-proclaimed rock of Yankee integrity, Senator Ralph Flanders, who previously had risen on the Senate floor in an attempt to smear the two-fisted McCarthy as a homosexual. These are merely a few of the affiliations of Paul Hoffman, who personally recommended Harlan Cleveland as head of the entire Far East program division of ECA.

In 1951, ECA activities were moved to the Mutual Security Agency (MSA), and Cleveland went to Washington as assistant director of MSA, in charge of its entire European operations. He was then 33 years old.

ECA and the Mutual Security Agency administered the $12-billion Marshall Plan and the Point-4 Program. If most Americans really do not understand the Marshall Plan, they are not alone. On September 26, 1953, Senator A. Willis Robertson of Virginia wrote a letter saying that Marshall himself had been asked by former Senator Tom Connally of Texas what the Marshall Plan was all about. Robertson says Marshall's reply was, "I will be damned if I know."

The Marshall Plan—so called because Marshall first proposed it in a speech at Harvard on June 5, 1947—was set up to bring postwar economic prosperity to certain countries of Western Europe (not including Spain, a staunch anti-Communist bastion which had beaten the Reds in a shooting war, and a nation impoverished because the Communists had fled to Russia with most of Spain's gold), and it set the pattern, along with UNRRA and our early give-away schemes, for our massive foreign aid programs which have drained a colossal $120 billion out of the pockets of American taxpayers since the end of World War II, depleting our gold reserves to the lowest in modern history. If the nations to which we have given foreign aid were to call in their promised gold tomorrow, our country would be strapped financially.

After the war, starting in 1947, we gave military aid costing $400 million to Greece and $150 million to Turkey under the Truman Doctrine, which was blueprinted by the very able and foresighted anti-Communist James Forrestal. The Truman Doctrine emphasized military aid to those countries, with just enough compensatory money to get them on their feet to help themselves. Today, Greece and Turkey are staunch anti-Communist nations, ably staving off the threats of the neighboring Soviet Union. But the Marshall Plan was the opposite of the Truman-Forrestal plan. It consisted solely of economic aid for Europe, to make Europe prosperous, on the fallacious principle that communism and prosperity do not exist side by side.

The Marshall Plan and Point-4 certainly did set Western Europe on its feet economically after the war, to a point where the Western European economy is now booming as never before; but where are many of these countries today politically? Western Europe's economic boom certainly belies the myth that communism cannot flourish alongside prosperity. Italy, France and England are three good illustrations. In all three countries there was, of course, Communist infiltration, but no massive move to the left, before World War II. Italy, now enjoying the greatest prosperity in her history and consequently her highest standard of living, has the largest Communist Party in Europe, tightly organized right down to the precinct level. To-day, about one-fourth of the entire adult population votes the Communist Party ticket, not to mention the leftist coalition parties which put much control of the Italian government into the Communists' hands. France, too, is enjoying her greatest economic upsurge and highest standard of living in history, but her Communist Party is one of the largest and most militant in Europe, and France is well on the way to being a completely socialized nation. England, also enjoying an unprecedented economic boom and high living standard, is one of the most socialized countries in the world, with a large and militant Communist Party. In all three countries, the highest per-capita Communist vote is in the most prosperous area.

In 1953, during the Eisenhower Administration, Cleveland left the government until President-elect Kennedy chose him, in December 1960, as Assistant Secretary of State. What are Harlan Cleveland's views on U. S. foreign aid, after more than a decade of giving away American taxpayers' money in high-level positions?

A short while after he resigned temporarily from government service, Cleveland was called before the Senate Foreign Relations Committee, to give his views on our foreign aid program. What did Harlan Cleveland advocate? He advocated that all U. S. foreign aid should be given to the United Nations, which the UN would then distribute *as UN foreign aid*. How many Americans would also advocate *that?* This is the man who, today, is officially in charge of our UN affairs and of strengthening American participation in the UN. Of course, he has continued to advocate his foreign aid, bundles-for-the-UN idea from inside the Johnson Administration. In fact, he abolished the job of one of his budget officers who, Cleveland believed, had a hand in a Budget Bureau decision against a move to give our foreign aid funds to the UN for UN distribution.

When Cleveland left government service in 1953, he became executive editor of the ultra-liberal magazine *The Reporter,* owned by Max Ascoli. Cleveland had a perfect forum from which to voice his views, and they ranged all across the left half of the political spectrum, from a defense of big government, to unremitting attacks upon anti-Communists. Cleveland served as publisher of *The Reporter* from 1955 until the end of 1956, and a few months later he became dean of the Maxwell School at Syracuse.

While there, Cleveland did a study for the Special Studies Project of the Rockefeller Brothers Fund, and his study was published by the Maxwell School in 1956 under the title, *The Theory and Practice of Foreign Aid.* Cleveland urged that our country vastly increase its giveaways to "underdeveloped" nations, with no thought or mention that shoveling out more of our taxpayers' money would put us farther down the road to financial ruin, thus weakening our ability to defend ourselves against the Communist menace. In face, Cleveland's thesis was that the more money we pour into "underdeveloped" countries, the less chance these countries will have of becoming Communist, quite the contrary to the actual pattern exhibited by these Kremlin-leaning nations.

Cleveland's assumption was that the leaders of these emerging nations are naïve, that they fail to comprehend communism as a totalitarian system (ignoring, for only one thing, the fact that many of them were educated in the West, and that some of them were even trained in Moscow), and that the more money we pour into these countries, the more we build up their economies; ipso facto, says Cleveland, the Communist menace will be overcome.

It is the same old fallacious argument that Americans have been hearing for years: prosperity and communism cannot exist side by side. This basic error is so widespread and so important to refute, that it is worthwhile to quote here a very good explanation of the truth about poverty and communism, quoted from a leaflet by the anti-Communist Cardinal Mindszenty Foundation of St. Louis, Missouri:

> The single, most important error about Communism is the belief that it is caused by poverty, hunger and social injustice. This fallacy is, in fact, the principal reason for the failure of the West to understand the Communist conspiracy and to take effective steps to defeat it. The fallacy that "poverty causes Communism" is the false "stomach" theory of Communism. Communism is not a disease of the stomach; it is a disease of the mind and soul.

> Communism does not originate with the poor, the uneducated, the exploited or the working classes. Every major world Communist figure who became a Communist in a non-Communist country did so as a student intellectual, materialistic in philosophy and atheistic in faith. The list of important Communists who were well-fed student intellectuals includes, among others, Karl Marx, Friedrich Engels, Vladimir Lenin, Josef Stalin, Mao Tsetung, Chou En-lai, Chou Teh, Liu Shao-chi, Ho Chi-minh, Alger Hiss, Harry Dexter White, William Remington, Klaus Fuchs, Julius Rosenberg, Bruno Pontecorvo, Allan Nunn May, Guy Burgess, Donald Maclean, Bernon Mitchell, William Martin, Fidel and Raul Castro, Ernesto Che Guevara. It was not hunger for food that turned them to Communism, but hunger for power.

> In the United States, Communism has had its greatest appeal for men who enjoyed all the financial, educational and social benefits of the American high standard of living and free-enterprise system. The Communists have their largest numbers in our richest States: New York, California and Illinois; few or none are known to live in the relatively poor States of Arkansas and Mississippi. When a study was made of the entire early leadership of the U. S. Communist Party, it was found that only one man (Manning Johnson) came from the working class; he later left Communism and gave valuable testimony to our Government. The American Negroes and Indians have surely been the

victims of social and economic injustices. Yet, the Communists have had less success among the American Negroes and Indians than among any other social, racial, economic or national class.

The Communist-inspired riots which have occurred all over the world in the last several years have been student riots, a fact which graphically illustrates with whom the Reds are having their greatest successes. Whether the riots were in San Francisco, Turkey, Japan, Uruguay, South Korea or Panama, the rioters were always well-fed university students, not the hungry and poor. Communism has been so much more successful with the student intellectuals than with the less fortunate that the Communist conspiracy has had to take pro-Communist college graduates and send them to the workbenches of the factories in order to "colonize" the working classes.

The most vigorously anti-Communist countries in Europe are the poorest: Ireland, Spain, Portugal, Turkey and Greece. Czechoslovakia was one of the wealthiest and most democratic countries in Europe; yet it went behind the Iron Curtain without the firing of a shot. France is perhaps the richest country in Europe, yet has had one of the strongest Communist parties in Europe ever since World War II. In Italy, most of the Communists are in the more prosperous northern half, while poorer southern Italy has comparatively few Reds. Large Communist gains in the last Italian election came at a time when Italy was more prosperous than ever in her long history.

The most anti-Communist countries in Asia are also among the poorest: Pakistan and South Korea. Southeast Asia, which is falling to the Communists today, is the rice bowl of Asia. Kerala has the most advanced educational system of all the States in India; yet, when the people elected a Communist government in 1958, nine of the eleven members of the Communist clique which took control were the sons of Indian aristocrats or intellectuals. Every one of the top leaders of Red China became a Communist as a student intellectual, many of them in European universities. Not one of them was hungry for food; they were all hungry for power.

The former rector of Villanueva University in Havana for nine years until forced out by Castro, Fr. John J. Kelly, O.S.A., has confirmed beyond a shadow of a doubt that it was NOT poverty that caused Communism in Cuba. He states that "Cuba enjoyed a higher standard of living, on the average, than any other Latin-American country. In 1958 Cuba stood fourth among the twenty Latin-American republics in the per-capita income, and enjoyed a social legislation far in advance of our own: eight-hour day, forty-eight-hour pay for a forty-four- hour week, one month paid vacation, nine days paid sick leave per year, labor insurance paid in at least two-thirds part by the employer, three months maternity leave with pay, and both hospital and medical coverage. No employer could dismiss an employee except through the Labor Board, which usually decided in favor of the employee. The labor unions and the so-called proletariat had little to do with the rebellion against Batista; the middle classes, the professions, and much of the monied classes ousted Batista with a big assist from the ignorant or subversive sub-alterns in the State Department." No one denies that there was unemployment and poverty in areas of Cuba, but these poor people were NOT Castro's supporters. Castro was a well-to-do student intellectual who became a Communist while at Havana University.

This is the same pattern that is being used throughout all Latin America, and has already been used in the Communist take-over of British Guiana by American university-educated Dr. Cheddi Jagan and his wife. It is no answer to say the people of British Guiana are poor; the people of other Latin-American countries which are anti-Communist, such as Paraguay and Peru, are just as poor. The difference is that British Guiana is controlled by a Communist intellectual couple hungry for power, trained in American schools and financed by American money.

Some people argue that, even though it is not actually the poor and hungry who become Communists, nevertheless poverty is a cause of Communism because it leads good people to accept Communism in their desire to help the less fortunate. This argument fails to distinguish between what is a cause and what is simply a recruitment device to attract the gullible. The Communist promise to remedy poverty is a recruitment device just like the Communist promise of free love. These are the "carrots" which criminal conspirators use to attract gullible people to the fringe of their apparatus, just as the kidnapper uses candy to lure a child into his car.

It is just as silly to say we can stop Communism by feeding hungry people, as it would be to say we can stop Communism by giving people all the free love they want; or to say we can stop kidnappers by providing children with all the candy they want so they won't get into strange automobiles; or to say we can stop bank robbers by making it easier to get loans from the bank. No matter what human desires (whether legitimate or not) are satisfied, human nature is such that there will always be other desires the Communists can foment or exaggerate in order to advance their conspiracy.

If our program to stop Communism is solely economic and materialistic, that is, based on improving economic conditions, it is doomed to failure. If we raised the living standards of Asia and Latin America and Africa tomorrow by one thousand percent, it would not slow down the advance of Communism, because there would still be a whole host of human desires and grievances which the Communists could exploit. Envy is a primary Communist recruitment device. Communists are masters at sowing hatred, exploiting minor grievances, and creating grievances where none exists. Of course, to feed the hungry is a Christian act. But any delusion that feeding hungry people is going to roll back the tide of Communism is just as false as the delusion, which some people have, that all we need to do is to be good Christians, or be good Americans, and we shall be safe from the Communists. The history of the Communist conquest of Eastern Europe proves that this is not true. We will never be able to stop the advance of the Communist conspiracy until we start treating Communists as the criminals they are.

The Rockefeller Brothers Fund continued its study projects —concurrently with the Fund for the Republic's Gaither Committee—after the launching of Sputnik, to preach panic and defeatism to the American people. The identical thesis of the studies of these two groups was that, since Sputnik had made it "obvious" that the United States could not beat Russia technologically or militarily (even though many American scientists publicly declared that many of the Russian "space achievements" might be fakes) we must therefore seek "other solutions" in thinking about Russia—such as a vastly increased foreign aid giveaways—and even contemplate surrender to Soviet Russia.

The studies of the two groups were so unashamedly defeatist that vigorous protests were heard from many responsible quarters. *The Economist* of London said of the Gaither Committee studies (and might just as well have included the Rockefeller Brothers Fund studies in its indictment):

> Broadening its task almost beyond recognition, it concluded that the Soviet Union stands a good chance of gaining such a

military lead by 1961 that it could then neutralize or destroy the United States.

The Rockefeller studies concluded:

> It appears that the United States is rapidly losing its lead over the U.S.S.R. in the military race. . . . Unless present trends are reversed, the world balance of power will shift in favor of the Soviet bloc. . . . However, it is not too late if we are prepared to make the big effort required now and in the years ahead.

All of which meant shoveling out more U. S. taxpayers' money and U. S. gold for years to come. As the months went on, the men who guided both reports started Americans thinking about "peaceful coexistence," which culminated in "leaks" about the inevitably of American surrender to the Russians.

Sputnik had been launched on October 4, 1957, and on August 5, 1958, the liberal St. Louis *Post Dispatch* published an article by retired Brigadier General Thomas B. Phillips under the headline "Question of When United States Should Surrender in All-Out Nuclear Attack Studied for Pentagon," and under the subhead, "Scientists are proceeding on assumption Russia has achieved, or is rapidly gaining, intercontinental military superiority with missiles." Excerpts from the article read:

> Three non-profit scientific agencies working for the Defense Department or the services are making studies as to whether the United States can survive and continue to fight after an all-out nuclear attack. One is studying the conditions when surrender would be advisable, rather than to try to continue a war that is already lost. . . .
>
> A straw in the wind, showing the direction of some thinking, is the publication of a book, *Strange Surrender,* by Paul Kecskemetri, Stanford University Press, 1958. The book is a RAND Corporation study. The RAND Corporation is a non-profit scientific agency operated for the Air Force by a group of universities . . .
>
> "What present weapons portend," writes Kecskemetri, "is an extreme disruptive effect, which . . . points to the possibility of surrender of a different sort: surrender without fighting . . ."
>
> Kecskemetri's book also said: "One may safely say that the

maxim, 'In war there is no substitute for victory,' is totally erroneous."

The book concluded: "We shall have to revise some of our deeply-rooted traditional attitudes, such as our rejection of compromise, and our faith in extreme, ideal solutions."

Needless to say, the elected representatives of the American people in Congress damned the very notion of American surrender to the Communists. One Congressman revealed that two of the organizations mentioned in General Phillip's article as studying U. S. survival were the RAND Corporation (not to be confused with the Sperry Rand Corporation) and the Operations Research Office of Johns Hopkins University.

At the very moment the St. Louis *Post Dispatch* published the "surrender report," top-ranking members of the "three non-profit scientific agencies working for the Defense Department and for the services" referred to by General Phillips, were at the World Brotherhood Conference in Switzerland. The conference (attended by U.S. disarmament adviser John McCloy) issued a statement proclaiming that the United States should "try to eliminate the stereotype attitudes about, and suspicion of Communism. We must assume that the Communist side is not worse than, but merely different from, our side." Harlan Cleveland was an official of World Brotherhood Conference two years later, as we shall soon see.

Furthermore, if one examines the lists of the men involved in both the Gaither and Rockefeller studies, it will be readily seen that these same men are today deeply involved in disarming the United States. For example: John McCloy, a trustee of the Ford Foundation, is an official of World Brotherhood and until recently was government coordinator of disarmament; the director of the Rockefeller Special Studies Project, Dr. Henry A. Kissinger of Harvard's Center of International Affairs (which contributes many "advanced thinkers" to pushing disarmament of America and to disarmament think factories) is now a consultant to the U. S. Arms Control and Disarmament Agency; Dr. Thomas C. Schelling, also of Harvard's Center for International Studies and also a staff member of the RAND Corporation, is a consultant to the U. S. Arms Control and Disarmament Agency. Dr. James Perkins, vice president of the Carnegie Corporation, a consultant to the RAND Corporation, and a member of the Rockefeller Studies on Arms and Disarmament, is now a trustee of the Institute of Defense Analysis.

The Ford Foundation-financed (half a million dollars to launch it) Institute of Defense Analysis (IDA), is a high-level think factory which does studies under contract for the Defense Department and the Disarmament Agency. It is these IDA studies, primarily, which are spelling out America's disarmament policies throughout the federal government. IDA's ultimate objective—according to IDA's own literature—is to establish one-world government.

Three important themes are currently being pushed by the IDA, which will be seen to burgeon during 1964. First, the "split" between Soviet Russia and Red China is to be emphasized *in order to ease the United States into merger with the Soviet Union.* (To quote an IDA study memo of September 15, 1962: "China can be an asset in seeking military and political arrangements with the Soviets in Europe.") Second, the theme of unilateral disarmament is to be made respectable. (See IDA Study Memorandum of March 10, 1962 by Dr. Morton Halperin.) Third, one-world government is to be presented to the American people as the only alternative to nuclear holacaust. (See IDA Research Memorandum of October 6, 1961 by Dr. Lincoln Bloomfield of M.I.T.'s Center for International Studies.)

President of the IDA is none other than Richard Bissell, former deputy to CIA Director John McCone. Bissell, as the CIA representative in the planning and supervision of the Bay of Pigs landing, is one of the Inner Circle members chiefly responsible for the disaster. He was rewarded by being given an eight million dollar grant by Secretary McNamara and was named head of the IDA, at a salary of $45,000 per year. One of Bissell's recent projects is an IDA disarmament study in conjunction with Soviet scientists.

In May 1960, Harlan Cleveland served as an official of the World Brotherhood Conference on "World Tensions," held at the University of Chicago. Serving as conference officials along with Cleveland were: Adlai Stevenson; Ralph Bunche, who runs the UN in a troika with U Thant and a leftist Indian UN delegate, and who has a long, long history of serving leftist causes; the UN's Paul G. Hoffman; columnist Marquis Childs; and Norman Cousins, editor of the *Saturday Review.*

The officials of the conference reached these conclusions in their report:

1) The Communists are not interested in political subversion. They merely want "peaceful coexistence," and they have no plans to conquer the world.

2) The Communists want to trade with the United States, and we should trade on a big scale with them. [despite Lenin's prophecy: "When the capitalist world starts trade with us, on that day it will begin to finance its own destruction."]

3) The United States should *increase* its aid to "poor" countries by three *billion* dollars *per year.*

4) United States should seek "closer relations" with the Soviet Union and with all Communist nations.

5) The Connally Reservation should be repealed. [This is the eight-word reservation, "as determined by the United States of America," appended to Congress' 1946 acceptance of the jurisdiction of the Communist-dominated World Court, whose five judges are chosen by the U.N. The Connally Reservation is the only thing which stands between our American sovereignty and a complete takeover by "Socialist one-world government." The World Court could declare, for example—if the Connally Reservation were repealed—that our U. S. Constitution, our Bill of Rights and our Declaration of Independence are null and void. Ever since it was written into our laws, the Communists and all fellow travelers and leftists have, of course, been trying to get it repealed.]

On February 23, 1961, Cleveland took office as Assistant Secretary of State for International Organization Affairs and for UN affairs, a job in which he guides all American participation in the UN. Cleveland also guides all U. S. participation in international conferences, and whenever any matters affecting the United States are considered by international bodies, Cleveland and his staff prepare and guide the recommendations for the American representatives.

After he became a part of the Kennedy Administration, Harlan Cleveland enunciated the "Soviets-are-mellowing" slogan as clearly and as painstakingly as any other member of the New Frontier. One illustration is a speech he gave on December 20, 1961, in Binghamton, New York, in which Cleveland said:

> Somewhere along the line, we see new leaders of communism facing with realism the fact that their old dream of a Communist one-world is an obsolete and therefore perilous delusion. They may persist for a further time in trying to insulate themselves from the unifying forces of science, education and modern industry. Eventually, I am persuaded, they must open their society to the overwhelming benefits and requirements of a hopelessly *inter*dependent world.

This idea that the Communists are mellowing or are on the road to mellowing, persists in the utterances of Cleveland as much as it does in the utterances of Walt Rostow, one of the originators of the idea, and of most of the Inner Circle of "advanced thinkers" on the New Frontier. Neither Cleveland nor Rostow nor any other New Frontiersman offers a speck of concrete evidence in support of their far-fetched thesis. The fact is that there has not been the vaguest hint of Soviet "mellowing" during the entire 47 years since Lenin's Bolsheviks seized the Russian government in a bloody coup with the intention of conquering the world in brutal fashion.

Was there any sign of "mellowing" when Khrushchev crushed the valiant Hungarian freedom fighters with Mongolian divisions, Russian tanks and mass murders in Budapest in 1956? Certainly Khrushchev and the rest of the Soviet leaders did not exactly look with favor upon this attempt by the Hungarians to "open their society," as Cleveland blandly assures us is going to happen. There was no "mellowing" by the Soviets when they entrenched their missiles in Cuba in 1962 and aimed them straight at the United States.

Cleveland continued in his speech, describing our time as *"a time for a new categorical imperative of peaceful change"*

... it is a "peaceful time," he says, "because we want to survive," and a time for "change" he explains, "because we want to live."

Some Americans might just be inclined to interpret these words as a rendering of the Communist slogan "Better Red than dead." But most Americans prefer Patrick Henry's stirring summation of the patriotic sentiments which wrested our country from tyranny: "Give me liberty, or give me death!"

One does not believe that Harlan Cleveland means to push the Communist propaganda slogan, "Better Red than dead." Yet, is it not noteworthy how often these "men of good will," these "advanced thinkers," end up supporting a Soviet thesis?

CHAPTER EIGHT

Marvelous McGeorge Bundy

"Never was patriot yet, but was a fool."

. . . John Dryden—ABSALOM AND ACHITOPHEL

WHEN EX-GOVERNOR FOSTER FURCOLO of Massachusetts heard that President Kennedy had appointed McGeorge Bundy as Special Assistant to the President in the field of national security, his appropriate one-word comment was: "Incredible."

Governor Furcolo's comment was not without foundation. Bundy, then dean of the faculty of Arts and Sciences at Harvard, was on public record in *opposition* to federal security. His opposition to security was based on his elaborately worded assertion that the government's security program "creates needless confusion and fear, spreads confusion far beyond the range of reason, and tends to discourage that confidence and eager sense of participation which has so often distinguished the relationship between American scholars and their government since the day of Benjamin Franklin."

Second, in bundling politically with Bundy—now often referred to as "the other Secretary of State"—President Kennedy had taken as one of his chief advisers on both national security affairs and foreign affairs a man who, rightly or wrongly, was generally understood to favor unilateral disarmament—that is, our disarming in order to encourage the Communists to do the same, all the while standing defenseless like a crab which has just shed its shell.

Governor Furcolo, a Democrat, later recovered his composure enough to say "McGeorge is completely unqualified" to advise the President on security affairs vital to the nation's present and future safety.

In return, Kennedy let loose one of the characteristic verbal blasts with which he customarily flayed his political enemies and those who did not go along with the philosophy and policies of his aides. Unfortunately, he never employed similar tactics against the enemies of our nation, against Castro, Khrushchev or Mao Tse-tung.

Kennedy asserted, "I must say I am not going to be deferred from appointing someone who opposed someone else"— a reference to the fact that Furcolo had been opposed politically by Bundy.

But Furcolo's opposition to Bundy's White House appointment was hardly political sour grapes. In fact, the American public can join Mr. Furcolo in wondering and judging just how good Bundy is at protecting our national security as the Reds roll along virtually unimpeded from Cuba, to all of Latin America, to Laos and almost all of Southeast Asia, to Berlin, to the Congo, to Ghana, Mali, Guinea and virtually the entire African continent, while we make a completely unpoliced testban treaty with them.

The far-reaching importance of Bundy's job as the President's special assistant in charge of national-security affairs and foreign affairs was delineated in *The Saturday Evening Post* of March 10, 1962, which said ". . . there has never before been a White House job quite like it." According to the magazine, Bundy and his staff of nine specialists (which formerly included Walt Rostow as Bundy's deputy) "police for the President the significant activities of three Government departments—State, Defense, Treasury—and other Security agencies:

> In a given situation they employ interdepartmental task forces to research and explore all policy alternatives. They search out the facts; the President makes policy . . .
>
> Bundy's job is highly important. He is, of course, the President's chief staff adviser on foreign affairs. But his basement office in the west wing of the White House also serves as a vital communications center. Dispatches and cables which may warrant the President's attention go first to Bundy's office; departmental memoranda concerning security and foreign relations—a daily torrent of paper—go there, too. It is Bundy's task to filter the inflow and see to it that the President is properly informed. . . .
>
> In a real sense, Bundy is a custodian of the President's time, which must be strictly rationed. Security issues which can be settled later stay on Bundy's desk.

The same *Saturday Evening Post* story, written by Milton MacKaye, an old friend of Bundy's and a newsman sympathetic to the late President Kennedy, recounted an incident which revealed both the tremendous importance of McGeorge Bundy's job, and the extent to which the late President Kennedy left important decisions to his "advisers":

> I happened to be at the White House on two separate days when important world news broke. On the first occasion he [Bundy] rushed to the President's office with the news—from our monitoring of Soviet radio—that the Russians were about to renew nuclear testing. He came back an hour later with the chilling report from our atomic experts that the Soviets had actually exploded the first of a series of nuclear devices.
>
> It was midafternoon, and Kennedy was taking a nap. Bundy at once called to a White House meeting Arthur Dean, John McCloy, Edward R. Murrow and several others. . . . What sort of announcement should the President make to the world? When Kennedy awoke, his advisers were ready with their recommendations.

How many such "naps" of President Kennedy's permitted Bundy and other White House "advisers" to make important decisions is not known. But in this one case, the "nap" must have been of several hours' duration, as can be seen from the story.

Shortly after Bundy took over his job in February 1961, following Kennedy's inauguration, the President announced that he would hold no more meetings of the National Security Council. Deliberate Administration news leaks made it clear that, in President Kennedy's opinion, former President Eisenhower had worked too much through such organizations, a method not conducive to the best results and certainly not necessary now with the Kennedy genius operating. The President himself would now make the decisions, asserting the leadership which he had promised the nation.

The National Security Council—whose purpose is to keep the President informed about U. S. military power, to recommend policy to federal defense agencies, and to unify government policy—is composed of the President, the Vice President, the Secretaries of State and Defense, the Director of the Office of Emergency Planning, the Special Assistant and Deputy Special Assistant for National Security Affairs, and the Council's Executive Secretary.

During the Eisenhower Administration, the Joint Chiefs of Staff were almost always asked to attend the council's weekly sessions and to give their opinions and advice.

After the Cuban Bay of Pigs debacle in April 1961, President Kennedy suddenly resumed National Security Council meetings; under President Johnson the council still meets about once a week. However, many key Washington observers believe that since the Bay of Pigs the opinions and advice of the Joint Chiefs are neither asked for nor heeded at the council meetings.

The Skybolt abandonment almost knocked British Prime Minister Macmillan out of office because Defense Secretary McNamara acted on his own. With the National Security Council operating properly, the State Department would have asked for time to let the Prime Minister get prepared for the blow, particularly since trust of the U.S.A. on Skybolt had been the key to Macmillan's defense policy.

The council's role and power have, nevertheless, been superseded generally by the influence of the State Department, since the council's opinions about national security—often in opposition to those of the State Department—cannot be implemented without a U. S. foreign policy aimed at maintaining the strength of the free world and at attaining victory over communism. These two key objectives—maintaining our power, and attaining victory in the cold war—are now almost completely absent from American military and diplomatic strategy.

It is significant, also, that after the Bay of Pigs fiasco, President Kennedy never reactivated the Operations Coordinating Board. Under President Eisenhower, the OCB was responsible for executing the decisions of the National Security Council, and was headed by the Under Secretary of State who operated with an expert staff. Now, apparently, Presidential Assistant McGeorge Bundy is doing—or, better, not doing— the work of the Operations Coordinating Board. National Se-

curity Council decisions are now badly implemented, and sometimes not implemented at all.

McGeorge Bundy is said by Washington insiders to be
one of the most influential men around the President. He is
certainly close enough to the President day by day to coordinate
the work of Rostow, Yarmolinsky, Cleveland, Goodwin and
others. To employ a Runyonism, he is IT to the Harvards in
Government, and for that matter, to the ADAers and others
of like beliefs.

Washington observers have credited a major part of many
highly questionable Kennedy and Johnson Administration policies to Bundy's advocacy; most must have Bundy's approbation
as the President's major National Security adviser and as a chief
Presidential adviser on foreign affairs. These policies advocate
removal of our Thor rockets from England and scrapping of
our rocket bases in Turkey and Italy, scrapping of our Skybolt
missile, and the abandonment of what most Republicans regard
as vital safeguards to disarmament agreements.

All moves toward U. S. unilateral disarmament are widely
credited to McGeorge Bundy—as is the adoption as official
policy of the plan to liquidate U. S. armed forces and destroy
our weapons, while simultaneously building an all-powerful
UN army and accepting the UN's International Court, which
could then overrule our U. S. Congress.

Sections of this proposal bear the views of Bundy—the
chief Inner Circle adviser on disarmament. Other sections involve the "end of nationhood" pushed by Walt Rostow. In the
document's plan to make a supra-state of the United Nations
can be seen the policy sponsored by Harlan Cleveland, among
many other Inner Circle advisers. Some sections bear the hallmark of John McCloy as chief adviser of the U. S. Arms Control
and Disarmament Agency—which Representative John Ash-
brook has christened "the Surrender Agency"—which promotes
and implements the disarmament of the United States.

This shocking plan to do away with American armed
forces within approximately ten years while simultaneously
building an all-powerful UN army, is completely unknown to

most Americans—perhaps not to one American in ten thousand. Yet, it is the official, announced policy of the U. S. Government, and the plan is being implemented as assiduously by the Johnson Administration as it was by President Kennedy.

The plan was first publicly proposed as a U. S. program by the late President Kennedy in a speech to the United Nations on September 25, 1961. Later that month it was formally published in a little-noted and rarely available document, Department of State Publication 7277. Almost as soon as it was published and anxious citizens started applying for a copy, the State Department and the U. S. Government Printing Office announced it was "out of print" and would not be republished. (Photostated copies can be procured from The Bookmailer, P. O. Box 101, N.Y.C. 16, N.Y.)

Once little vocal opposition was heard, the plan was actually presented as a treaty proposal to the Geneva disarmament conference by U. S. Delegate Arthur H. Dean on April 18, 1962, together with a message of approval from President Kennedy. Two days later the Soviets displayed their contempt for anyone's naïve belief that the Soviets would disarm: the Soviets moved their nuclear missiles into Cuba; but our State Department officials—not Fidel Castro—assured Americans that these Soviets were only "technicians."

One of President Johnson's first official acts as President was to inform the American public that he was in total accord with our disarmament proposal at Geneva.

Anti-Communist spokesmen both in Congress and in the nation have emphasized one significant point with regard to the disarmament plan: many Americans, when informed of the plan, discount the program, believing it to be "so fantastic" that it must be merely a propaganda device of some sort, perhaps to assure the world that we are peace-loving, or to mollify the so-called neutral nations.

But the plan is not a propaganda device; it is the official, announced policy of the U. S. government, and it is being carried out by the Administration in Washington at this moment. The United States is being steadily disarmed under a plan which trusts the Soviets also to disarm; a plan which is steadily building a UN world army while U. S. armed forces are being liquidated; a plan which will empower the UN's Communist-dominated International Court to destroy the power of our U. S. Congress; a plan which will fasten one-world government upon the world. And the plan will be completed by 1973, coincidentally the year Lenin designated more than 40 years ago as the date for final Soviet conquest of the world.

If Americans doubt that this plan is the official policy of our government, conceived and spearheaded by our "advance planners" in Washington, they need only know of a few quotes from the highest-ranking men who are implementing it:

The late President Kennedy, announcing at a press conference on April 18, 1962, that he had put forth the plan at the Geneva disarmament conference, declared: "It provides a blueprint for our position on general and complete disarmament as well as elaboration of the nature, sequence and timing of specific disarmament measures. . . . I want to stress that with this plan the United States is making a major effort to achieve a breakthrough on disarmament negotiations."

Adlai Stevenson: "It is presented in dead earnest."

Arthur H. Dean: "We are not primarily discussing measures to calm the international scene or to facilitate partial disarmament . . ."

William C. Foster, Director of the U. S. Arms Control and Disarmament Agency: "U. S. disarmament proposals are, most emphatically, not intended for propaganda purposes."

Senator Joseph D. Clark, Democrat of Pennsylvania, informed the Senate on March 1, 1962: This three-stage disarmament plan "represents the fixed and determined policy of the Executive arm of the U. S. Government."

Conservative leaders in Congress have repeatedly warned of the impending disaster inherent in the disarmament plan. Senator Richard Russell, Democrat of Georgia and Chairman of the Senate Armed Services Committee, stated flatly: "It would put this country at the mercy of the Soviet Union."

Senator Strom Thurmond declared in Congress:

> This disarmament plan should be of concern to all Americans because it proposes not only the creation of a super United Nations armed force . . . but also that we lay down our arms in an agreement with a nation which is controlled by an ideology—communism—whose leaders have sworn to bury us, and whose leaders have broken 50 of the 52 major agreements they have entered into since World War II.

The *Arizona Republic* voiced the sentiments of most conservative newspapers, in an editorial entitled "Blueprint for Surrender":

> The disarmament plan is a blueprint for the destruction of American sovereignty. It is a chart leading to World Government dominated by Communists and neutralist nations.

The announced goal of the plan is "a world which has achieved general and complete disarmament under international control and a world in which adjustment to change takes place in accordance with the principles of the United Nations." (The veto is not mentioned.)

To achieve this goal, all nations must carry out the following, which are quoted from our Geneva disarmament proposal:

> 1) Disbanding of all armed forces; dismantling of all military establishments, including military bases; cessation of the production of armaments and the liquidation of all armaments.
> 2) Elimination of all stockpiles of nuclear, chemical, biological and other weapons, and cessation of production.
> 3) Elimination of all means of delivery of weapons of mass destruction. Destruction of air force and naval transports.
> 4) Abolition of the organizations and institutions designed to organize the military efforts of states; cessation of military training; closing of all military training institutions.
> 5) Discontinuance of military expenditures. The parties to the Treaty would halt all military expenditures and would annul legislation concerning military establishments or service.

In concrete terms, what this means for the United States is that we shall, within approximately seven years, liquidate our U. S. Army, Navy, Air Force and Marine Corps. We shall destroy our nuclear stockpiles. We shall shut down the U. S. military academies at West Point, Annapolis and Colorado

Springs. We shall discontinue all U. S. military training, abolish the draft law and ROTC units in all schools. We shall stop all U. S. production of weapons and missiles of all kinds.

The plan also provides for the simultaneous building up, while nations are weakened militarily, of a UN army.

The whole plan is to be completed in three stages, covering approximately ten years. Stage One is to take place in three one-year steps, "which would significantly reduce the capabilities of nations to wage aggressive war":

> All states would have adhered to a treaty effectively prohibiting the testing of nuclear weapons. [This has already been partly achieved.]
>
> The production of fissionable materials for use in weapons would be stopped and quantities of such materials from past production would be converted to non-weapons uses. [President Johnson has announced a significant reduction in U. S. production of fissionable materials—40 per cent of our uranium and 20 per cent of our plutonium—for use in U. S. nuclear weapons.]
>
> States owning nuclear weapons would not relinquish control of such weapons to any nation not owning them and would not transmit to any such nation information or material necessary for their manufacture. [The U. S. has refused to give Skybolt nuclear missiles to the British Royal Air Force; we have consistently refused to give any nuclear weapons, information or material to any non-nuclear nation, especially to West Germany, so feared by the Soviet Union.]
>
> Strategic nuclear weapons delivery vehicles of specified categories and weapons designed to counter such vehicles would be reduced to agreed levels by equitable and balanced steps; their production would be discontinued or limited; their testing would be halted or limited. [Now partly accomplished by the U. S., unilaterally.]
>
> Peaceful uses of outer space would be promoted. [Proposed by President Kennedy, and seconded by President Johnson.]
>
> UN "peace-keeping" powers would be strengthened. [See Katanga.]
>
> An international disarmament organization would be established for effective verification of the disarmament program. [The UN has established a ten-nation committee on disarmament, composed of five Western nations and five Soviet nations —a neat arrangement for the Soviets. Later this group was ex-

panded to include the seven following so-called "neutral" nations, most of whom consistently vote against the United States and for the Soviet Union in the UN: Brazil, Burma, Ethiopia, India, Mexico, Nigeria, Sweden and the United Arab Republic. This is another clear example of where the United States will be when the entire disarmament plan is completed and we find ourselves under the domination of the UN.]

The United States has apparently taken most of these Stage-One steps unilaterally. In addition to reducing the strength of the U.S. armed forces, Stage One calls for a 30 per cent reduction in such U.S. armaments as our nuclear jet bombers and fighter planes, our Atlas, Titan and Polaris missiles, our missile launching pads, anti-missile missile systems, aircraft carriers, battleship, cruisers, submarines, etc.

Stage Two will further reduce national armed forces, armaments, military establishments, strategic nuclear weapons delivery vehicles and countering weapons. The permanent UN army will be established. Production of chemical, bacteriological and radiological weapons will be halted, subject to the findings of the UN "Experts Commission." All stocks of such weapons will be reduced or converted to peaceful purposes; stocks of nuclear weapons will be reduced. Certain military bases and facilities "wherever located" will be dismantled or converted to peaceful purposes. The UN Disarmament Organization will be strengthened and enlarged.

It is significant that Stage Two also provides:

> The parties to the treaty would undertake to accept *without reservation,* pursuant to Article 36, Paragraph (1) of the Statute of the International Court of Justice, the *compulsory jurisdiction* of that court to decide international legal disputes.

This means that only five judges, chosen by the UN and sitting on the UN's International Court, could declare null and void our U.S. Constitution, our Declaration of Independence and our Bill of Rights. Is it any wonder that Senator Russell declares that this plan "will put this country at the mercy of the Soviet Union"? To describe the International Court (sometimes referred to as the World Court), presided over by a Communist from Red Poland, as heavily weighted in favor of Communists and pro-Communists would be putting it mildly. A good example is the U.S. member, appointed by Eisenhower, Philip Jessup. The evidence of Jessup's pro-Communist sympathies is overwhelming. Briefly, Jessup was one of the foremost members of IPR working in close association with the notorious Communist, Frederick Vanderbilt Field. He was a sponsor of many Red front organizations, a protégé of Dean Acheson and a close friend of Alger Hiss, and a character witness for Hiss at the two Hiss trials. He was a vigorous supporter of Owen Lattimore, and he was caught red-handed lying under oath to a Senate Committee. To top off Jessup's record, the Senate in 1951 refused to confirm his appointment by President Truman as U.S. Ambassador to the UN, because of his pro-Communist activities. Even a quick rundown of the Communist and pro-Communist backgrounds of the other 14 members of the International Court would unearth facts equally as astonishing. Only nine judges constitute a quorum. And yet, this is the organization to which the Administration in Washington plans to turn over the "compulsory jurisdiction" of U. S. legal proceedings. Its implications are frightening.

Stage three of the plan will complete the disarmament of the "world," while the UN army has "sufficient armed forces and armaments so that no State could challenge it." All nations will "have at their disposal only those forces and organizational arrangements necessary . . . to maintain internal order."

One columnist commented: "Letting the Communist-dominated UN rule the world with an all-powerful army, while allowing us to retain forces capable only of 'maintaining internal order,' is exactly comparable to allowing criminals to run wild, while our police force may only give traffic tickets."

In case patriotic Americans, Frenchmen, Italians or patriots of any nationality balk at their nation's sovereignty being destroyed and their country's being placed under UN one-world government controlled by a UN army, the plan contains a proviso which will neatly dispose of them:

Those parties to the treaty which had not already done so

would . . . enact national legislation in support of the treaty, imposing legal obligations on individuals and organizations under their jurisdiction and providing *appropriate penalties for noncompliance.*

In this regard, two events might be noted. One is the bill before Congress to forbid all American citizens from buying and keeping arms, except those registered with the FBI. Now, in the first place, this is in direct conflict with the Second Amendment to the Constitution, which states: " . . . the right of the people to keep and bear arms, shall not be infringed."

It is clearly unconstitutional and illegal, and criminals would always get guns on the black market. In the second place, refugees from behind the Iron Curtain explain, to anyone who will listen, that when the Communists took over their countries, they simply went down the government's list of those possessing arms and fired the arms at the citizens' heads. The populace thus had no way of defending itself from Communist terror.

The second event that might be noted in connection with this proviso of the disarmament plan is that in April 1962, immediately after the plan was presented at Geneva, the U.S. Army announced:

> Special emphasis will be placed by the Army on counterinsurgency. . . Every individual in the regular Army, the Reserve, the ROTC and the cadets at West Point must be indoctrinated or trained in counterinsurgency just as soon as physically possible.

What does "counterinsurgency" mean? It means putting down citizens' rebellions, or, in the words of the commanding general of the U.S. Army Continental Command:

> An action including all military, political, psychological and sociological activities directed toward preventing and suppressing resistance groups whose actions range in degrees of violence and scope, from subversive activities to violent action by guerrilla elements. . . .

Why are our troops being trained to put down citizens' rebellions, and not being trained to fight Communist armed attack? Is this a foreboding of things to come for American citizens who will most certainly rebel violently against a UN army and one-world UN government?

At the end of the Third Stage of the plan, the UN army will be the only army in the world. It will be supplied with arms by the world's nations, who will keep none for themselves except those necessary "to maintain internal order." No nation will have nuclear weapons; all the nuclear weapons of individual nations will have been destroyed or given to the UN army. Only the UN army will possess nuclear weapons. The UN army will be staffed by citizens of different nations who shall be drafted into the UN army by the leaders of their countries. This could mean that the disarmed American citizenry could be up against a UN army including African savages such as those who massacred the populace of Katanga and even ate some of them, or those who at the moment of this writing are, dope-crazed by Communist revolutionaries, dismembering Christian missionaries and Matusi warriors in Africa.

Now, where and when did this three-stage plan for disarmament originate? Did it originate in 1962, when on April 18 Arthur Dean proposed it as a U.S. treaty at Geneva? Did it originate in late September 1961, when the State Department published it as U.S. policy? Did it originate on September 25, 1961, when the late President Kennedy proposed it to the UN?

Curiously enough, this three-stage proposal for world disarmament was not originally proposed to the UN by President Kennedy. Two years previously, on September 15, 1959, Nikita Khrushchev had proposed *exactly* the same three-stage plan for "world" disarmament to the UN. But the plan goes back even farther than that.

It originated—lock, stock and barrel—in Soviet Russia in 1927, when it was proposed to *the meeting of the worldwide Communist Party by Russian Foreign Commissar Maxim Litvinov.* The two plans—the 1927 Soviet plan, and the present-day U.S. plan—are exactly the same.

At the Sixth World Congress of the Communist International the following year, in 1928, the Communists spelled out their disarmament proposal a bit more clearly as a Soviet weapon for conquering the world, by disarming the free nations while the Soviets gear for smashing the world with their clenched fist:

> ... The disarmament policy of the Soviet Government must be used for purposes of agitation much more energetically and to a wider extent than has been done hitherto. ... [It must be utilized] to eradicate all pacifist illusions and to carry on propaganda among the masses in support of the only way toward disarmament and abolition of war, *viz.,* arming of the proletariat, overthrowing the bourgeoisie and establishing the proletarian dictatorship. [The last passage means, of course, the Communist domination of the world.]

Let us compare both disarmament proposals: first the Kennedy-State Department-Geneva proposal; and then the "Scheme for General and Complete Disarmament" (the same words used in the U.S. Administration schemes) first proposed by Litvinov in 1927:

Plan for U. S. Disarmament —Today:	*Communist proposals —1927:*
1) Dismantling of all armed forces. Dismantling of all military establishments, including military bases. Cessation of the production of armaments and the liquidation of all armaments.	1) The dissolution of all land, sea and air forces. The destruction of fortresses and bases. The destruction of all weapons, military supplies and all other forms of armaments.
2) Elimination of all stockpiles of nuclear, chemical, biological and other weapons, and cessation of production.	2) The destruction of all weapons, military supplies and all other forms of armaments.
3) Elimination of all means of delivery of weapons of mass destruction. Destruction of air force and naval transports.	3) The scrapping of all military plants and factories.
4) Abolition of the organizations and institutions designed to organize the military efforts of states. Cessa-	4) The discontinuance of calling up citizens for military training, either in armies

Plan For U.S. Disarmament —Today:	*Communist Proposals —1927:*
tion of military training. Closing of all military training institutions.	or public bodies. Legislation for the abolition of military service, either compulsory, voluntary or recruited. Legislation for prohibiting the calling up of trained reserves.
5) Discontinuance of military expenditures. The parties to the Treaty would halt all military expenditures and would annul legislation concerning military establishments or services.	5) The discontinuance of assigning funds for military purposes.

Robert Morris, former chief counsel to the Senate Internal Security Subcommittee, who has also served as counsel to the Senate Foreign Relations Committee and officer-in-charge of Advance Psychological Warfare on Guam and Officer-in-Charge of Counterintelligence for the Third Naval District, wrote of the U.S. disarmament plan soon after it was announced:

> This incontrovertibly means that the combination of forces which ran the invasion of Katanga, killing innocent women and children, would be supreme, and we here in the U. S. would be subject to them. We seem to be forging our own chains. . . . This is the surrender of our Constitution, our Bill of Rights, the religious and spiritual heritage of our freedom. This disarmament program outlines the steps for liquidation of the U.S.A. . . . It makes this liquidation the official policy of our government today.

Dr. Morris also presented an excellent capsule explanation of how the Soviets will soon dominate the UN, which is especially enlightening for those well-meaning Americans who regard the UN as "our hope for peace," thanks to the flood of such UN propaganda spewed constantly across our nation from coast to coast:

> There is no denying that Soviet power in the United Nations is growing stronger every day. Perhaps it has not *yet* directly taken over, but by its infiltration of non-Communist governments, its ruthless diplomacy and its own inflexibility added

to its own strength, it is the dominant force driving the UN to do its bidding. And this trend is continuing. By the time the State Department enacts its "Program," the admission of Red China and further Soviet takeovers in Africa, Latin America and Asia will give the Soviets a clear preponderance in the UN.

Is this what Americans want for themselves and their children—a world ruled by a Communist-dominated UN? A Communist slave world? The Communists' unceasing and successful drive to dominate the UN, coupled with their ceaseless efforts to disarm the free world and place it under UN control can mean only one thing: that the Communists plan to control the world through the UN. And under the Administration's three-stage plan for U.S. disarmament and domination of the world by a UN army, every American man, woman and child will be under total UN domination within approximately seven years. The terrible nightmare of our being Communist slaves is no longer just an awful dream. It may soon be a reality unless the American people are jolted into reversing this suicidal policy.

The chief editorial writer of the Dallas *Morning News,* Kenneth Thompson, in a column headlined "One, Two, Three —Surrender," called the U.S. disarmament plan:

> . . . one of the most incredible documents ever to emerge from the foggy corridors of the State Department . . . [It] completely and unabashedly advocates the surrender of American rights and sovereignties . . . It certainly is one of the most fantastic, harebrained blueprints for surrender on record. Old Nikita himself might just as well have written it.
>
> And if more of the American people knew about this scheme, there would be a nationwide uproar that would make the reaction to the Alger Hiss scandal look like another era of good feeling by comparison.

In 1963, Representative James B. Utt, Republican of California and an authority in Congress on the United Nations, declared:

> The people have to be visibly and actively aroused before there will be any change. At the rate we are going, I feel *very certain* that we will be under an international control *within*

the next seven or eight years. That would be the United Nations, which, I think, is a godless organization.

If this nation ever turns its back on the God that created us, we are certainly going to pay the penalty.

There used to be a word for plotting the destruction of American sovereignty. The word was treason. The penalty was hanging. Have we as a nation forgotten the brave men who bled and died at Valley Forge, in the Argonne Woods, on Okinawa? Have we accepted so completely the "Better Red than dead" brainwashing that we have lost sight of the convictions that made ours the greatest nation in the world? Consider the difference between the Communist "Better Red than dead" slogan and: "Is life so dear, or peace so sweet, as to be purchased at the price of chains and slavery? I know not what course others may take, but as for me, give me liberty, or give me death!" . . . "My only regret is that I have but one life to give for my country." Have the people of the United States of America been so completely duped by leftist propaganda about "accommodating" the Soviet Union, about the "mellowing" Soviet slavemasters, that they will not protest en masse against an insidious plan which may make us the slaves of Communist terror and tyranny?

While the leaders of our government disarm the United States, the Soviets publicly renew their vow to bury us. Are we so demented as a nation that we will not turn out these leftist egghead planners? Are the shapers of this disarmament policy so blind that they cannot see what they are doing to our nation? Is "blind" the correct word?

To insure that today's American children, and their children's children, are totally brainwashed in the precepts of the coming one-world, UNESCO (the United Nations Educational, Scientific and Cultural Organization), headquartered in Paris, has enacted a program which, says Robert Morris, "fits into this grand design for surrender." It is a blueprint for a monolithic, worldwide system of atheistic education which professes to tolerate "independent education" but only if it "conforms" to the master plan and "promotes the UN."

The nuclear test-ban treaty signed in August 1963 is in line with Stage One of the disarmament plan, which states: "All states would have adhered to a treaty effectively prohibiting the test of nuclear weapons."

Published statements past and present reinforce the realization that the test ban is being used by the Kremlin to further Soviet interests. Beginning with the Sixth World Congress of the Communist International resolution of November 28, 1928, the Communists have emphasized:

> The aim of the Soviet [disarmament] proposals is . . . to propagate the fundamental Marxian postulate that disarmament and the abolition of war are possible only with the fall of Capitalism . . . There is no contradiction between the Soviet government's preparations for defense and for revolutionary war, and a consistent peace policy.

"Peace," of course, in Soviet terminology, means the complete absence of any resistance to communism; it means the final Communist conquest of the world. This is the most basic word in the Communist lexicon.

Ever since 1928, the Communists have pushed for "disarmament" to conquer the world, and even as the U.S. was preparing to sign the test-ban treaty, Khrushchev publicly told the world's Communist leaders:

> The test-ban treaty will perpetuate not the American nuclear monoply, but the fact of its liquidation.

Within two or three days after our American "leaders" went ignominiously to Moscow to sign the test-ban treaty, Khrushchev wrote an open letter to the leaders of the Red Chinese, in which he declared:

> This [test-ban treaty] is a victory for communism.

The letter was duly reported in our nation's press; yet the U.S. Senate ratified the treaty because they were afraid that their constituents would interpret a vote against the treaty as a vote "against peace," and they would not be re-elected.

One of America's most brilliant military strategists, General Douglas MacArthur, once uttered these fateful words which are certainly applicable to our nation's signing the nuclear Test-Ban Treaty:

> Peace, indeed, can be obtained at least temporarily by any nation, if it is prepared to yield its freedom principles. But peace at any price, peace with appeasement, peace which passes the dreadful finality to future generations—is a peace of sham and shame which can end only in war or slavery.

When the late President Kennedy sent our American representatives to Moscow to sign the treaty the Chicago *Tribune* wrote one of the hardest-hitting questionings of Kennedy's purposes ever to appear in print in this country. The editorial declared flatly:

> We sometimes wonder whether the Kennedy Administration is committed to national suicide or whether it is conducting a planned drive into surrender to communism.

As Robert Morris put it:

> When all the pieces are put into place, our policy calls for an affirmative drive toward a mammoth "accommodation" with Soviet power . . . Our whole policy reflects, despite steadfast Soviet intransigence, a determined drive to effect what has been called a "peaceful merger with the Soviet Union."

The top men of our Administration who are planning our "peaceful merger with the Soviet Union" do not have to search long or hard to find the constantly reiterated, primary doctrine of the international Communist conspiracy: the Communists intend to conquer the world. For example, on July 14, 1963, even while the Administration was pushing for the test-ban treaty, the Soviet Russians wrote an open letter to the Red Chinese, saying:

> We fully stand for the destruction of imperialism and capitalism. We not only believe in the inevitable destruction of capitalism, but we are doing everything for this to be accomplished *as soon as* possible.

If we consider that the Communists plan the "destruction of capitalism . . . as soon as possible," and then consider U.S. disarmament steps to date, we have cause for the deepest concern. We are being given a series of little Munichs, so we won't rebel as we would against a big Munich. We can only hope that there will not be a nuclear Pearl Harbor at the end of the road down which the men around Johnson are leading us.

This is abundant evidence from our highest-echelon military leaders, from nuclear scientists and from Congressional leaders, that the signing of the test-ban treaty is a step down the road to a big Munich or a nuclear Pearl Harbor.

In the first place, all the members of the Joint Chiefs of Staff were on record in opposition to that treaty. It was only when the White House did some painful arm-twisting that some of the Joint Chiefs were forced to backtrack for public consumption to some extent. In a position paper on the treaty, the Joint Chiefs had declared.

> 1) Militant communism remains dedicated to the destruction of our society.
> 2) The U.S.S.R. is ahead of the United States in the high-yield—tens of megatons—technology, in weapons-effect knowledge derived from high-yield explosives, and in the yield/weight ratio of high-yield devices.
> 3) If . . . both sides faithfully observe its provisions . . . United States would not be able to overtake the present advantage which the U.S.S.R. probably has in the high-yield weapons field; whereas the Soviets, by underground testing, could probably retrieve any lead which we may presently have in the low-yield tactical field.

Among the highest-ranking nuclear scientists in complete opposition to the treaty was Dr. Edward Teller, whose research in nuclear fission spearheaded development of the hydrogen bomb. After giving the Senate committee extensive documentation of the disasters for the U.S. inherent in the treaty, Dr. Teller declared:

> The proposed test-ban treaty . . . would endanger our security and help the Soviet Union in its plan to conquer the world.

Among Senators opposed was Senator Barry Goldwater, who, unlike most of his Democratic colleagues and many of his Republican colleagues, announced he would vote against the treaty "even if it means political suicide for me." Goldwater, in proposing that the Senate, if it did vote for the treaty, condition it on Russia's removal from Cuba of all military and technical forces and equipment, appealed to his fellow Senators:

> If you must vote for this treaty, then in your nation's name and in the name of the trust your nation has placed upon you, demand at least this single, honorable, appropriate and meaningful price. Such a moment may not be ours again. God help us if we cannot claim it now, in the name of peace and in the name of freedom.

The Senate voted against Senator Goldwater's proposal 75 to 17.

Among Congressmen opposing the treaty was Representative Craig Hosmer, Republican of California. Hosmer is accepted as one of the most knowledgeable men in Congress on nuclear matters, and is a former attorney for the Atomic Energy Commission in Los Alamos. As a leading member of the Joint House-Senate Committee on Atomic Energy, Hosmer called the treaty ". . . the Administration's sure-lose test-ban strategy of gradual nuclear self-mutilation."

Immediately before the treaty was approved by the Senate, retired Rear Admiral Chester Ward summed up its probable effects:

> The U.S. Senate will ratify the so-called "limited" test-ban deal with Moscow. This will freeze the U.S. in second place to Russia in the technology of strategic nuclear weapons. U.S. nuclear strike capability will be reduced so fast relative to the Soviet's mushrooming superweapon strength, that *within 18 months* we will have lost our power to deter a Soviet surprise attack, or to retaliate effectively against the overwhelming military power of their superweapons of annihilation.
>
> If this prediction is allowed to come true, *it will be the end of our country.*

But the United States has signed a completely unpoliced nuclear test-ban treaty with Moscow which will guarantee Soviet nuclear superiority over the world. We have this assurance from the lips of the late President John F. Kennedy himself. On March 2, 1962, he told the American public.

. . . a new agreement without controls would enable them [the Soviets] to prevent the West from testing while they prepare in secret . . . We now know enough about broken negotiations, secret preparations and the advantages gained from a long test series never to offer again an uninspected moratorium.

It should be remembered that the terms of the treaty are to be interpreted by the UN's World Court, and the preamble to the treaty states that its purpose is "general and complete disarmament." It is not a "partial nuclear test-ban treaty"; it is a disarmament treaty. And it is entirely in keeping with the Administration's grand design for disarmament of the United States in three stages.

It should also be noted that, under the terms of the treaty, the United States must give ninety days' notice that it plans to resume nuclear testing. But on the Soviet side—quite aside from the probability that the Soviets are testing in secret, or in their satellite nations, which are not bound to the treaty—Section (o) of Article 49 of the U.S.S.R. constitution states that the Soviet Presidium "ratifies and denounces international treaties of the U.S.S.R."

This means that the 33 men of the Soviet Presidium can break any treaty made by the U.S.S.R. They would not have to do it publicly. The Soviet Union could merely break the treaty, resume clandestine nuclear testing—and "neglect" to inform the free world that it has resumed nuclear testing.

Even though Defense Secretary McNamara has scrapped U.S. first-strike weapons, he continues to assure the American public that we have weapons which "can absorb the first blow" and "hit back at the Soviets." As late as February 1964, he reiterated his statement and declared that we have intercontinental ballistic missiles "in dispersed and hardened sites, safe from atomic attack." These are "second-strike" weapons.

Quite aside from the fact that the American people, in conflict with Mr. Rostow and Mr. McNamara, would have preferred to retain our first-strike weapons which deterred Soviet aggression upon us, there is now strong evidence that the Soviets may have destroyed even our second-strike nuclear capability.

Frightening evidence of this possibility was presented—as a probability—in the September 16, 1963, issue of the magazine *Missiles and Rockets,* which is highly respected by nuclear scientists and engineers throughout the country. The magazine prefaced its revelations by announcing that it was deliberately breaking "the highest national classification," top secret, because this information was being dangerously and deliberately kept from Congress and the public.

Missiles and Rockets disclosed that the Soviets had conducted tests which revealed the existence of a hitherto completely unknown effect known as the "electro-magnetic pulse" —*which is capable of crippling, at long range, the electronic firing mechanism of missiles, so that they cannot be fired from their silos.*

The magazine explained that the electro-magnetic pulse (EMP) was discovered by the Soviets' double-crossing breach of the nuclear test-ban moratorium. The discovery is of transcendental importance to the survival of the United States.

It may mean that the United States, explains the magazine, "has invested billions of dollars in a 'Maginot Line' of Atlas, Titan and Minuteman missiles" which could be rendered useless by the Soviet development.

According to *Missiles and Rockets,* the Soviets declare they have developed a superbomb which discharges the electro-magnetic pulse. The magazine also revealed that, in his censored testimony during the Senate's treaty hearing, General Thomas S. Power, Commander of our Strategic Air Command, expressed grave fear that the Soviet claim may be true, and that the Soviets may now possess the ability to destroy the electronics of our silo-based missiles and wipe out the ability of the United States to retaliate against attack. Power is slated for removal at the end of his current term.

The pattern of U.S. unilateral disarmament can be seen in the entire picture of the state of America's defenses. In the spring of 1962, a group of ultra Liberals collaborated on a book entitled *The Liberal Papers,* edited by Representative James Roosevelt. This book, when re-examined today, was clearly a blueprint for Kennedy's and Johnson's foreign policy and defense program. Here are examples:

The Liberal Papers proposed the dismantling of American missile bases in Europe. The Kennedy Administration scrapped our Jupiter missile bases in England, Turkey, and Italy.

The Liberal Papers proposed a "non-provocative" attitude toward Russia on the theory that Communists would "play fair" if only we showed that we trust them. The Kennedy and Johnson Administrations have ordered censorship of speeches by military men to cut out such phrases as "the Communist conspiracy" and reference to the Communist objective of world conquest.

The Liberal Papers proposed unilateral disarmament by the U.S., declaring that the Communists would also disarm unilaterally "if we set a good example."

The Kennedy and Johnson Administrations accordingly have ordered "phasing out" of our long-range bombers. Both Administrations have ordered a halt to development of a nuclear aircraft engine, even though Russia is developing one. Although the Soviets may already possess an anti-missile missile, the Administration has scrapped our new Nike-Zeus missile system. Skybolt has been scrapped, the space platform program emasculated and no new weapons come from U.S. drawing boards.

While the Communists develop satellites to put nuclear warheads into orbit (a 100 megaton bomb exploded 100 miles in space over the United States would incinerate almost the entire North American Continent) our Administration has slowed down programs for the *military* use of space. We are virtually defenseless in the area 100 to 500 miles above the earth, on which the Soviets are concentrating.

We have also retreated from our original U.S. demand for 20 on-site inspections. We have now signed a treaty that makes no provisions for policing, a treaty prohibiting testing in the atmosphere, where the U.S. is behind, but which permits underground testing, where Russia is now behind.

It is true, then, that Walt Whitman Rostow has gone far in implementing his theory that victory in the nuclear age is "impossible" and that "we do not expect this planet to be forever split between a Communist bloc and a free world. We expect this planet to organize itself in time on the principles of voluntary cooperation among independent Nation-States dedicated to human freedom." If the Russians don't agree, what happens?

How far the men around Kennedy and Johnson have succeeded in U.S. military disarmament can be realized by comparing the nuclear arsenal of America as planned by the Eisenhower Administration for the mid-1960's, with the Kennedy-Johnson Administration's plans for the late 1960's. This graphic comparison was published by *U.S. News and World Report* in its August 5, 1963, issue:

HOW AMERICA'S NUCLEAR ARSENAL IS TO BE "STREAMLINED"

	From this—as planned by the Eisenhower Administration for the mid-1960's	*To this*—as planned by the Kennedy Administration for the late 1960's
B-47 bombers	1,100	0
B-52 bombers	630	0
B-58 bombers	80	0
Thor missiles	60	0
Jupiter missiles	45	0
Atlas missiles	126	0
Titan missiles	126	54
Polaris missiles	464	656
Minuteman missiles	600	950+
Nuclear weapons and delivery systems equaling:	30 to 40 billion tons of TNT	2 billion tons of TNT

Radical cutbacks, as a result, have been put into effect where nuclear weapons systems are concerned. What the record shows: *B-47 bomber:* Already cut back from 1,100 to 650. Will be down to 300 by next summer, entirely abandoned by 1966.

Power of the B-47 bomb load is more than 10 megatons; this is equal to more than 10 million tons of TNT.

B-52 bomber: Production has halted despite Congressional desire to continue, and the operational fleet was frozen at 630 planes. Some models will be scrapped inside 5 years; others presumably can be kept flying a few years after that. In the latest model, the H-series, the B-52 will carry more than 50 megatons over a 10,000-mile range.

B-58 bomber: The production line was shut down last autumn—also over Congressional opposition—after about 80 planes were earmarked for combat-type duty. This plane carries a 15 megaton load at supersonic speeds.

RS-70 bomber: Planned by the Air Force as bomber of the 1970's, but held up in development stage. The Joint Chiefs of Staff and many members of Congress want to see it in production, but chances are slim.

Thor missile: Four bases in England, with 60 medium-range missiles capable of reaching into Russia, were ordered dismantled shortly after Soviet Russia withdrew its missiles from Cuba.

Jupiter missile: Bases in Italy and Turkey, with a total of 45 missiles, were ordered abandoned. They had just become operational at a cost of $555 million.

Skybolt missiles: Designed to extend the life of the bomber force well into the 1970's, this project was killed, although Britain, which was to share the missile, protested strongly.

Nike-Zeus "missile killer": Army requests to put this anti-missile missile around U.S. cities were refused, over strong protests from Gen. Maxwell D. Taylor, Chairman of the Joint Chiefs of Staff. The project has been scrapped in the search for a substitute.

Military satellites: The Midas "spy satellite" was killed after a decision that 15 extra minutes' warning of missile attack was not worth the millions still required to perfect it. Numerous other military space projects have been abandoned or delayed.

Navy carriers: Signs point to a cut of as much as one-third in the Navy's fleet of 15 attack carriers. Construction is being delayed on an additional new carrier authorized by Congress last year.

Overseas bases: Flying bases in England, Morocco, Spain, France, Guam, and elsewhere have been or will be shut down. Prospects are for further withdrawals from overseas, possibly involving 1 of the 2 Army divisions in Korea and some 50,000 men in Europe.

Atomic production: The aim is to shut down half of the Nation's 14 major plants manufacturing nuclear materials for weapons. The Administration feels that the present stockpile is bigger than any demand it can foresee.

Nuclear test ban: The United States alone took the initiative in suspending atmospheric tests in June as evidence of good faith before formal test ban talks with Russia. Military requests to continue testing were set aside.

At Congressional hearings on the fiscal year 1964 defense budget, three members of the Joint Chiefs of Staff—Admiral George W. Anderson, General Curtis LeMay and General Earl G. Wheeler—opposed defense budget cuts proposed by President Kennedy's civilian "experts" on national defense stationed in the Pentagon.

General LeMay declared: "I think it is a dangerous philosophy to say 'Well, a stalemate is going to exist. We cannot do anything about it; therefore, we will do nothing.' If we accept mutual deterrence *this will,* I think, *inevitably lead to defeat.*"

The following trenchant summary of how the President's advisers are disarming the United States was given by Dr. Stefan T. Possony, director of the International Political Studies Program of Stanford University, in the August 26, 1963, issue of *U.S. News & World Report:*

By hook or crook we are abandoning the nuclear race.

The pattern has been that, with the exception of a minor beefing-up of our guerrilla capabilities, the ordering of a joint Air Force-Navy fighter and the contracting of Titan III—not for a military space program but as a "building block," should such a program become necessary in the dim future—Mr. McNamara, during more than two years in office, has not authorized a single new weapons system. He is slowing down our technological progress deliberately.

If we allow the Soviets to acquire vastly superior nuclear firepower; if we confront a mixed Soviet strategic force, consisting of missiles as well as aircraft, with only missile force; if we do not have the missile defenses while the Soviets possess a capability to shoot down our missiles; and if the Soviets achieve military space capability against which we cannot defend ourselves and for which we have no offensive equipment—then there is no doubt that we would be defeated or could win only at the price of excessive American casualties.

The fact that we presently are investing in research and development 50 cents of every dollar we are spending on procurement means that we are financing many exploratory research programs. It does not mean that we are modernizing our decisive weapon systems.

Perhaps the philosophy of "the biggest bang for the buck" had its faults. But the present philosophy of "the least bangs for the most bucks" courts disaster. All things considered, it does not look as though under the stewardship of Robert Strange McNamara, the United States is being equipped to forestall a nuclear and technological Pearl Harbor.

Let us look at the background of Presidential Assistant McGeorge Bundy, to whom the origin of much disarmament of the U.S. is widely credited.

Looking at Bundy's background, we find that, although he endorsed Kennedy in the 1960 campaign, he says he is a Republican and notes that he collaborated on the late Henry L. Stimson's memoirs, *On Active Service,* from 1946 to 1948, while he lived on Stimson's Long Island estate. Stimson was a Republican who entered Franklin D. Roosevelt's World War II Cabinet and could be admired by Bundy as a fellow internationalist.

Bundy's father, Harvey, was nominally a Republican— an Assistant Secretary of State in Herbert Hoover's Administration—but from 1941 to 1945 he served as special assistant to Secretary of War Stimson under FDR. Yet McGeorge Bundy's general views are directly opposed to Republican beliefs as they were delineated in the 1962 "Declaration of Republican Principles."

Bundy majored in mathematics at Yale, where he obtained his A.B. in 1940, and soon after graduation he was defeated at the polls by an obscure Democratic opponent in a heavily Republican district for the Boston City Council, the only elective office Bundy has ever sought.

Bundy's interest has always been in international affairs.

After McGeorge completed work on the Stimson memoirs, he worked briefly in Washington, helping to set up the Marshall Plan, and then worked in 1948 and 1949 as a political analyst for the Council on Foreign Relations. This organization boasts of respectable members and impeccable names, but its policies since its inception have been entirely internationalist. Bundy and others of his type have used it as a clearing house for their peculiar kind of internationalist views. Touch the disarmament program at any point, and you hit a member of the Council on Foreign Relations.

McGeorge Bundy joined the Harvard faculty in 1949. Bundy had compiled a brilliant academic record at Yale. He moved up fast at Harvard where he fitted like a hand in a tight glove. Bundy was at first a visiting lecturer from 1949 to 1951, an associate professor in 1951, and by 1953 he was Dean of Arts and Sciences, a post he held until his 1961 entrance into the Kennedy Administration. Bundy headed about 1,000 professors at Harvard, and their responsibility included instructing 5,000 undergraduates and 1,800 graduate students. His own course was a most popular one—"The United States in World History."

The Keynesian philosophy of economics promulgated in this country by men such as J. Kenneth Galbraith has been the foundation of much of the Socialist trend in our government today. McGeorge Bundy's sentiments about Keynesism can be seen in the following account written by veteran reporter Chesley Manly of the Chicago *Tribune:*

> Four years ago this reporter asked McGeorge Bundy, then dean of the Harvard faculty, now Special Assistant to President Kennedy, whether his economics department was not dominated by Keynesians.
>
> He responded archly, "Aren't all economics professors Keynesians?"

Reports persist that 47-year-old McGeorge is "one of Washington's half-dozen major movers and shakers" and attribute his appointment to the intercession of columnist Walter Lippmann, the oracle and den mother of the Kennan-Bundy school of international affairs. In fact, it is said that Kennedy actually considered making Bundy Secretary of State and, after pressures from Washington *Post* Publisher Philip Graham led to the appointment of Dean Rusk, it is reported that Kennedy proposed Bundy for Under Secretary, only to have Rusk veto Bundy for this particular post.

And what does this man, one of the most influential figures in our U. S. Government, think about patriotism?

Bundy, when contributing a chapter to the book *Zero Hour* in 1940, wrote:

> We are taught at an early age to salute the flag, to be patriotic *and to believe a lot of lies.*

Later, however, in 1951, McGeorge published his own book, *The Pattern of Responsibility.* His introduction to this study of Dean Acheson included selections from Acheson's public statements and documents. (It also duly noted that McGeorge Bundy's brother, William, now Assistant Secretary of State for Far Eastern Affairs, is married to Acheson's daughter.) The introduction contains a number of interesting comments:

About then-Secretary Acheson's statement that he would "not turn my back" on Alger Hiss after Hiss' conviction by a federal court, Bundy remarked:

> In the vexed question of Alger Hiss, I think it entirely understandable that Mr. Acheson should have felt it right and necessary to say everything that he said, but I also think it plain that Alger Hiss, even on the difficult assumption that he was wrongly convicted, has not honorably or candidly repaid his friendship and compassion.

Speaking of Mr. Acheson's convictions about Soviet Russia, Mr. Bundy wrote:

> If the charge against him is that in 1944 and early 1945 he was hopeful of Russian good intentions, than I believe he must plead guilty along with most of his countrymen, *myself among them.*

Bundy also penned in his book a record understatement

about the Chinese Communists, whom the State Department had called "agrarian reformers": "I do not believe that our policy toward China from 1945 to 1950 adequately assessed the probable character of the Communist regime in that country."

Ignoring the fact that the United States had cut off military supplies and economic aid to the anti-Communist Chinese Nationalists, and had forced truces between them and the Communists whenever the Nationalists were scoring victories, Bundy blithely opined: "That does not imply I think Nationalist China could have been saved. I do not."

Now no one cared what McGeorge Bundy thought before he was given his present job with its tremendous import to the security of the nation. But such airy ignoring of demonstrable facts scarcely instills confidence in him.

One written statement of Bundy's may well be indicative of his general attitude toward the world struggle against communism. In his book about Dean Acheson, he wrote:

"I think he has shown a tendency to promise definite results in an indefinite world."

Bundy has neither promised "definite results" nor attained any at all, except in the realm of appeasement. One wonders if President Johnson is right when he says "Let McGeorge do it."

CHAPTER NINE

Bouncing George Ball

"Victory at all costs, victory in spite of all terror, victory however long and hard the road might be; for without victory there is no survival."

. . . Winston Churchill, Speech in House of Commons, May 13, 1940.

"We attempt to prevent the development of situations which can result in direct confronation of the great powers."

. . . George Ball

UNDER SECRETARY OF STATE GEORGE W. BALL has been a conspicuous failure in two public tests of trying to justify State Department policy since he was named to the second highest State Department post by the late President Kennedy.

The first public test Ball failed was in February and June of 1962 when he tried ineffectually to explain to the Senate Special Preparedness Subcommittee why State Department censors had consistently emasculated speeches of our highest-ranking U. S. generals and admirals by deleting anti-Communist phrases like "beat the Communist challenge," "achieve victory," "destroy the virus of communism," "emerge victorious," and adjectives describing communism as being "godless," "vicious" and "tyrannical." However, at these "muzzling the military" hearings, Mr. Ball did give the Senators and the American public a firsthand glimpse of the reasons why we are losing the struggle against the international Communist conspiracy.

Later in the year, Under Secretary Ball again flubbed badly as a State Department apologist when he was confronted with criticisms of State Department policies by 200 Democratic candidates for elective office, meeting in Washington at the start of the 1962 political campaigns. According to one newsman who covered the event, Ball's replies to the candidates added up to reiterating that ours is "a complex world, and that the problems the United States has to deal with are beyond anyone's capacity to solve."

Ball had been put to an earlier 1962 public test of explaining State Department policies when he was called before the Special House Committee on Export Control and was asked to hand over a copy of his co-called "Secret Ball Report," which urged stepped-up U. S. trade with Communist countries. On that occasion, however, Ball preferred to side-step his role as State Department spokesman. Ball simply refused to answer all questions the Congressmen asked him about it.

Nevertheless, Dean Rusk's right-hand man has proven himself adroit at handling his many-faceted job. Ball's law firm is registered as a highly paid foreign agent for the European Common Market; yet Ball has been permitted to act as an official New Frontier lobbyist for lowering tariffs in connection with the same European Common Market.

When Ball was called to the Senate's "muzzling the military" hearings, he was not questioned about his relationship with the "Uncrowned King of the Pentagon," Adam Yarmolinsky, even though Ball had taken Yarmolinsky into his Washington law office—Cleary, Gottlieb, Steen and Ball—and even though the Ball-Yarmolinsky relationship went back to still earlier times.

Also, the man charged with censoring speeches under the organizational format at State—until just before the Senate hearings, at any rate—was, by custom, the Deputy Assistant Secretary. The man holding this post, Philip Stern, left the State Department precipitately just prior to the Senate investigations. Philip Stern and George Ball had been associated with Clayton Fritchey on the Northern Virginia *Sun,* an extremely liberal newspaper published in Arlington County, Virginia, in the District of Columbia suburbs. The Senate investigating committee could have questioned Ball about this relationship, too.

When confronted with examples of censorings during the

hearings and asked point-blank why the deletions had been made, Ball, the State Department's spokesman, backed down and pleaded that he thought the censorings were "inartistic," "inaccurate," "fatuous" and "foolish," in almost every case. This was rather rough on Ball's so quickly removed former associate, Phil Stern. It reminded one of the old Mutt and Jeff chestnut about a group of people passing through the turnstiles at a baseball game, each pointing behind him with the words, "He's paying."

Surely, Stern, the quickly vanished former Deputy Assistant Secretary, was not there to defend himself from his former chief's slurs. Neither was Stern's former immediate boss, former Assistant Secretary Roger Tubby, who, after earlier testimony, had been quickly and conveniently shipped out of the country to Geneva, as the (hitherto nonexistent) "Special Ambassador" to no one or nothing in particular. Tubby had been a law partner of ADA Ambassador Loeb before the New Frontier.

Before Ball became either the luckiest or most adroit Administration official alive, he had been one of the many liberals who made a good deal of money from their Washington experiences without its affecting their liberal views. Born in Des Moines, Iowa, December 21, 1909, Ball graduated from Northwestern University in 1930, and from its law school in 1933. George Wildman Ball joined the early New Deal Department of Agriculture as an attorney, along with his future Chicago law partner, Adlai Stevenson. Later Ball was shifted from the Wallace department to Henry Morgenthau's Department of the Treasury (1933-1935), at a time when Henry Glasser, later an associate of Harlan Cleveland with UNRRA in Europe, was a chief aide in the Treasury Department. At the same time, Cleveland's predecessor at the Maxwell School of Syracuse University, Paul Appleby, was moving from Agriculture to the Bureau of the Budget, surely unaware that he would one day be a pawn (or perhaps in comparison, a bishop or knight) in the chess-like moves of New Deal, Fair Deal and New Frontier officials from Syracuse to Washington and back.

As Under Secretary of State, Ball has done considerably more than merely avoid trouble by rapid shifting of gears. Whenever the Secretary of State is away from Washington, Ball acts in his place, and it was as Acting Secretary that Ball flew in the face of the evidence that the Rosenbergs, Golds and others convicted by U. S. courts of doing so, had truly stolen our atomic secrets and transmitted them to Russia.

"We could," Acting Secretary Ball said in a communication sent to members of the Foreign Service abroad, "envisage a future in which preponderant American strength might provide the guarantee for a new era of peace, a golden age in which the new technology could be harnessed not only to the rebuilding but the reshaping of the world.

"Then, almost overnight, the temperature of the world dropped. We lost our monopoly of the nuclear weapon that had transformed the concepts of warfare."

Ball then ventured into the familiar "black-is-white, upside-down" dissertation typical of New Frontiersmen.

"We went," Ball said, "through an agonizing phase of believing that these changes could have occurred only because we somehow had been betrayed by treason in high places. We went through an unworthy period of seeking for scapegoats, failing to recognize the realities, refusing to recognize that while we might have a temporary monopoly of a weapon, we did not have a monopoly on brains—nor, for that matter, of will and determination."

Did Soviet scientists develop nuclear power, or did the Soviets steal our nuclear secrets? What about the Rosenbergs? What about Harry Hopkins shipping 50 cases full of secret documents about our atomic research, and later complete materials for construction of the atomic bomb, through Great Falls, Montana, to our enemies in Soviet Russia? By creating a red herring in ignoring the Soviet threat when he served as Acting Secretary, Ball perpetuated the atmosphere within the State

Department which later caused a Foreign Service Officer to write
to Walt Whitman Rostow:

> Whom are you trying to kid with all this pseudo-optimism?
> . . . As long as the naïve intellectuals continue to lose themselves
> in their own jargon and to evaluate the world situation through
> rose-colored glasses, we will most certainly be following the pink
> markers along the road to socialism . . . Beware the Ides of
> Marx.

Under Ball's verbal dexterity, facts become myths. To
Ball, the whole vast network of thievery of our nuclear secrets
never existed. One of our top scientist's girls was never the
mistress of Steve Nelson, a top Communist official in the U. S.
It was all "mythology." Ball is right, however, in saying that
the Russians exercised "brains," "will and determination." They
certainly did in stealing our nuclear secrets. He might have
added the word "organization."

Ball continued his verbal mythology when he said about
the period during which 800 million of the world's people
were enslaved by Communist aggression and subversion,
"America's postwar conduct in world affairs was marked by a
high degree of wisdom and success."

Ball then voices the line of President Johnson's chief
advisers:

> The knowledge that this struggle, now characterized by the
> cold war, may flame into hot wars in remote corners of the
> globe and that these hot wars may escalate into thermonuclear
> holocausts is a kind of brooding omnipresence over all our affairs.

Then Ball makes a classic outline of the policy which the
Kennedy-Johnson advisers have developed: "We attempt to
prevent the development of situations which can result in direct confrontation of the great powers. While we have been
firm, *we have not been inflexible."*

Then Ball asserts that the Inner Circle's policies are based,
at least in part, on the assumption that the Soviet Union will
disarm, either entirely or in part:

> "It is not unlikely therefore," states Ball, "that at some

point the Communist power will be forced to make the hard choice between insistent demands for a better standard of living and the spiraling costs of a continuing arms race."

Yet Ball went before the Senate Preparedness Subcommittee and denied that "victory" had been dropped as an American concept in the Inner Circle's foreign policy.

Ball contradicted himself. The word "victory" had been expurgated from a spech prepared by Brigadier General John W. White, because, according to a State Department explanation transmitted to the committee with a letter signed by Ball himself, the word had a "militaristic and aggressive ring" and "also implies an all-or-nothing approach leaving no room for *accommodation.*"

The year-long Senate Special Preparedness Subcommittee hearings were authorized by the Senate Armed Services Committee and ended in October 1962. They were held to investigate "the use of military personnel and facilities to arouse the public to the menace of the cold war, and to inform and educate armed services personnel on the nature and menace of the cold war." The Senators examined 161 censored speeches which had been prepared for delivery by our highest-ranking admirals and generals—on communism, the Communist threat and the cold war. Almost all censoring of these speeches had been done by the State Department, which has been censoring military men's speeches since former President Harry Truman ordered it on December 5, 1950, when Truman and General MacArthur were conflicting publicly about our no-win policy in Korea. Under Secretary George Ball testified at the subcommittee hearings as spokesman for the State Department to explain the censorings.

Ball's testimony was summed up by Senator Strom Thurmond—who did about 90 per cent of the questioning of Ball, and who had questioned the Under Secretary at length about his knowledge of communism and Communist tactics—in these words, in Thurmond's section of the subcommittee report:

> There can be no more vivid demonstration of the need for widespread education on Communist techniques than this—that

the number two officer in our State Department can demonstrate such ignorance and incompetence in the field of Communist tactics.

Is it ignorance? Most left-wingers in the Administration seem to be, or have been, connected with George Ball, Adlai Stevenson's former law partner. George Ball seems to be at the center of a web.

Also after his lengthy questioning of Ball, Senator Thurmond declared: "The State Department has made a concerted effort, to the limit of its power, to keep the facts [of the Cold War] from both the Congress and the people . . ."

During the hearings, when Ball had almost finished his testimony, Senator Thurmond declared:

> Mr. Secretary, despite your very articulate attempts to explain it away, there is just too much in the written replies of the State Department supporting the conclusion that our policy is one of accommodation, containment of aggression—as the term is defined and limited by the Department of State—and paralysis induced by the specter of escalation toward nuclear war, to be dispelled by your testimony.
>
> The best evidence is the policy papers themselves. It appears that newspapermen are being given access to some of these policy papers.
>
> As a matter of fact, indications are that an integral part of our policy is systematically to expose to the Communists and to the public the broad outlines of our policy in order to dispel whatever fears the Communists may have of us, and to re-orient the thinking of the American public toward a favorable attitude to our policy.

Trying to find out from Under Secretary Ball about our State Department policies in combatting the Communist menace proved to be like trying to spar with feathers. Ball's interrogators were hard put to get a straight answer out of him, and he gave consistently what Senator Thurmond termed "studiously evasive answers" to almost every question put to him about the State Department's role in the cold war.

Ball's first appearance as spokesman for the State Department was on February 27, and in a prepared statement which he read to the subcommittee, Mr. Ball stated that the State Department censorings were made basically for two reasons: to avoid offending the Communists when "events of foreign policy significance" were going on; and to avoid allowing the Communists to "distort public statements by representatives of the American government, whether civilian or military," but especially, Ball pointed out, military men's statements.

In his opening statement, Ball then took a slap at the growing ranks of critics of the State Department's "no-win" policies, saying: "Nothing can be gained by oversimplifying the problems before us. The characterization of a policy as a 'win' or 'no-win' policy does not reflect the realities of to-day's world. The cold war is not an adult game of 'cops and robbers.'"

Ball then produced a letter from President Kennedy to Secretary Rusk, dated February 9, 1962, in which Kennedy said:

> I therefore direct you and all personnel under the jurisdiction of your Department not to give any such testimony or produce any such documents . . . which would enable the Senate's Special Preparedness Subcommittee to identify and hold accountable any individual with respect to any particular speech that he has reviewed.

In other words, President Kennedy had directed all State Department censors to plead Executive Privilege—or the "Executive Fifth Amendment," as it has been aptly described—if they were called by the subcommittee to explain why they had censored speeches of the military. George Ball appeared as the spokesman for the State Department, and he refused to allow State Department censors to appear, saying they were exempted by Mr. Kennedy's Executive Fifth Amendment directive.

However, when the Senators proceeded to ask State Department spokesman Ball why deletions had been made, Ball refused to discuss them. He said, instead, that he wanted to go back to the State Department and submit written explanations to the Senate subcommittee. Senator Thurmond reminded Ball that he had had weeks to prepare his answers, and said, "You want to go back and work on them and *get* the answers."

One matter of paramount importance was made eminently clear by Mr. Ball during his first, otherwise unsatisfactory, testimony: that "the speech deletions and changes are the result of a knowledgeable application of our foreign policy to the speeches, to insure conformity with our foreign policy."

After a morning of trying to get straight answers out of Mr. Ball, Senator Thurmond said in exasperation: "Mr. Secretary, we are asking a lot of questions here that we want answers to, and, obviously, you are not answering the questions . . . I think it is a waste of time to ask them because you are not answering the questions."

A couple of examples of Mr. Ball's testimony might serve to explain the Senators' exasperation with the Under Secretary:

> *Senator Smith:* Mr. Secretary, [communism] being the threat that it is, then why can we not call it by its proper name and why cannot the military leaders call it communism instead of a vague platitude such as "adversary of freedom"?
> *Mr. Ball:* I cannot answer that question, Mrs. Smith, because I really do not know to what your remarks are addressed.
>
> *Senator Thurmond:* Mr. Secretary, in the Department of Army Pamphlet 30-101, it is stated: "If . . . people realized the vicious objections of communism, they would no doubt oppose it and rededicate their lives to its destruction." How would you modify a statement such as this in the time of sensitive negotiations?
>
> *Mr. Ball:* This is the kind of hypothetical question which is impossible to answer. As I say, these questions could be answered in specific terms in the context of a whole series of circumstances, a whole series of conditioning factors. I cannot do it otherwise.
>
> *Senator Thurmond:* Then why is the word "victory" consistently deleted from these speeches?
> *Mr. Ball:* As I say, Senator, if you will give me the instances where these deletions have been made, we shall endeavor to explain them.
> *Thurmond:* But you would have to get the answers from someone else, would you not?
> *Ball:* I would have to get the answer by referring to the condi-

tions that existed at the time and all the other surrounding circumstances and discuss them with the Department.
Thurmond: You cannot answer this yourself?

Ball: My answer today would be speculation as to why any particular deletion was made.

This was the type of evasive answer given to every question put to Ball about the censorings, even though, as Senator
Thurmond pointed out, Ball had had the opportunity to prepare himself for weeks: "This book of deletions has been
available for weeks. The *Congressional Record* has been available for over a week that has the deletions in it, and he is not
prepared to answer the questions about these matters."

The subcommittee's chief counsel, James T. Kendall, then
tried his luck in eliciting an answer from Mr. Ball about State
Department policies. Since Mr. Ball had said that the censorings had been made in conformity with State Department foreign policy, Mr. Kendall began by asking Mr. Ball for his definition of State Department foreign policy. Ball's answer was:

> "Foreign policy in the State Department with respect to
> any particular area of policy is made out of the bits and pieces
> of the everyday business of the Department in its relations with
> foreign governments, the decisions that are made with respect
> to specific matters, the long-range positions that are adopted,
> many of which are expressed in papers and in the instructions
> given at staff meetings, and so on. It is a very complicated busi-
> ness. There is nowhere that you can find a book which contains
> or covers the foreign policy of the United States. It is a contradic-
> tion in terms."

Mr. Kendall then asked Mr. Ball what was "the general
proposition of our policies with respect to world communism,
Sino-Soviet communism." Ball replied "Again, they are policies
in a shifting scene."

The Senators dismissed Mr. Ball, and on March 29, Under Secretary Ball sent to the subcommittee a list of explanations defending the State Department's censorings. Ball's covering letter to the subcommittee stated: "The explanations
herewith furnished to the committee have been prepared by

specifically assigned officers *working under my personal direction.*"

On June 4 and June 7, Mr. Ball again appeared before the subcommittee to discuss the State Department censorings.

In his opening statement, Mr. Ball declared that the State Department "has not sought to discourage the use of the word 'victory'." But Senator Thurmond then proceeded to show Ball example after example of State Department censorings of military men's statements that the United States wants victory over communism. When confronted with the deletions, Ball did an about-face, disavowed his lengthy written explanations justifying the deletions, and pleaded limply in virtually every case that the deletions were mistakes. For example:

When Senator Thurmond asked Mr. Ball why Admiral H. D. Felt, Commander in Chief of our Pacific Fleet, had been prevented by the State Department from telling Congressional hearings that Communist strategy is one of "economic and psychological warfare," and of "subversion and armed revolution supported from outside the target nation," Ball replied:

> "The only explanation that we could find for this—frankly I would not have deleted it myself—is the context of the time. I would have been, I think, inclined to say that we have no explanation as to why that particular change was made. It represents, I think, an overzealousness."

Strangely enough, Mr. Ball's lengthy written explanation submitted to the subcommittee on March 29 had made no allusion to anything like "overzealousness," or to the idea that Mr. Ball himself "would not have deleted it."

When Mr. Ball was asked why Lieutenant General Arthur D. Trudeau, Chief of Army Research and Development, was not allowed to say in a spech, "We must win this struggle, or we lose the world," Ball squirmed:

> "I would say, Senator Thurmond, I think this is one of those marginal cases where it would have been just as well if the State Department reviewer had not made this particular recommendation."

Again, it was strange that Mr. Ball had submitted a written justification of the censoring to the subcommittee, but it was only when confronted with the deletion by the Senators that he decided the censoring could "just as well" not have been made.

Again, Ball was asked why Brigadier General John W. White was forbidden by the State Department from saying, "Victory on each of the four battlefields of the Cold War is essential to the survival of freedom." The word "victory" had been deleted by the State Department and replaced by the words "defeat of Communist aggression." The reason given for the deletion to the subcommittee by the State Department, over Mr. Ball's name, was:

> The word "victory" has a militaristic and aggressive ring, less suited than the substituted word to describe our national objective. It also implies an all-or-nothing approach leaving no room for accommodation.

This was a corker, and Senator Thurmond said: "What about this, Mr. Ball?" Ball writhed and replied:

> ". . . this explanation . . . is perfectly fatuous. I do not know why it was put there . . . I think it is a foolish statement . . . inartistic and inaccurate."

Again, it was strange that, far from writing to the subcommitte on March 29 that the censoring was "perfectly fatuous," "foolish," "inartistic and inaccurate," Mr. Ball had submitted to the Senators that the word "victory" has "a militaristic and aggressive ring" which does not describe our national objective, and that it left "no room for accommodation."

When Ball was asked why Brigadier General M. W. Schewe, Deputy Assistant Chief of Staff for Reserve Components, was not allowed by the State Department to say, "On the outcome of the conflict depends the nature of the free world order. Ultimately, either totalitarian communism will prevail or the freedom familiar to the societies of the West will expand . . ." Mr. Ball replied:

> "As I say, I think that there has been some overzealousness

at one time or another . . . I must say that I think this is one of those marginal instances where, I think, the reviewer could very well have passed this."

When Mr. Ball had submitted his explanation of this censoring to the subcommittee he had defended it in a two-part statement, which emphasized that "the stress placed on the all-or-nothing character of the conflict by a high military officer might have been used to undercut the sincerity of the President's mission [to confer with Khrushchev in Vienna]."

When Ball was asked by Senator Bartlett why Major General Edwin B. Broadhurst had not been allowed by the State Department to quote a boast by Khrushchev about the Soviets' shooting down an American airplane, Ball replied:

"I would say, Senator Bartlett, that this is certainly a marginal case of, perhaps, overzealousness on the part of the reviewer.

And when Mr. Ball was asked why Lieutenant General Arthur D. Trudeau had been forbidden by the State Department to say, "Witness the steady advance of communism for over a century," with the State Department censor's noting: "It is only the externally aggressive type—Sino-Soviet—which the United States is committed to check," Mr. Ball's reply was:

"I think that the comment, however, is a little bit foolish . . . I think that is a very poor explanation for the change . . . Frankly, I do not understand the State comment in this case . . . Let me say again that I think this represents a kind of overzealous editing on the part of the State Department reviewer, and that this is much too subtle."

When Ball was asked by Senator Bartlett why General George H. Decker, Chief of Staff of the U. S. Army, had been forbidden by the State Department to criticize those who say they would "rather be Red than dead," Ball replied:

"I must say I don't think that this was necessary."

Mr. Ball's written explanation to the subcommittee had made no mention of the idea that Ball disapproved of the deletion. In fact, the written explanation said the deletion was made because it "was thought undesirable to popularize this slogan." It would appear that General Decker was, in fact, attempting to depopularize it.

The State Department censors had repeatedly struck out the word "vicious" in descriptions of communism by military men, and Mr. Ball's explanations had upheld the strikeouts. However, when Senator Stennis took the censors to task for deleting the adjective and said it should not have been deleted, Mr. Ball declared:

"I would concur in exactly what you say, Mr. Chairman."

When Ball was asked why General S. E. Anderson was not allowed by the State Department to say "the Communist world," or "the world struggle we call the Cold War," Mr. Ball answered:

". . . I think [it] perhaps oversubtle . . . But I think it is a highly subtle change, and perhaps overly subtle . . . I find these particular changes are oversubtle . . . I think this is an oversubtle, overelaborate change."

When Under Secretary Ball was asked why the State Department prevented Rear Admiral Simmes from saying, ". . . two powerful and ruthless dictatorships—Soviet Russia and Red China — whose avowed and frequently announced purpose is to impose upon the free world their squalid and tyrannical system," with the State Department terming this "invective," Ball answered:

". . . I see no particular virtue in the use of these words just for the sake of using them. I think that, to the extent we win the battle for men's minds, we do so by persuasion and not by invective . . . I think it is a question of whether it serves our national purpose at the time."

As one last example of Mr. Ball's equivocating, one answer which he offered should stand as a classic. When Ball was asked why in a speech in New Zealand, General Herbert B. Powell was not allowed by the State Department to call communism "the anti-religious cult that opposes us" and "a Godless cause of a few million atheistic fanatics," Ball replied:

"It would seem questionable wisdom, in a foreign country, to inject the religious note into this."

Virtually every time Mr. Ball was confronted with a deletion and was asked to explain it, instead of defending them in public, he disavowed the deletions as being "foolish . . . overzealous . . . inaccurate . . . inartistic." But it was Ball himself who had taken the responsibility for previously defending the deletions in lengthy written explanations to the subcommittee.

In other words, the Under Secretary of State adopted a strategy which permitted him to avoid defending the State Department's virtually indefensible muzzling of our military leaders, which is part of the State Department's overall policy of accommodation and "no-win" in the face of the Communist onslaught.

As for Mr. Ball's declaring that military men's anti-Communist statements have to be deleted because the Communists take them out of context and distort them for propaganda purposes, Senator Thurmond showed Mr. Ball a sentence out of Ball's own opening statement to the subcommittee, and showed how it could be taken out of context for Red propaganda. Ball had told the subcommittee in his opening statement:

> "One of the pernicious myths that the Soviet propaganda machine seeks to spread around the world is that America is dominated by a bloodthirsty and irresponsible military clique prepared to unleash atomic destruction unless kept in check by Communist might."

Senator Thurmond showed Ball how the Communists might use a part of this paragraph for propaganda purposes:

> "America is dominated by a bloodthirsty and irresponsible military clique prepared to unleash atomic destruction unless kept in check by Communist might."

Mr. Ball hastened to assure the Senator that the Communists have a fastidious respect for the truth in using quotes for propaganda. He said:

> "I think that you will see the examples we will bring to this committee that what they do is to quote words accurately—I

mean, whole paragraphs accurately, but put them in distorted context, and this is the technique which they follow."

Ball supplied 27 examples of Communist propaganda to the subcommittee. However, of the 27 examples, 14 contained no quotations whatsoever from U. S. sources; only two contained a quotation of as much as a paragraph; three contained quotations of whole sentences; five of the examples contained quotations of less material than one complete sentence; and three were characterizations of an official statement by newsmen of the non-Communist world.

Ball declared that the Communists need genuine quoted words from the statements of U. S. spokesmen. Senator Thurmond then asked: "Don't they lie; don't they make any statement they want, to carry out their ends? That is what I am getting at."

Ball replied: "You will find very little evidence of their inventing quotations from people."

Thurmond's retort to this pipe dream of Mr. Ball's was: "Mr. Ball is, to say the least, poorly informed."

In his section of the subcommittee report, Senator Thurmond noted that on June 2, 1961, Richard Helms, Assistant Director of the CIA, had testified before the Senate Internal Security Subcommittee on the subject of "Communist Forgeries." Helms had related in his testimony, and documented, "how the Communists forge any number of types of documents, including U. S. State Department cables, letters from State Department officials, and State Department directives—all of which were planted and used in Communist propaganda. Not only scattered quotes, but whole documents were 'manufactured.' Such false documents were planted, for the most part, in the press of the Western nations and then immediately picked up and used by the Communist propaganda machine."

"The complete history, in detail, of such forgeries is available in sworn testimony along with reproduction of the forged documents," Thurmond pointed out. "The authenticity of this type activity by the Communists is attested to by a high official of the official Intelligence agency of the U. S. Government. What is more incredible is that many of these forgeries involved the State Department."

Senator Thurmond cited Mr. Ball's declaration that the Communists do not manufacture quotations as one example of his "ignorance and incompetence in the field of Communist tactics," and declared that this instance "is most revealing about what is wrong with our foreign policy and why State Department personnel repeatedly try to play down the Communist threat . . ."

The Senator concluded that Mr. Ball's "attempt to justify censorship actions on the theory that by censoring statements of Defense personnel, the Communists' propaganda machine would be reduced to paraphrasing and characterizing, rather than quoting, statements of such personnel for their propaganda efforts, illustrates the totally unsatisfactory nature of the explanations."

The Senators did manage to extract from Under Secretary Ball some clues to his thinking on the total warfare the Communists are waging against us in their unceasing drive to enslave the world. Anyone interested in ascertaining something of the powder-puff, beclouded policies of our State Department toward the international Communist conspiracy need only to read Mr. Ball's testimony before the subcommittee. As the former chief counsel of the Senate Internal Security Subcommittee once phrased it, "No wonder we are losing." Here are a few examples:

Under Secretary of State Ball on "Are we at war with the Communists?"

> In a figurative sense we have an opposition of ideologies, and we have a need to defend, to protect our vital interests around the world. When you say we are at war, this is an expression which, as I say, has figurative and literal meanings. We are not literally at war . . .
> This is a quarrel over an ideology. To call it war is a figurative use of the term. It is like saying we are at war with the devil or we are at war with sin . . . Let us say that it is a contest, it is a struggle that is going on, on many fronts. The word "war" has historically a very definite military meaning. The word "war"

Constitutionally has a military meaning. It is a figure of speech when we use it in any other sense.

Under Secretary of State Ball on "What country is the enemy of the United States?":

Again, you have two kinds of uses of a word. You have a figurative use; and you have a literal use. I would say that, as regards the literal use of the term, I would want to look at those countries where we had a state of war existing between us. So far as the figurative use of the term is concerned, I could name a number of countries. If you say "potential enemy," you are much more accurate. From my point of view, I would think that would be better. In my judgment, it would be better to use some expression which indicates the antagonism [*sic*] which we feel toward the Communist system, the danger which we foresee in the aggressive inclinations of international communism, without using a word which is subject to such misinterpretation.

Under Secretary Ball on terming the Communists our "enemy":

"To speak of war with communism, or of Communists being an enemy, is a figure of speech . . . To say that the Communists are our enemy, or that the Soviet Union is our enemy, or that the Communist bloc is our enemy, is a figure of speech which, to my mind, serves no useful purpose for it to be used by a high military man and it is certainly subject to misrepresentation."

Under Secretary Ball on the Soviets' saying communism and the free world pose "an irreconcilable conflict of systems":

Let me say that you can have an irreconcilable conflict of systems and you can still have accommodation of mutual interests in limited areas of the world . . . to keep constantly probing to see what the possibilities were of relieving tensions in local situations by trying to find solutions to local problems.

Under Secretary of State Ball on an "all-or-nothing" approach to the State Department's fighting communism:

Senator Thurmond: I want to ask you this: Is it U. S. policy to reject or not to reject what the State Department characterizes as the "all-or-nothing approach"?
Mr. Ball: Well, asked in a vacuum, I find it impossible to answer.

I mean I do not know what "all-or-nothing approach" means. What are we talking about?

Senator Thurmond: Well, it has been used over and over again in explanation of the censoring of these speeches. You ought to know about it unless someone else prepared your answers.

Mr. Ball: No, with reference to different points.

Senator Thurmond: Can you cite us some instances where it *does* represent State Department policy?

Mr. Ball: An "all-or-nothing approach"?

Senator Thurmond: Yes, sir. It has been used by the State Department in your reply over and over, and I want to know if you have any instances where it *does* represent State Department policy.

Mr. Ball: Well, I would suppose that in our foreign policy dealings around the world there are many instances where we do *not* use an "all-or-nothing approach," where it would be totally inappropriate.

Under Secretary Ball on military assistance and scientific aid to Communist Yugoslavia:

> *Senator Thurmond:* Since Yugoslavia is a Communist country and Tito has as his goal, as you said, the communization of the world, are we wise in approving the training of Communist sailors and airmen in our military establishments and training their scientists and giving them uranium?
>
> *Mr. Ball:* First of all, with regard to the matter of training I would say, to the extent that some of the Yugoslavians are subject to the United States, that the process of Westernization which is going on there is speeded up and expedited, and that this is particularly true in connection with some of the technicians who have come over here under the technical assistance programs . . . Now, on this question of the military, it has been the policy of the Government for a great many years to try to enable President Tito to maintain the independence of Yugoslavia from the bloc for the reasons I have given. This is the basis for such military assistance as has been provided.

Under Secretary Ball on the Communists' goal of conquering the world:

> *Senator Thurmond:* Would you not agree that the goal of a Communist world or even the prediction of a Communist world is the cornerstone of Marxist ideology?

Mr. Ball: I think that is probably right. I think that certainly he put his greatest emphasis [*sic*] on the international character of the Communist movement . . . [But] we have Marxist countries that have had Marxist societies or we have had Communist societies that have not depended on an international goal . . . I would suppose right now that in a sense Yugoslavia is in that position. It is not a part of the bloc as such.

(Mr. Ball had said previously in his testimony: Tito "shares the ultimate ambition of a Communist world." Then he said, above, that Yugoslavia is a Communist country that does not depend "on an international goal.")

Under Secretary Ball on telling the American people whether or not the State Department intends to save the key southeast Asia nation of Laos from communism:

Senator Thurmond: Mr. Ball, are we going to win Laos?
Mr. Ball: Mr. Chairman, I think that, if we are going to continue this dialogue, it should be done in executive [i.e., secret] session.
Thurmond: Whether we are going to win in Laos ought to be in executive session? You are not willing to tell the American people in open session whether we are going to win in Laos?
Ball: Senator Thurmond, I will say to you that we are going to pursue the policies which, in our judgment, are in the best interests of the United States in the protection of our vital interests.
Thurmond: And whether these policies are going to win in Laos is going to be withheld from the American people?
Ball: I am afraid that the problem is much more complicated than that, and I really think—
Thurmond: I do not think it is so complicated, Mr. Secretary, that the American people fail to have intelligence to understand it. If the State Department people have the intelligence to explain it, we think we have the intelligence to understand it.

(Mr. Ball's reluctance to tell the American people whether or not the State Department intended to win in Laos is understandable. Precisely one week after Mr. Ball's testimony, our State Department succeeded in forcing Laos into a "coalition government" with the Communists in key positions—a time-honored Communist tactic for taking over a country—and Laos went down the drain to communism. Khrushchev immediately dispatched a cablegram to President Kennedy, hailing the Laos "coalition government" as a victory—for communism.)

When Mr. Ball was asked about the international Communist high command, "whether or not it is evolving into a peaceful state," whether or not Khrushchev's goals are different from Stalin's, he replied:

Mr. Ball: I think I would hesitate, Mr. Chairman, to comment on this at this point.

Senator Thurmond: Let me ask you, to be sure you understand the question: Are Khrushchev's goals any different from Stalin's —his goals of world domination and enslavement? Now, do you think you need to go into executive session on that?

Mr. Ball: I would prefer to go into executive session on it.

Under Secretary Ball on the Communist prime minister of British Guiana, Cheddi Jagan: (Jagan is a head of the Communist Party of British Guiana.)

He is pro-Communist in the sense that he sees the future of his country, I think, much more in Communist terms than in others. The question in my mind is whether he was actually a member of the Communist Party. I must say that I spent a morning talking with him, and I have a rather confused impression as to just where he does come out.

One final illustration to show the upside-down thinking of our State Department leaders:

Senator Thurmond: Mr. Secretary, we have troops in Korea today. They are there for some purpose. Who is the enemy? Who is our enemy in Korea today up on the front lines?

Mr. Ball: The troops that are in Korea today are there to sustain the Korean Government and to help protect the integrity of Korea, but there is no shooting going on there.

Senator Thurmond: Who is the enemy? There must be some enemy there or we would not have troops there.

Mr. Ball: Well, no. We have troops in many places in the world where there is no enemy but where there is a potential danger.

Thurmond: Name some place where we have troops where there is no enemy.

Ball: We have troops in Berlin.

Thurmond: There is no enemy in Berlin?

Ball: Let us be quite clear. We have troops in Berlin which were put there under the occupation arrangements which were made after the war. What we are doing in Berlin is to insist on the maintenance of our troops there in order to protect our vital interests in Berlin. Now, to say that we have an enemy in Berlin is to use a figurative expression or to use an expression not in its literal meaning.

Thurmond: Would you consider it a correct statement if anyone said that we are at war with communism?

Ball: I would consider it a figuratively correct statement. As a literal statement, being at war implies a state of war which is declared by the U. S. Congress. To say that we are at war with an abstraction, with an ideology, is a figurative use of the term.

These absurdities of George W. Ball, the second-ranking official of the U. S. Department of State, are eloquent testimony to what is wrong with our State Department.

Another occasion on which Under Secretary of State Ball had a difficult time explaining State Department policies was in September 1962, when Ball appeared as Acting Secretary of State before a Washington meeting of 200 Democratic candidates for elective office. The candidates asked many critical questions about State Department policies throughout the world, and Ball had a rough time trying to dodge them.

Mr. Ball's performance at this session was a lesson in the State Department's own "fatuous, foolish, inarticulate and inaccurate" black-is-white, upside-down mythology.

The third public test in which Undersecretary Ball was asked to explain State Department policies was early in 1962, when a House committee asked him to hand over a copy of his "Secret Ball Report" which was a blueprint for stepped-up American trade with Communist countries. Even though the U. S. House of Representatives had established the Special House Committee on Export Control for the specific purpose of investigating the Ball blueprint, Mr. Ball appeared before the Congressmen and simply refused to give a copy to the American people's representatives. He also refused to answer any and all questions about it, even though the New York *Times* had already published a rather complete news leak about it in January 1962.

When Representative Steven Derounian, Republican of New York, managed to get hold of a copy of Ball's secret blueprint, he sent a copy to President Kennedy and demanded to know whether or not the Administration intended to implement

Ball's recommendations. Mr. Derounian received approximately the same treatment from Kennedy which the House committees had received, but couched in more evasive language.

Later in the year, however, the House committee and Mr. Derounian received an eloquent answer from the Administration that the Ball blueprint was, indeed, being implemented, when in September the Commerce Department approved sale of the following vital items to Communist countries:

U.S.S.R.: A completely new type of mining equipment, which Representative Glen Lipscomb, one of the nation's most knowledgeable experts on East-West trade relations, described as of strategic importance to the Soviets; steel and iron staples, glass products, asbestos fiber, saw blades, heavy-duty industrial equipment, textile machinery and parts.

Yugoslavia: Electronic tubes, copper cable, aircraft and automotive parts, iron and steel scrap, steel pipe, petroleum products, electronic testing machines and arts.

Hungary: Radioactive isotopes; chemical specialties, medical and pharmaceutical preparations, technical data.

Cuba: Technical data, medical equipment, radio transcriptions, office machinery.

East Germany: Semiconductors, surgical and medical equipment, synthetic resins, technical data, radioactive isotopes.

Of course, the previous Administration had lavished gifts on Communist countries, such as a $200,000 nuclear reactor to Yugoslavia; and to the Communist nations in the UN, through the UN's International Atomic Energy Agency, it made available 5,000 kilograms of the nuclear fuel Uranium-235. However, in the autumn of 1963, when President Kennedy announced the wheat "sale" to the Communists (a "sale" backed by long-term credits of the Export-Import Bank, which, in turn, is financed with American government money), the public finally heard, loud and clear, that Under Secretary Ball had scored a direct hit with his secret report.

As the Ball blueprint is being implemented for all-out trade with Communist nations, the American people might take heed of the dire prophecy of Lenin:

When the capitalist world starts trade with us, on that day it will begin to finance its own destruction.

The New York *Daily News* voiced the sentiments of all Americans opposed to the wheat trade, and to all trade with the communists, when it said: "Why not a concerted free world effort to choke international communism quietly to death? Why bail out the Reds from their present troubles so that they can make a renewed effort to bury us?"

Former German Chancellor Konrad Adenauer pointed out that, far from trading with the Soviets, the free world should cease all trade with the Communists at the precise moment in history when "all the foundations of Khrushchev's control are shaky." By trading with the Communists, the German statesman pointed out, the West is bolstering the Communist empire. In an interview in *Look* magazine, the former chancellor declared:

I do not believe Soviet Russia has the strength to carry out the many programs that challenge her today . . . And she has only one place to turn for the assistance she must have—to the West. I can tell you, from studies our experts have made, that I know how desperately she needs chemical plants, fertilizers, synthetic-textile mills, heavy farm machinery, clothing and many other lacks in her present economy. Her request for wheat was merely a symbol of far broader needs.

That is why I say *we of the West now have the upper hand. Soviet Russia needs our help.* She can find it nowhere else. But if the free nations deliver to Russia the help she needs, they should do so only on certain clear conditions: that Russia shows *through deeds, not only through words,* that she has changed her policy toward the West.

We now have the opportunity to insist on concessions in exchange for assistance. To help the Russians become stronger and more prosperous without making such stipulations can be suicidal for us.

But the Kennedy and Johnson Administrations have insisted on no such concessions from the Communists. Instead, they have opened wide the door to all-out U. S. trade with the Communist empire, a policy which is suicidal for us.

CHAPTER TEN

*Arthur Schlesinger, Jr. — His Father's Only Son

"Diogenes struck the father when the son swore."

. . . Robert Burton—ANATOMY OF MELANCHOLY

IN 1952, THE REPUBLICANS ran on a slogan of "Communism, Corruption and Korea." However, they made a mistake by referring to a young Harvard professor writing speeches for Adlai Stevenson as "Red Front Schlesinger" in a series of press releases. Arthur Maier Schlesinger, Jr., also a writer for James Wechsler's New York *Post,* became so upset that he issued a statement of denial which said in effect and quite accurately, if unfilially: "It wasn't I; it was my father."

For Arthur Schlesinger, Jr., has never belonged to any Red front organization. But his father, also a Harvard professor, has been affiliated with, or sponsored, many Communist fronts, and has quite accurately been described as one of the most prominent fellow-travelers in intelligentsia circles in the nation. No son is responsible for what his parents have done, although this parent problem has also plagued Pierre Salinger and Adam Yarmolinsky.

The Republicans have never formally corrected the record, apparently feeling that Arthur, Jr.'s, writings clearly show him to be in left field, as for example, "I happen to believe that the Communist Party should be granted freedom of political action . . ."; and that while not one of Schlesinger's words openly supports communism, he frequently ends up advocating the current Party Line—innocently, of course.

Those were the days when Republicans also publicly as-

* Although the subject of this chapter withdrew from the Johnson Inner Circle early in 1964, the impact of his presence during the Kennedy years, and its continuing impact on the Johnson Administration, is important enough to warrant inclusion in this book.

sailed Adlai Stevenson, now the New Frontier's UN delegate, pointing out that he had served with Alger Hiss as an Associate Counsel of the Agricultural Adjustment Administration, and that three days after Hiss took over the UN division at the State Department, Adlai entered it. In the papers which the FBI picked up in a New Hampshire barn, Hiss recommended that Adlai represent the United States at a meeting of the Institute of Pacific Relations, later declared by the Senate Internal Security Subcommittee to be dominated at the top by Communists.

The connections between Stevenson and Arthur, Jr., made it natural that Adlai would choose the younger Schlesinger for his public relations staff. After all, both were connected with Americans for Democratic Action—Schlesinger as a founder and prominent member and Stevenson as a founder of an ADA chapter in Illinois which went under the name "Independent Voters of Illinois." Besides, Schlesinger's writings for the left-wing New York *Post* made him an ideal candidate for the position.

Under Johnson as well as under Kennedy, Arthur Jr., conceived in Socialist thought and dedicated to the proposition that Socialism should rule America, was in the White House as a trusted Special Assistant to the President, where he helped to make and enunciate American policy at home and abroad by drafting speeches and memoranda. Schlesinger and Adolph Berle are widely credited with (or blamed for) assisting in the final planning of the ill-fated Bay of Pigs landings. Both had earlier made a swing around Latin America for our government, although Arthur, Jr., had no more experience in Latin America than he had at the South Pole. The two made the ultimate mistakes of taking over invasion planning from seasoned diplomat Whiting Willauer and of forgetting to debrief Willauer as to what the former General Claire Chennault associate had planned for handling Castro's planes during the landings. It was these Castro planes which smashed the invasion.

A look at the frothy intellectual background and amazing political views of "Dr." Arthur Schlesinger, Jr., court egghead and historian of the New Frontier, who is widely believed to have been perhaps the most influential Presidential adviser to both Kennedy and Johnson, is certainly important for the American public.

Arthur Schlesinger, Jr., was born in Columbus, Ohio, on October 15, 1917, and was graduated from Harvard in 1938 with a bachelor's degree (A.B.). He has never attained a higher academic degree. He does not even hold a master's degree. The "Dr. Schlesinger" appellation of which is he so fond is based upon honorary degrees bestowed upon him by Muhlenberg College (in Allentown, Pennsylvania), by Bethany College (located in Bethany, Oklahoma), and by the University of New Brunswick, Canada.

After graduating from Harvard, Schlesinger served as a junior member, from 1939 to 1942, of Harvard's Society of Fellows, which financed him in research for a series of 1941 lectures entitled "A Reinterpretation of Jacksonian Democracy." Schlesinger's book, *The Age of Jackson,* published in 1945, is based on these lectures.

In 1942, Schlesinger joined the Red-riddled Office of War Information (OWI), and the following year he joined the equally Red-infiltrated Office of Strategic Services (OSS). As World War II drew to a close, the 28-year-old Schlesinger served briefly in the Army during 1945.

In 1946, Schlesinger, holder of only a bachelor's degree, became an Associate Professor of History at Harvard, and a full Professor of History in 1954. He held his professor's rank at Harvard until the advent of the Kennedy Administration, when JFK made him a Presidential adviser.

The puzzle of Schlesinger, Jr.'s, holding—with only an A.B.—first an associate professorship and then a full professorship in the history department of Harvard might be solved in one easy sentence: his father was head of that department.

Unfortunately—and unlike his son—the elder Schlesinger can write lucid prose, and he has wielded his pen to produce utterly leftist history textbooks which subvert traditional American beliefs, such as *New Viewpoints in American History* and *Political and Social History of the United States*. In his history books, Schlesinger, Sr., excoriates our Founding Fathers as rich chiselers who did in the poor folk; he denounces our American Constitution as a bulwark of "privilege"; and he sneers as States' Rights as a bourgeois "fetish."

The junior Schlesinger has obtained, largely through the trumpetings of the Liberal Establishment, a reputation as an intellectual—a reputation with little or no basis in fact, according to many objective scholars. His writings abound in factual errors, misrepresentations and distortions which if compounded by a non-Liberal, would see the author laughed off the intellectual and literary scene. Schlesinger's chief claim to intellectual fame rests on his book *The Age of Jackson,* published in 1945 by Little, Brown, which received the Newspaper Guild Award for best book of 1945 and the Pulitzer Prize in 1946.

It is interesting to note that *The Age of Jackson* was published during the brief period Mr. Schlesinger was in the U.S. Army. The book was presumably written in that year or sometime during the previous year (the foreword is dated May 7, 1944). Inasmuch as Schlesinger was in the OWI and OSS from 1942 to 1945, and in the Army in 1945, *The Age of Jackson* was written on taxpayers' time while Mr. Schlesinger was in government service.

In writing his biographical sketch for *Who's Who,* Schlesinger neglects to note several significant facts pertinent to *The Age of Jackson.* He notes that the book "received the Newspaper Guild Award for the best book of the year 1945"; but he fails to mention that at that time the Newspaper Guild was so notoriously dominated by Communists and Communist sympathizers that a full-scale clean-up of the organization was launched the following year. Schlesinger also fails to mention that there is nothing in the charter, articles of incorporation or by-laws of the Newspaper Guild which provides for such an award as Mr. Schlesinger received—and that no such award for a book had ever been made before, or has been made since by the Newspaper Guild.

Schlesinger's manuscript for *The Age of Jackson* had gone the rounds of many publishing houses and had been rejected. Finally it was accepted for publication by Little, Brown and Company, the editor-in-chief of which was then Angus Cameron. Mr. Cameron had been identified as a Communist by several witnesses before the Senate Internal Security subcommittee. The U.S. House of Representatives Committee on Un-American Activities cites Mr. Cameron as affiliated with about 20 Communist fronts, including the notorious Waldorf-Astoria Peace Conference which denounced the United States, praised Soviet Russia as a citadel of peace, and called for civil disobedience against our government.

Despite the ballyhoo and the awards, *The Age of Jackson* is regarded by many competent historians as an absolutely unreadable book, a montage of quotations glued together by the 28-year-old Schlesinger in an effort to make a name for himself. Certainly, like all of Schlesinger's biased and glue-job books (which always wind up as a plea for socialism), *The Age of Jackson* could never be taken seriously as an historical work, or even as a Ph.D. dissertation, by any board of scholars.

One result of the ballyhoo for *The Age of Jackson* (much of which came from leftist publications) was a commission for Schlesinger to write two articles on communism for *Life* magazine, for a whopping price. Schlesinger hired a New York *World-Telegram* writer, Nelson Frank, to dig up the information, and paid him a minimum fee for his labors. Schlesinger then carefully weeded out from Frank's material any items which might prove embarrassing to Schlesinger, Sr., to various in-laws of Schlesinger Jr. and to Junior's particular friends.

J. B. Matthews pointed out that in his articles, Schlesinger, Jr., had condemned as "Communist menaces" long-forgotten, obscure and comparatively innocent fronts; but that Schlesinger had omitted a host of really subversive Red fronts with which the elder Schlesinger, as "one of the most prominent fellow-traveling academicians in the United States," was actively affiliated. Matthews added that Schlesinger, Sr.'s, Communist fronts are listed in reports of the House Commit-

tee on Un-American Activities, then known as the Dies Committee, and Matthews says this apparently accounts for "the
younger Schlesinger's intense dislike for the Dies Committee,
expressed half a dozen times in the *Life* articles."

Matthews described Schlesinger's conclusion to his *Life*
articles as "abominable," and not a few Americans might agree.
Schlesinger's conclusion was this: "The way to detest them
[the Communists] is . . . to correct the faults and injustices
in *our* present system which make even freedom-loving Americans look wistfully to Russia."

In 1947, while at Harvard, Schlesinger wrote an article
for the avant-garde, left-wing *Partisan Review* which, in addition to its stunning leftist avowals, hurled insults at Christians
and at Christian beliefs. Official liberalism, wrote the junior
Schlesinger, "dispensed with the absurd Christian myths of
sin and damnation and believed that what shortcomings man
might have were to be redeemed, not by Jesus on the Cross,
but by the benevolent unfolding of history. Tolerance, free
inquiry, and technology, operating within the framework of
human perfectibility, would in the end create a heaven on
earth, a goal accounted much more sensible and wholesome
than a heaven in heaven."

In 1962, Scripps-Howard columnist Henry J. Taylor,
former U.S. Ambassador to Switzerland, asked Schlesinger
if he now disavowed the sentiments he expressed in his 1947
article. Schlesinger's retort was, "I neither withdraw nor
apologize."

Two years after the *Partisan Review* article, in 1949, the
32-year-old Schlesinger set himself up as the high priest of
"the non-Communist Left" with his manifesto *The Vital Center.*
Briefly Schlesinger's theme song was that capitalism, or free
enterprise, must be destroyed. It must be replaced by socialism.
Paying his usual lip service to anti-communism, Schlesinger
says that communism should be rejected because it does not
assure freedom. But the historical precedent of socialism's
paving the way for engulfment by communism in country after
country does not figure in Mr. Schlesinger's reckonings. Neither

does Schlesinger bother to explain how men can be free in a socialistic society, where every facet of the citizen's public and personal existence is dictated by a Big Brother government.

Schlesinger added to his accomplishments in 1951 by doing a hatchet job on General Douglas MacArthur in a book entitled *The General and the President.* Schlesinger's co-author on the book was Richard Rovere, whose distortions are for sale to a variety of left-wing publications such as *New Masses* and *The Nation,* who now wields his pen for *The New Yorker,* and who has distinguished himself as one of the nation's foremost hate-mongers—of the late Senator McCarthy in particular, and of anti-Communists in general.

By any fair assessment, *The General and the President* is a contemptible piece of writing, hastily patched together within two months of General MacArthur's triumphal return to the United States when the general awakened the American populace to the dubious machinations of the State Department and called for victory over the Communists in Korea. Replete with innuendo and smear attempts against MacArthur, the book carries on to an inglorious finish with a thoroughly unfactual account of the Korean War and of the Senate's MacArthur Hearings. Fortunately the American people, with their characteristic good sense, prefer General Douglas MacArthur as a hero to the shabby Schlesinger-Rovere duet.

Schlesinger's next contribution to furthering socialism in America was a trilogy entitled *The Age of Roosevelt,* a premature attempt, in the eyes of many, to write history so soon after the death of FDR. The public was treated to the trilogy in three doses: *The Crisis of the Old Order,* 1957; *The Coming of the New Deal,* 1958; and *The Politics of Upheaval,* 1960. The trilogy is a monument to pseudo scholarship, consisting for the most part of clippings from left-wing journals, with almost no allusion to impartial or primary sources, attempting to show by sweeping and unfactual generalizations that "the capitalist class" must be extirpated and replaced by (you guessed it) socialism.

Shortly before the 1960 Democratic convention which

nominated Senator Kennedy for President, Schlesinger drafted a document aimed at Democratic leaders which bore the title, "The Shape of National Politics to Come." As usual, Schlesinger's one-note theme song comes through loud and clear: socialism must take over the United States. Businessmen, wrote the junior Schlesinger, exist to be pushed around by the government and should be "disciplined," since businessmen's "aggressive pursuit of their own advantages imperils the general welfare."

An incisive summary of Schlesinger's pre-convention document was written in 1962 by M. Stanton Evans, editor of the Indianapolis *News,* in *The Fringe on Top,* co-authored by Allan H. Ryskind and William Schulz:

> In matters of economics Schlesinger's writings are invariably a superficial confection of whatever happens to be prevalent among the liberal intellegentsia. His memorandum to the Democratic leaders . . . is in fact a sort of retail version of Galbraith's theories, devoid of Galbraith's wit or economic expertise.
>
> Schlesinger seems to be completely innocent of the forces which make our economy run. The prosperity of America, produced by the free enterprise system, he takes as a sort of given— something which is simply there, to be chopped up and redistributed according to whatever plan "intellectuals" like himself happen to devise . . .
>
> Responsibility for affluence, in Schlesinger's view, evidently depends upon how you want to evaluate it. If you want to describe it in its aspects of materialism and "greed," then you pin it on Conservatives; but if you want to invoke its great creative potencies, then you claim it for Liberalism.
>
> It is a disingenuous game Schlesinger is playing; but while his arguments may change with the winds, his objectives do not: the aggrandizement of government power, and the reduction of individual choice—these are the lodestars of his policy, in 1962 and in 1947.

Arthur Junior had played a prominent role in sponsoring the left-wing cause, as a founder and co-chairman of the ADA, which is, in the words of a Senate Republican Policy Committee report, "a group of left-wing Democrats who hope, as either the senior or junior partner of a labor alliance, to capture the

Democratic Party and bring about a system of National Socialism in America." Today, in the words of Representative Steven B. Derounian (Republican of New York), "The ADAers are morbidly fascinated by the U.S.S.R., and anything accomplished by the Communists is acclaimed by the ADA as superior to anything accomplished by the United States of America." The annual national platform of the ADA, another Congressman declared, is hardly distinguishable from the annual platform of the Communist Party, U.S.A., as published on the pages of the Communist *Worker*.

This is the organization which former Presidential Adviser Arthur Schlesinger, Jr., helped to found, the organization of which he is former co-chairman, and the organization for which he is one of the nation's foremost spokesmen and wheelhorses.

From his White House aerie, Arthur Junior supervised our Alliance for Progress, which is paid for by the American taxpayers to the tune of $20 billion over a ten-year period from 1962 to 1972—a neat sum added to the almost $8 billion which the United States has given to Latin America since the end of World War II. When President Kennedy announced the Alliance for Progress in 1962, he made clear that its purpose was to stop the spread of communism in Latin America by stimulating private enterprise in those nations.

The fact of the matter is that, after only two years, the Alliance for Progress, far from stopping communism and boosting free enterprise in Latin America, is engaged in the wholesale financing of socialism throughout all of Latin America, and while American taxpayers' dollars are flowing into those countries, private capital is flowing out at a faster rate. For example, since the Alliance for Progress began, almost $1 billion in private funds have been taken out of Brazil, with about the same amount taken out of Venezuela. In the words of Senator John Tower, who charges that the generosity of the American taxpayer is being betrayed, "U.S. aid money is being used to harass and drive out free-enterprise capital by financing government seizures of private business" and to "cover Latin

American government losses caused by deficits in nationalized industries. In short, we are underwriting socialism."

As one example of the hoax being perpetrated upon the American taxpayer, Senator Tower explained, in the January 1964 *Reader's Digest,* that South American governments are seizing property of U.S. corporations in Latin America, and then the South American governments turn around and pay compensation—with Alliance of Progress dollars.

As a Mexican businessman, quoted by Senator Tower, summed up the Alliance for Progress in an interview with an American newsman: "Your Alliance is giving governments the money to buy up and operate as money-losing Socialist state monopolies, scores of businesses that were formerly tax-paying parts of the free enterprise system. It seems remarkable to some of us that the wealth of the American people should be used to undermine the very system that produced it."

To some American observers, it does not seem so "remarkable" in view of Arthur Schlesinger, Jr.'s, role in the Alliance for Progress.

Arthur Jr., a careful practitioner of words which often convey meanings without flat assertions, once slipped badly. In 1953, after Attorney General Brownell exposed the late Harry Dexter White, a former Morgenthau aide, as a Communist agent, Schlesinger protested this exposure with a harsh letter to President Eisenhower on November 20, 1953. Writing as co-chairman of ADA, Schlesinger said the exposure of White "threatens to make the United States Government the laughingstock and despair of the entire free world. It has already undermined the respect of the American people in their representative form of government. Continued events of this nature will do nothing but tear our nation apart."

Where does a statement of this nature leave Schlesinger's "anti-communism" and that of the allegedly anti-communist ADA of which he has long been a leader? For Schlesinger this letter defending a Communist agent was a bad mistake.

Schlesinger wrote this letter in 1953, when he was ADA co-chairman; and as imprudent as this was for Schlesinger personally, it hardly affected U.S. prestige abroad. However, it appears that Schlesinger took his imprudence with him to the White House, where it had worldwide repercussions in eroding respect for our nation. In 1961, as a Presidential adviser, Schlesinger had a major role in planning the disastrous Bay of Pigs invasion of Cuba. The Cuban blunder so seriously diminished respect for the U.S. in the eyes of the world, that Edward R. Murrow ordered the USIA to stop publishing its polls taken around the world of plummeting American prestige.

But supervision of our Latin American affairs—in our all-important backyard where Castro maintains a Soviet-Red Chinese bastion and where communism advances daily—was only one facet of Schlesinger's job. As one of the White House advisers to Presidents Kennedy and Johnson, Schlesinger played one of the most powerful roles in the nation.

Just how capable of shaping the destiny of millions of Americans and of human beings throughout the world is the bow-tied, bespectacled, pseudo-intellectual Arthur Schlesinger, Jr.? An estimate of Schlesinger's ability, with which a large segment of observers would wholeheartedly agree, was presented in the Richmond, Virginia, *News Leader* in January 1961, as the eggheads of the New Frontier galloped onto the American scene:

> The New Frontier was traced, recently, across the television screen, and it took the shape of a vicious circle. Board Chairman of Mr. Kennedy's Brain Trust—Arthur Schlesinger, Jr.—"faced the nation," and, in one half-hour, explained absolutely everything that has happened in the past half century, and all that is to come in the next two decades . . .
>
> In one half-hour, in a caricature of history, the bank of the Kennedy Brain Trust was opened to our scrutiny; and the vaults are empty.

CHAPTER ELEVEN

ADA Runs The Show

". . . the liberal deviseth liberal things."
. . . Isaiah xxxii., 8

AMERICANS FOR DEMOCRATIC ACTION shapes the Johnson Administration's policies and supplies President Johnson and his Inner Circle of advisers with leaders, plus arms and legs to carry out their bidding—just as in the Kennedy Administration. To illustrate the massive influence of the ADA on Administration policies, a few striking examples might be cited.

It is unfortunate for the nation that both the late President Kennedy and President Johnson—with Harlan Cleveland and Arthur Schlesinger, Jr., cheering, though barely, from the sidelines—bought ADA's dangerous 1960 platform proposal "gradually to replace national armed forces," which includes liquidating our U.S. military forces, and to create instead "a United Nations Armed Force." This was made official U.S. government policy by President Kennedy in September 1961, less than one year after the proposal was made by the ADA, and is now being implemented by the Johnson Administration.

In 1960, and again in slightly different words in 1962, the ADA platform declared: "We oppose the transfer of nuclear weapons to other nations at this time while crucial negotiations are in progress" with the Soviet Union. Is it a coincidence that shortly afterwards the Kennedy Administration pulled out our 60 powerful Thor rockets from England, where they looked down the throat of Soviet Russia, protected the U.S. Mediterranean Fleet, and deterred Soviet attack on the United States? The Kennedy Administration's scrapping of the Skybolt missile, which we had agreed to give to Great Britain, is additional evidence of the New Frontier's adherence to ADA policies.

Senator Joseph S. Clark of Pennsylvania, an ADAer, let

the cat out of the bag when he said to 600 ADA members and their friends at a Pittsburgh meeting on March 9, 1962:

> I am convinced that the struggle for the mind of the President has been won by those who believe in disarmament.

In its 1962 platform, the ADA declared, "We support the U.S. 'Program for General and Complete Disarmament in a Peaceful World'." This program, of course, is nothing but the ADA 1960 program which, Senator Clark reveals, was sold to the President.

In April 1962, the ADA called for a U.S.-Russian agreement banning nuclear tests "without inspection provisions." Is it a coincidence that four months later, in August 1962, Assistant Secretary of State Harlan Cleveland (who has absolutely no experience in atomic matters) appeared before the Joint Atomic Energy Committee of Congress as a representative of the Kennedy Administration, and officially advocated that the U.S. and Russia ban nuclear tests without inspection provisions? Is it a coincidence that there is no inspection provided for in the Test-Ban Treaty?

ADA's 1962 Annual Convention was held in Washington, since 41 of its members, or former members, then held top federal government posts and hundreds more were distributed in key posts throughout sensitive agencies and departments. At this convention, James Wechsler — a founder of ADA, a former paid official of the executive committee of the Young Communist League and writer for the fellow-traveling *PM* and for *The Nation,* and now editor of the far-left New York *Post*—delivered an ADA tribute to Presidential Adviser Arthur Schlesinger, Jr., who had just been re-elected vice-chairman. Wechsler said that Schlesinger "cares profoundly for the immediate condition of man." Earlier, the *ADA World* had paid front-page tribute to Assistant Secretary of State Harlan Cleveland and to the Administration's UN Ambassador Adlai Stevenson (who recently distinguished himself as guardian of America's interests against the Soviets by publicly upbraiding Americans for distrusting Soviet Russia).

Former President John F. Kennedy, had once declared in a June 13, 1953, *Saturday Evening Post* interview, "I'm not a liberal at all . . . I'm not comfortable with those people," when referring to the ADA (despite the fact that his speech writer, chief assistant and alter ego was then-ADAer Theodore Sorenson). Nevertheless, in 1963, President Kennedy sent an expanded message of greeting and approbation to ADA's 16th Annual Convention. Moreover, while the ADA was meeting in the nation's capital, Kennedy invited the ADA national chairman and ADA's 20 chapter leaders to the White House. At this White House meeting, according to James Wechsler's New York *Post* report of the conference, the President devoted "notable attention" to their "care and feeding."

From the time the Presidential bug infected him in 1956 Kennedy did a turnabout in views and had a perfect ADA record in the Senate voting charts; and from the moment he was nominated for the Presidency, he surrounded himself with ADA aides and advisers. As President, he never fired one ADAer, and the only ADAer he ever demoted was Chester Bowles, whom he kicked upstairs with the all-embracing title of "Special Representative and Adviser on African, Asian and Latin American Affairs." However, Kennedy later promoted Bowles, appointing him as U.S. Ambassador to India, although it does seem a come-down from his previous exalted title.

What is the ADA? It is an organization of arch-liberals, many of them with long histories of membership in socialistic organizations. It proclaims itself as a "national, independent liberal organization . . . for progressives, dedicated to the achievement of freedom and economic security for all people everywhere, through education and democratic political action." Membership is open to anyone who declares his belief in the ADA program, pays five dollars in annual dues, and joins an ADA chapter, if one exists in his locality. The ADA functions like a political club, paralleling the French Revolution's Jacobin Club of Robespierre, whose members attained complete revolutionary power by gaining control of the Committee for Public Safety. ADA members work for ADA-endorsed candidates in precincts, in elections, during registration drives and at political conventions, in order to attain their ends.

In 1958, the Senate Republican Policy Committee staff undertook an intensive study of the origins, platforms and policies of the ADA, and concluded:

> The ADA is a group of left-wing Democrats who hope, as either the senior or junior partner of a labor alliance, to capture the Democratic Party and bring about a system which would amount to National Socialism in America.
>
> The ADA's perennial statist program represents a distinct parallel to that of the Communists.
>
> The ADA is the intellectual and political vanguard in the United States of the so-called "third force" in the political spectrum [which is] laundered communism in white tie and tails masquerading as the welfare state or "dynamic democracy." But beneath the uplift lingo and the self-righteous accents, the doctrine is socialism still—slow and deliberate and economic paralysis; the chloroform of hope, pride, enterprise, self-respect, initiative and individual liberty of thought and action.

Americans for Democratic Action was inaugurated at a dinner in Washington on January 4, 1947, the offspring of an earlier organization known as the Union for Democratic Action (UDA). UDA had been founded in the spring of 1941 to help mold American public opinion toward our entry into World War II, and to push the Socialist program of the New Deal. Its membership, according to political analyst James Burnham, was "a kind of grab-bag, pro-war, 'anti-fascist' united front of intellectuals, writers and publicists of the Left, combining Liberals, Socialists and Communist fellow travelers," and, it might be added, Communists. Many of UDA's members, according to the Senate Republican study, "had been collaborating with the Communist front in what they deemed worthy causes."

When World War II ended, UDA ostensibly went out of business, gave birth to the ADA in 1947, and UDA members transferred wholesale to the ranks of ADA. The reason for the founding of ADA, according to a former ADA national chairman, Francis Biddle, was "to split from the liberal movement in America those elements of communism and fellow travelers which . . . certainly up until 1945, did great harm to the liberal movement."

The supposed purification rite ended with the founding of the ADA; however, the "purified" ADA speedily wrote platforms and espoused causes which are, in the words of the Senate Republican report, "hardly distinguishable from the party line emblazoned on the pages of the *Daily Worker.*"

Among the principal founders of ADA were James Wechsler; James Loeb, Jr., (former national director of the UDA, appointed by the late President Kennedy as U.S. ambassador to Peru and now U.S. Ambassador to Guinea); and Joseph L. Rauh, Jr. (a Washington attorney who later defended convicted Communist perjurer William Remington; Rauh is now General Counsel for fellow ADAer Walter Reuther's United Automobile Workers). Also among ADA's founders were jobless New Dealers like Leon Henderson, Wilson Wyatt and Paul Porter; labor union leaders such as Walter Reuther, James Carey and David Dubinsky; a number of young ambitious politicians (who subsequently owed their campaign success to precinct work by ADA and/or the ADA subordinate, the National Committee for an Effective Congress) like Hubert Humphrey of Minnesota and Richardson Dilworth of Pennsylvania; liberal newspaper columnists like Kenneth Crawford, Stewart Alsop and Marquis Childs; various liberal intellectuals like J. Kenneth Galbraith and Arthur Schlesinger, Jr.; and, of course, Mrs. Eleanor Roosevelt and her son, FDR, Jr.

Its membership today? While lists are hard to come by, the following officials high in the Johnson Administration or formerly close to the JFK Inner Circle are now, or have been, ADA members:

STATE DEPARTMENT:

JONATHAN B. BINGHAM—U. S. Representative to UN Trusteeship Council. ADA alumnus.

CHESTER BOWLES—U. S. Ambassador to India. Former Under Secretary of State. Former head of OPA. Former Governor of Connecticut. Former Congressman. One of principal owners of defunct leftwing newspaper *PM*. Former Chairman of Democratic National Committee. ADA founder.

J. KENNETH GALBRAITH—Former U. S. Ambassador to India. Now returned to Harvard as Professor of Economics. Was deputy to Bowles in OPA. ADA founder; ADA policymaker.

JAMES LOEB, JR.—U. S. Ambassador to Guinea. Former Ambassador to Peru. ADA founder. Was full-time paid Executive Secretary of ADA from 1947 to 1951; had held same position with parent group, UDA (Union for Democratic Action).

MRS. KATIE LOUCHHEIM—Deputy Assistant Secretary of State for Community Advisory Services. Was Assistant Secretary of State for Public Affairs. Former special assistant to Bowles. Former Vice Chairman of Democratic National Committee. Former ADA member.

ADLAI STEVENSON—U. S. Ambassador to the UN. The *ADA World* (the official ADA organ) identified Stevenson as "one of the original founders of ADA," and as "a charter member of ADA." (The record is not clear.)

G. MENNEN WILLIAMS—Assistant Secretary of State. Former ADA member.

EXECUTIVE DEPARTMENTS:

MRS. JIM G. AKEN—Former Congressional Liaison Officer of Health, Education and Welfare Department. (Now married to Rep. Richard Bolling.) Former ADA member.

JOHN A. BAKER—Director of Agricultural Credit Services, Department of Agriculture. ADA alumnus.

FREDERICK C. BELEN—Deputy Postmaster General. Former ADA member.

WILBUR J. COHEN—Assistant Secretary for Legislative Affairs, HEW. Former ADA member.

ARCHIBALD COX—Solicitor General of the U. S. Current ADA member.

THOMAS K. FINLETTER—Assigned to International Organization USRO Paris. Former member of ADA's National Executive Board.

HENRY H. FOWLER—Under Secretary of the Treasury. Former ADA member.

ORVILLE L. FREEMAN—Secretary of Agriculture. Former Governor of Minnesota. Active ADA member. Protégé of ADA founder and Vice Chairman, Senator Hubert Humphrey.

ROBERT G. LEWIS—Deputy Administrator for Price Supports, Department of Agriculture. ADA alumnus.

CHARLES S. MURPHY—Under Secretary Department of Agriculture. Former aide to President Truman. ADA alumnus.

MRS. ESTHER PETERSON—Assistant Secretary of Labor and Director of Labor Department's Women's Bureau. Appointed by President Johnson as Special White House Advisor for Consumers. ADA member.

ABRAHAM B. RIBICOFF—U. S. Senator from Connecticut. Former Secretary of Health, Education and Welfare Department. Former ADA member.

CHARLES H. STODDARD—Director of Bureau of Land Management, Department of the Interior. Former ADA member.

GEORGE L. P. WEAVER—Assistant Secretary for International Labor Affairs, Department of Labor. Former head of CIO Committee to Abolish Discrimination. ADA founder.

GOVERNMENT AGENCIES:

JACK T. CONWAY—Former Deputy Administrator of HHFA. ADA alumnus.

GEORGE DOCKING—Former Director of Export-Import Bank. ADA member.

FRANK W. McCULLOCH—Chairman National Labor Relations Board. Chairman of ADA's National Executive Committee.

THEODORE C. SORENSON—Deputy Director of Plans and Policy, U. S. Information Agency. Former Special Counsel to President Kennedy. Was active in ADA's campus auxiliary, Students for Democratic Action. Was hired by Kennedy on recommendation of Senator Paul Douglas and Douglas' former aide, Frank W. McCulloch, both of whom were founders of ADA.

WILLIAM TAYLOR—General Counsel of Commission on Civil

Rights. Since 1959 has been paid lobbyist for ADA on Capitol Hill.

ROBERT C. WEAVER—Administrator Housing and Home Finance Agency (HHFA). ADA alumnus.

SIDNEY H. WOOLNER—Former Commissioner of Community Facilities, HHFA. ADA alumnus.

SUPREME COURT:

ARTHUR J. GOLDBERG—Associate Justice of U. S. Supreme Court. Former Secretary of Labor. ADA member.

Although ADA claims loudly that it is "anti-Communist," it has consistently advocated the following extreme left-wing programs:

1. Unilateral disarmament of the United States.
2. The establishment of a world government.
3. A "conciliatory" U. S. policy toward Soviet Russia, and "accommodation" of the Soviets.
4. Red China's admission to the UN, and U. S. diplomatic recognition of the Chinese Communists.
5. An uninspected nuclear test-ban agreement with Soviet Russia.
6. Appeasement of the Castro Communist dictatorship.
7. Abolition of the House Committee on Un-American Activities, and abolition of all anti-Communist loyalty oaths.
8. Breakaway inflation and exorbitant federal spending programs for left-wing welfare projects.
9. Socialized medicine, socialized education and socialized electric power.
10. The crushing of pro-Western leaders in Africa, Latin America, Europe and Asia.
11. Massive American aid to Communist countries.

The ADA is officially registered in the Lobby Index as interested in influencing legislation on Capitol Hill which promotes the social and economic programs of the New Deal, Fair Deal and the New Frontier; but, more important, ADA lobbys nationwide for its left-wing programs, as the lodestar of what Francis Biddle termed "the liberal lobby"—a host of subsidiary liberal organizations with interlocking directorates chaired and manned by ADA stalwarts.

The influence of ADA can be seen in the platform and resolutions adopted by the Democratic Party, ranging from the party's national platforms since FDR's second term, to those of grass-roots Democratic organizations today throughout the nation, with the exception of the South generally, where the conservative principles of the genuine Democratic Party still hold sway. This is not to say that the national platforms of the Republican Party adopted since 1952 under the influence of the "liberal" northeast wing of the GOP—many of whose members are political bedfellows with the most "liberal" of the "liberal" Democrats—are not imitations of the Democratic national platforms, but the grass-roots Republican sentiment otherwise is strongly conservative and generally untainted by ADA-type liberalism.

An instance of the ADA's influence on the grass-roots Democratic Party organization could be seen in the summer of 1963, when the Young Democrats organization held its Thirteen Western States Conference in Berkeley, California, and passed resolutions which demonstrated that the youthful wing of the Democratic Party is weaned on the far-left pap of its political matriarch, the ADA. Among the 32 resolutions passed by the Young Democrats were demands for: resumption of U.S. diplomatic relations with Cuba; withdrawal of U.S. troops from South Viet Nam where they were fighting Communists; a nonaggression pact between NATO and the Warsaw Pact Communist countries; abolition of the House Committee on Un-American Activities; and repeal of the McCarran Internal Security Act.

Republican National Chairman William E. Miller, like many other observers, pinned on ADA the responsibility for the left-wing sentiments of the Young Democrats. Miller asked his opposite number, Democratic Party National Chairman Bailey—who had recently charged that the Republican Party was being taken over by the "radical Right"—What about your "radical Left," the ADA, of whose influence there is no doubt?

Miller drew a parallel between the platform of ADA

and the resolutions of the Young Democrats, and pointed out the prominent ADA members who hold the highest Administration posts—in the Cabinet, on the White House staff, in the State Department, three Under Secretaries of three government departments, the U.S. Solicitor General, the Assistant Secretary of Labor, the Assistant Postmaster General—and added: "There are others in key positions, not to mention uncounted underlings and flunkies. The Democratic side of the Senate is literally crawling with members of the Americans for Democratic Action, and the House of Representatives has a liberal quota."

Miller concluded: "I would urge Democratic leaders to repudiate the resolutions adopted at the Young Democrats' meeting, and then to take steps to reassure the American people by purging from high office the radical Left of the Democratic Party and the Administration."

From Chairman Bailey there was a resounding silence on both counts.

In a syndicated newspaper column, Senator Barry Goldwater noted that "when cornered about the Young Democrats' extremism, Democratic Party leaders expressed only mild disagreement, saying in effect that kids will be kids and that they —the older Democrats—could not possibly agree with such things."

However, said Goldwater, "the facts somehow belie such disclaimers, and make the youngsters look like a watered-down version of the real thing":

> Most policies of the New Frontier, for instance, are shaped by current and former members of Americans for Democratic Action. Their views on just about every major issue, domestic or foreign, go at least as far as the Young Democrats went, and in many cases further.
>
> Of the 50 current and former members of ADA brought into government by Kennedy, many hold the highest policy-making and advisory posts and have pressed consistently for ADA programs . . .
>
> Other ADAers are key New Frontier spokesmen in the Senate, the House, in industry, business, organized labor, civic

and fraternal organizations and just about every other field imaginable. That they influence the policies of and speak for the Administration is undenied.

There is also the question of the now infamous collection of essays, *The Liberal Papers,* compiled under the guidance of present and former liberal Democrats in the House which has been labeled by Republican National Chairman William E. Miller as "going beyond the Communist line." The Administration has stated publicly that the views expressed are "contrary" to its own, but nevertheless has pressed forward on many programs it recommends.

The elder Democrats of the West in particular would do well to refer to a typical example of their own views—the platform of the Washington State Democratic Party adopted at Bellingham, Wash., June 23, 1962—and compare it with the document of the young Westerners. A delegate to the Washington Convention which adopted it stalked out, saying: "What they have here is the Communist Manifesto. If I had stayed and voted with them, I would have been excommunicated from my church."

The ADA since its inception has advocated U.S. friendship with the Soviet Union, and virtually all ADA foreign policy programs flow from this thesis. The first ADA charter program stated:

> We firmly believe in the urgent need for breaking out of the vicious cycle of mutual distrust between ourselves and Russia. We favor a policy based on an understanding of the legitimate aspirations of the Soviet Union.

Through the years, the ADA policy toward Soviet Russia has been the same, and today the current program declares:

> Policy toward the Soviet Union should be guided by the concepts of defense without provocation, and conciliation without appeasement.

The ADA platform does not make clear, however, how one attains "conciliation without appeasement"; nor does it explain how civilized men can conciliate ruthless Communist revolutionaries who are bent upon conquering the world.

James Burnham has done one of the most incisive analyses

of the ADA, in *National Review* on May 7, 1963. Mr. Burnham wrote in part:

Nowhere in ADA literature is the Soviet Union identified as an enemy. ADA's war is "against injustice and inequality." "A bold program of economic stabilization, rising living standards and improved distribution" will win the war, which *"must not be directed against the Soviet Union* or any other nation." Suitably conciliated, the Soviet regime will prosper and relax; the era of universal peace and plenty will begin. The ADA should be granted a clear patent for invention of the No-Win policy.

The 1961-1962 version of the [ADA] platform declares that "support of the principles of the United Nations"—not the national interest of the United States—"is the cornerstone of our foreign policy." ADA proposes to strengthen the UN in every way, give it a permanent armed force, remove restrictions (like the Connally Amendment) on U.S. acceptance of decisions by international bodies, etc.

Granted the ADA's dedicated internationalism, it is not surprising that in its periodicals and other literature, we never come across *any* words, article or symbols that could be called "patriotic." No flag ever appears, no patriotic quotations or slogans; no reference to patriotic memories, holidays or observances. This is natural enough, since ADAers regard themselves as citizens of humanity and the world, bound to a higher loyalty than any mere national patriotic ties. They celebrate UN Day, not the Fourth of July.

Since 1950, the ADA had held that "the United States should immediately withdraw recognition of the Chiang Kai-shek government as the government of China" and undertake "initiation, together with our allies, of negotiations toward diplomatic recognition of the Peiping regime and its accreditation to the UN as the government of China."

The 1962 program suggests "de facto recognition of East Germany" in return for a Soviet guarantee on access to Berlin, replacement of NATO troops in Berlin by a "UN presence," and "standing authority" for the President "to extend loans and grants to the Communist countries of eastern Europe."

From 1950 until the present day, ADA has called for the abolition of the House Committee on Un-American Activities, and has attacked HUAC in the sharpest manner. But you will search a long while before you find in ADA publications any sharp attack on the hundreds of Communists and Soviet agents, from Alger Hiss to the organizers of the Fair Play for Cuba Committee, who have been exposed by HUAC. The Senate's Internal Security Subcommittee and the FBI are also cherished targets—but not the Communists and Soviet spies whom these two agencies have unearthed.

There has been no change over the years. Last July, Prof. John Roche, as ADA National Chairman, wrote to the *New Republic* concerning the approaching trial—after years of legal jockeying—of the Communist Party leadership: "It is deplorable that Attorney General Kennedy has . . . launched legal proceedings against Gus Hall and a dozen others for refusing to register under the Communist Control Act of 1954 . . . We believe that the Communist Control Act is both unconstitutional and unworthy of a free people." ADA has many times delivered the same judgment on the Smith Act and the Internal Security Act.

With the Soviet Union, ADA can show infinite patience. "An understanding of the legitimate aspirations," "negotiations," even "conciliation" are the proper approaches to Moscow, while waiting for "relaxation and greater personal freedom within the Soviet Union."

There is no ADA summons to support the peoples of captive eastern Europe in a struggle for freedom. How different is the ADA outlook on Franco's Spain (which furnishes bases indespensable to our defense)! Over the years, ADA platforms thundered: "We unequivocally condemn the fascist regime in Spain. We favor political and economic support to the government-in-exile and to the democratic forces within Spain."

But ADA greeted Castro's takeover [of Cuba] hopefully and sympathetically. Prof. Robert J. Alexander explained in the April 1960 issue of *ADA World,* fifteen months *after* Castro had come to power, that Castro's denunciations of the U.S. were deserved, because they are "largely due to the recent history of our relations with the Latin American countries." Nothing about communism; nothing about a threat to the United States. "The Cuban crisis," an editorial stated in October 1960, "will be solved . . . as the Cubans realize that the rest of Latin America is moving forward with our help . . . Castro's hold in Cuba comes from *what he has done for his people, not what he has done for the Russians."*

[In February 1962] ADA stood unmoved as Cuba was rapidly being transformed into a Soviet military base: "Action by the U.S. to intervene militarily or to support military invasion by Cuban exiles or by others in violation of the Charters of the UN and the OAS would be not only wrong but self-defeating . . . [This is] no time to take unilateral economic sanctions against Cuba." Sanctions against the Right, Si; against the Left, No!

On every *specific* issue in every field, ADA supports government control, planning, financing or takeover . . . "by bold long-range programs for the development of our resources, the rebuilding of our cities, the elimination of our slums, and the provision of full and equal opportunities for health, education and security for all our people." "Government subsidies and financing and, if necessary government plants must be used to provide more power, more steel and other vitally necessary raw materials." "The government needs increased authority over the amount of bank credit and bank resources." *"Housing goals must be set by the Federal Government."* "The leadership of the Federal Government is central to the achievement of growth and full employment."

These are typical demands that appear and reappear in ADA manifestoes, platforms, articles and speeches from the beginning to its present day. In January 1962, *ADA World* demanded, along with government Medicare and care of the aged, "a broad and comprehensive federal program . . . for schools, hospitals, cultural and recreational centers, mass transit and water supply systems."

ADA is critical of the indirect or "representative" democracy defined by the Constitution and favors steps toward direct "plebiscitary" democracy. It favors eliminating seniority in choosing chairmen of congressional committees; equalizing election districts *by federal compulsion;* abolishing the electoral college in favor of direct popular election of the President and Vice President.

To guarantee the ADA version of the rights of free speech and assembly, ADA advocates strict limits on congressional investigations and government security proceedings; no restrictions on passports; abolition of loyalty oaths; repeal of the Smith Act, Internal Security Act and Communist Control Act.

Mr. Burnham finished his analysis with a point-for-point enumeration of the ADA programs which have been adopted by the New Frontier:

ADA long advocated "a broad-scale federal program to aid education"; this is today Administration policy.

Demands always featured in ADA propaganda—such as abolition of the loyalty oath requirement for student grants; open "confrontation of the accuser" in government security inquiries (i.e., exposure of confidential sources); court and executive action to compel reapportionment of state legislature districts; federally enforced anti-discrimination in housing—have been put into effect [by the Kennedy and Johnson Administrations].

General Medicare financed through Social Security is a long-time ADA doctrine. Today it has high priority in the Administration program.

The proposal for a Department of Urban Affairs was an ADA plank before it was taken up by the White House.

ADA influence is undoubtedly responsible for inclusion of distinctly left-wing "social and democratic reform" in the Alliance for Progress program.

A popular front solution for Laos, with Western withdrawal, was advocated by ADA before the Administration embraced it.

While pressing for force against rightist tyrannies, ADA has from the beginning opposed forceful actions against Castro. ADA people and thinking played a major, probably decisive, part in the Bay of Pigs shamble.

Increasing orientation on the UN (for instance, in support of UN interventions in Angola, South Africa, Rhodesia) follows explicit items in ADA programs, as does formation of a special disarmament agency.

Exploiting "areas of overlapping interest" with Red bloc nations; relying on "tides of history"; drawing Communist countries into a hoped-for "world community of free nations"; barring talk of Cold War "victory" or liberation of Communist-held peoples—the whole present rhetoric of coexistence is in the ADA mood.

When Sal E. Hoffman resigned from the ADA in December 1950, because of ADA's position on Asia, its consistent advocacy of U.S. recognition of Red China and its admission to the UN, he said:

"The most kindly and charitable interpretation I can place on the position of the ADA Board is that their opposition to Communists and communism, so strongly proclaimed when I joined in founding ADA in January 1947, does not extend to the remote areas of the world.

"Opposition to communism with exceptions is no opposition at all today . . . The road of world history is strewn with wrecks and tombstones of those who thought they could compromise with totalitarianism. In the circumstances, I must bid ADA adieu."

Representative Gordon H. Scherer of Ohio, then ranking Republican on the House Committee on Un-American Activities, charged flatly on January 30, 1958, that the ADA is "the hard core of the Communist conspiracy."

Perhaps the hardest-hitting attack ever made on ADA as an organization which aids communism was made by the late Congressman Kit Clardy of Michigan in the House of Representatives on June 2, 1954:

> They have urged a continuation of diplomatic relations with all Communist nations. They have opposed the rearmament of Germany. They urged withdrawal of our recognition of the Chiang Kai-shek government. They fought adoption of the Subversive Control Act . . .
>
> If they have ever openly attacked the Communist Party position on any subject, it has not been called to my attention. They deny the existence of an internal threat and speak softly about the problem in far-off lands.
>
> I challenge anyone to name a single Communist tracked down and exposed by ADA. While I can cite many instances where ADA members have defended Communists exposed by others, I have never found them on the firing line where Communists were being uncovered . . .
>
> Their opposition to communism is only skin-deep. If embracing a large segment of the Communist Party line makes one anti-Communist, then they qualify.

Representative Clardy quoted a statement by FBI Director J. Edgar Hoover to the effect that "the pseudo-Liberal can be more destructive than the known Communist because of the esteem which his respectability invites."

Clardy charged, "This ADA has, in my opinion, done as much, and probably more, than any other group in the nation to foster and promote many of the aims of the Communist Party—even as it loudly proclaims that it is anti-Communist."

Representative Clardy pulled no punches in telling the House:

> ADA continually waxes indignant over the exposure of Communists—but never against proved cases of infiltration and subversion. They never grow indignant at traitors even when exposed.
>
> They occasionally have a word or two to say in general terms of disapproval of communism, but never do they attack a Hiss, a Remington, or a Lattimore. In fact they have been found speaking for the defense.
>
> ADA sometimes speaks of communism beyond our shores as dangerous—but it cannot see or sense the presence of a grave threat in our own land. They would have us believe that there is no Communist threat in our midst. They continually speak of the threat of communism in America as a phantom. They continually deride those who are trying to alert the Nation to the terrible danger of communism. They seek to lull the Nation into believing there is no internal danger. They have never admitted the guilt of Alger Hiss.
>
> But to come back to this group of left-wingers—this group of ADA members—this propaganda front—writing columns and appearing on radio and television programs. The cumulative effect of their continuous barrage against the things many of us stand for is bound to have a tremendous effect.
>
> Not knowing of their background and purposes, their utterances are accepted by many as the unbiased viewpoint of impartial observers. Their membership in ADA is, I suspect, known only to a small fraction of one per cent of those who read or listen to them.
>
> They pose as Liberals. They are continually applying that term to each other in a sort of mutual admiration society performance. And so I think it is high time the public was made fully aware of the fact that these gentlemen are left-wing members of a left-wing outfit doing their best to sell socialism to America. They are the kind of fake liberals Mr. Hoover must have meant when he said they could be more destructive than the known Communist because of their cloak of respectability.

Clardy concluded: "Consciously or not, they are building the foundation for the communization of this country. If we followed their advice, the Communist conspiracy would soon take over."

Today, President Johnson and his advisers are following the ADA's advice close to completely. How else can one explain, for example, the following 1963 incidents:

1. President Johnson's personal bestowal December 2— 11 days after he became President—of the Atomic Energy Commission's 1963 Enrico Fermi Award of $50,000 tax-free (paid for by the American taxpayers) to J. Robert Oppenheimer, the controversial wartime director of the Los Alamos atomic energy project, "in recognition of Oppenheimer's work in atomic physics."

The news that Oppenheimer was to receive the award was leaked from the White House in early April 1963, as evidenced by carefully planted stories in key newspapers, and the award was originally scheduled for presentation by the late President Kennedy, who had paved the way for Oppenheimer's receiving the award by inviting the scientist to dinner at the White House earlier in the year.

Is it a coincidence that this announcement followed a 1962 ADA policy declaration (chorused by pacifist and left-wing groups throughout the nation) that Oppenheimer should be reinstated with a top-security clearance, and that he was foully slandered in 1954 when the Atomic Energy Commission deprived him of access to atomic secrets on the grounds that he was a security risk?

Anyone who had hoped that Lyndon Johnson might display a bit more hard anti-Communist sentiment than had the late President Kennedy, was rudely awakened at Johnson's aggressive attempts to give the award personally to Oppenheimer. With Kennedy's death President Johnson could easily have bowed out of the ceremony, but he went out of his way to present the award and to praise the physicist at the ceremony, declaring that "one of President Kennedy's most important acts was to sign the award." Johnson added that it was with "great pleasure and pride" that he bestowed it, and declared: "It is important to the nation that we have constantly before us the example of men who set high standards of achievement. This is a role you have played, Dr. Oppenheimer."

Declared Senator Bourke Hickenlooper, Republican of Iowa, ranking minority member of the Joint Atomic Energy Committee, who refused "in good conscience" to attend the ceremony: "I fail to see how anyone who has respect for the security system of the United States could support this award." Admiral Lewis L. Strauss, former chairman of the Atomic Energy Commission, also refused to attend the Oppenheimer award ceremony.

Although the Oppenheimer award ceremony received much attention in the press, the award was given at the precise moment when another event, little noted but a probably more disastrous erosion of our national security, was taking place: eleven Soviet officials, led by Andronik Petrosyants, chairman of the Soviet Union's Committee on Utilization of Atomic Energy, had just wound up a two-week tour of U.S. atomic installations. To label this tour of Soviet scientists through our atomic installations as "fantastic" would be, in the minds of most Americans, an understatement. But to the ADA master planners of a "new world," it is merely another step in the implementation of the ADA platform of "breaking out of the vicious cycle of mutual distrust between ourselves and Russia . . . a policy based on an understanding of the legitimate aspirations of the Soviet Union."

God knows what the ADA-infested New Frontier gave to the Soviet scientists; but if the Administration hoped to give Oppenheimer "backdoor clearance" by this award, and by the late President Kennedy's inviting him to dine at the White House, it overlooked the fact that the public realizes the denial of a security clearance to Oppenheimer was not, as an ADA spokesman said, "a bad hangover of McCarthyism." The Atomic Energy Commission panel, headed by educator Gordon Gray, had painstakingly sifted every aspect of Oppenheimer's case and exercised the very antithesis of so-called "McCarthyism."

The AEC panel discovered that Oppenheimer was a softie in giving critical jobs to scientists who might have been dupes of the Communists. Oppenheimer himself had friends who were either admitted Communists or fellow-travelers and had made specific contacts with them. In the words of the AEC panel, Oppenheimer's associations with known Communists "extended far beyond the tolerable limits of prudence and restraint."

In a letter to J. Edgar Hoover, Oppenheimer was described as follows by William Liscum Borden, former Executive Director of the Congressional Joint Committee on Atomic Energy:

"More probably than not, he [Oppenheimer] has been functioning as an espionage agent; and more, probably than not, he has since acted under a Soviet directive in influencing U.S. military, atomic energy, Intelligence and diplomatic policy."

Oppenheimer's wife and brother were both members of the Communist Party, and it is known that he himself regularly contributed a sizable portion of his salary to Communist coffers right up to 1939, when the first stage of the atomic energy project opened at the University of California at Berkeley, where Oppenheimer was a leading physicist in the radiation laboratory. Moreover, Oppenheimer was "less than candid," in the words of the Gray committee, in testifying about his "old pals of Berkeley, California, days," among the large and militant Communist Party membership on the Berkeley campus and specifically in the atomic radiation laboratory.

In following ADA dictates, the Kennedy and Johnson Administrations must have "forgotten" that "Oppy" and other brilliant physicists, whose knowledge was vital during the war in order to push the atomic bomb to conclusion, were expendable after 1945, along with the necessity of employing brilliant physicists who happened to be political innocents. "Oppy," moreover, opposed U.S. development of the hydrogen bomb after we ceased being allies of the Soviet Union.

2. On March 19, 1963, the State Department announced it would abandon its opposition to a UN decision validating the credentials of Hungarian delegates. This could mean acceptance of their credentials by the UN General Assembly before Congress has any chance to consider our apparent drastic change of policy toward Communist Hungary. The State De-

partment then issued a memorandum saying that the Kadar regime has eased its savage repression of Hungarians who bravely resisted their Communist masters, while the New York *Times* editorialized on May 14, 1963, "We believe . . . that there is good cause now for [restoring normal diplomatic relations with Hungary] and hope that the State Department will follow through with its apparent present intention."

Ohio Senator Frank Lausche, a Democrat, noted that *The Economist* of London had forecast this change a year before, stating that the Russians would vote for "neutralist" U Thant as permanent UN Secretary General, only on condition that the U.S. would agree to shelve the Hungarian issue at the United Nations. A clear horse swap by the Communists on both counts.

Nikita Khrushchev surely was not "mellowing" when Russian tanks rolled over Hungary in 1956, and today Soviet troops still prowl throughout that land, while thousands of political prisoners still languish in Hungarian jails. Yet, Walt W. Rostow wrote in early 1963 that, while he could "understand and sympathize" with those who remember Budapest in 1956, he had not changed his belief that the state of world affairs had undergone "quite a radical change," supposedly for the better, in the past two years.

This move by our State Department, conceived by the ADA and nurtured by Rostow, can irreparably damage U.S. prestige throughout the free world, and cast despair into the hearts of the Eastern Europeans still under the Communist heel, to say nothing of outraging the 35 million American citizens of Eastern European descent who yearn for the liberation of the Soviet slave satellites.

3. A vast crusade by left-wing groups, including the ADA and COPE (the Committee on Political Education of the AFL-CIO), is attempting to smear Conservatives in America. One concrete example of this smear effort can be seen in the organizing of Group Research, Inc.

What is Group Research, Inc., and how is it abetting the

denigration of Conservatives and of conservative organizations in America?

Group Research is an organization incorporated in Washington, D.C., January 30, 1962, professedly "to gather, collate and distribute information concerning organized efforts to affect governmental and economic policies."

But, in fact, Group Research, Inc., devotes itself exclusively to compiling dossiers on American Conservatives and on conservative organizations, and—by channeling its dossiers to organizations such as the AFL-CIO's COPE—it instigates witch-hunts on these anti-Communists and anti-Communist groups throughout the nation. Evidently, Group Research does not regard Communists, Communist fellow travelers, Red front organizations and Lunatic Left dupes and organizations as part of what Group Research terms "organized efforts to affect governmental and economic policies."

Group Research, Inc., did not spring to life full-blown on January 30, 1962, when it was incorporated at its office at 1404 New York Avenue, N.W., in Washington. It was really born on December 19, 1961, 42 days before, when ADA bigwig Walter and brother Victor "Carry-on-the-fight-for-a-Soviet-America" Reuther presented the "Reuther Memorandum" to Attorney General Robert Kennedy. The Reuther Memorandum is a blueprint for destroying the nation's rapidly growing conservative, anti-Communist rebellion against the far-left policies of the ADA, the New Frontier, the New Deal, the Fair Deal, and now the Fast Deal, and it stipulated that private organizations would be established to harass and "expose" Conservatives and conservative organizations and to besmirch all of them as "radical Right" fanatics and groups.

When Group Research was in business, six weeks later, it got to work drawing up a wide range of prominent Conservatives as its targets, such as: Admiral Arleigh Burke; Captain Eddie Rickenbacker, hero of World Wars I and II and, until recently, head of Eastern Air Lines; ex-Congressman and former medical missionary Dr. Walter Judd; William F.

Buckley, Jr., publisher of the respected *National Review* magazine; and film star Ronald Reagan.

Group Research also compiles dossiers on members of conservative and anti-Communist organizations such as the American Security Council; Young Americans for Freedom (YAF), and the Intercollegiate Society of Individualists (ISI).

If anyone had doubts about the continuance of the ADA's shaping our Administration's policies when President Johnson assumed office, they were quickly dispelled when the new President announced that he intended to follow faithfully all the policies of the Kennedy Administration, and did not fire a single ADAer. To prove his devotion to ADA, he promptly named ADAer Mrs. Esther Peterson, Assistant Secretary of Labor, to the new post of White House Adviser for Consumers. He followed up this ADA appointment by promoting ADAer Carl Rowan from U.S. Ambassador to Finland, to the post of Director of the United States Information Agency.

The announced policies of the ADA, as they are being followed by the President of the United States and by his advisers, surely represent gambling with this nation's future as we have never seen it before.

CHAPTER TWELVE

The House That Jack Built

"Then they huffed, and they puffed, and they blew the house down."

     ... Adapted from THREE LITTLE PIGS

THE AMERICAN PEOPLE are uneasy. Every thinking American is alarmed by a Communist bastion 90 miles from American shores. Many are concerned because of the failure of the New Frontier to win a single victory in foreign affairs and its consequent attempt to peddle "peace" through appeasement. Some sense a movement toward federal regimentation and controls. Many are deeply concerned about our very survival, fearful that our days are numbered and that our chances for surviving are being thrown away by our officials.

There can be little doubt of the existence of this uneasiness from the Atlantic to the Pacific and from Canada to the Mexican border. But on one matter nearly all uneasy citizens are in agreement—that President Johnson must get rid of the strange men around him.

For the American people are instinctive. They are right in their judgments on basic issues far more than they are wrong, and they know something is drastically wrong. Attempts to call black "white" and white "black" have not confused them but have instead alarmed them.

One indication of this is that Senators and Congressmen, Democrats and Republicans alike, have been cutting down Administration domestic legislative proposals despite their awareness that if they thwart the President, he may punish them with all the power at his command.

"If only," one Congressman lamented, "this Administration were as tough with Castro as it has been with us."

It is a good bet that had the American people known in 1960 what these obscure planners and plotters stood for, and that in effect they were going to run the federal government, the number of Americans who voted against Kennedy and Johnson, in 1960—and the majority of voters did vote against them, counting all votes cast for all Presidential candidates—would have been much larger.

Ask yourself whether any of these men could have run for elective office successfully if their programs had been exposed by an opponent: McGeorge Bundy? Adam Yarmolinsky? Walt W. Rostow? Jerome Wiesner? George Ball? Dean Rusk? Harlan Cleveland? The idea is ridiculous.

Yet these are the men running the United States, with the acquiescence and support of the President. No wonder they believe in an appointed bureaucracy which they can control, instead of a government by the elected representatives of the people.

Edward R. Murrow, former official spokesman overseas for the insiders, as director of the United States Information Agency, was publicly quoted as explaining that he did not want to run for the Senate from New York, "because I don't really like people." Neither did Ralph Bunche, the favorite UN official of Adlai Stevenson, who said, "I don't like kissing babies."

All of these insiders are more effective operating from under rocks than from out in the open. They often prefer to leave the public exposition of their views to the Marquis Childs, the Walter Lippmanns, and the "Scotty" Restons.

These Presidential advisers make their speeches to selected audiences with little fanfare. Rostow was clearly unhappy that his "new foreign policy" did not get leaked to and accepted by the American people before he was publicly called before the Senate Foreign Relations Committee. He was clearly sad that public opinion forced him to take the Executive Fifth Amendment. Pierre Salinger was not directly quoted as saying one word in Moscow during the "Nicky and Pierre" show, the Comedians' Summit Conference. Adam Yarmolinsky seldom makes public pronouncements. The one exception to this low-key operation has been the junior Schlesinger—writing books and articles for the general public.

These men are, for the most part, amateurs and certainly theorists in government. Most of them are arrogant and do not bother to hide it. They take the view that they know what is best for you and me, and that they are going to give it to us, whether we like it or not. A pounding stream of favorable propaganda, combined with censorship amounting to attempted brainwashing, covers their most brazen actions—such as their plan to liquidate our armed forces and our armaments in the face of the Communists' unswerving determination (represented by their recent attempt to get an atomic "drop" on us from Cuba) to conquer us.

Certainly in our Republic, our citizens have an inherent right to express unpopular views. If one says that continued deficit spending is the key to prosperity, even though all history protests, that is his right. If he wants to advocate opening up the world's greatest single market to free trade by lower-paid workers in other nations with a standard of living far lower than America's, it is his right. If he wants to speak in favor of starving his family to feed the neighbors, his family may have him examined for sanity, but as long as he does not break a law, such statements are his right.

Americans may even advocate ending our present system of government and replacing it with another by legal means, as long as they do not call for overthrowing it by force or violence.

In effect, the men around Johnson advocate all these legitimate procedures with differing degrees of forthrightness. Yet one does not feel that they themselves believe in genuine freedom of expression.

For example, at a Democratic Party meeting on the West Coast, the party national chairman, John M. Bailey, defended the right of the Fund for the Republic's vice chairman, "Ping" Ferry, to attack J. Edgar Hoover and the FBI, encharged with our internal security. By doing this, Bailey not only endorsed this particularly reckless abuse of the privilege of free expression, but he also invited similar abuses from opponents of Hoover and the FBI. (Parenthetically, "Pink" Ferry was already on record in *Monthly Review* magazine as advocating U.S. surrender to the Communists as preferable to nuclear war.)

The men around Johnson are outside the mainstream of American thought, conviction and tradition.

How many Americans, for example, want "an end of nationhood"? How many of us want "a decade of austerity"? How many in the U.S. believe we are merely "an island off the coast of Eurasia," with "marginal" influence in the world? How many believe that today's tight-knit world can long exist half slave and half free? Or, for that matter, how many would assert, particularly in view of Cuba, that the Soviet Union is "mellowing"?

How many of us want to give up the American way of life, or to surrender the economic system which has given us by far the highest standard of living in the history of the world? How many of us want our lives managed by either federal or foreign regimentation and control?

How many Americans favor disarming when other nations do not disarm? How many want their children, or grandchildren, to be Soviet slaves and brainwashed atheists?

If it were laid on the line to the American people that they could throttle the world Communist conspiracy by our ceasing to help it, and by other nonbelligerent acts, every patriotic American would vote to do it. But this little group around the President contends that the choice is either disarmament or eventual nuclear disaster; and they imply that almost anything is preferable to what they believe is almost certain death.

This same little group was responsible for yanking our rockets out of Great Britain without notice, offering an excuse disputed by the real experts. They gave the rockets' mission to the already overloaded Strategic Air Command and to the Polaris submarine force.

Despite Russia's breaking her nuclear test-ban agreement with us in 1961, they have made a nuclear Test-Ban Treaty with Andrei Gromyko, who, Mr. Kennedy said publicly in October of 1962, lied to him. Moreover, it is an unpoliced ban.

They propose melting our sovereignty by quick stages into a United Nations world government. They have destroyed federal security programs aimed at preventing treacheries by the sort of subversives who stole our atomic and other secrets. Now, they have effectively smashed these security organizations.

Whatever their motives, their words and actions have had the effect of aiding world communism. Certainly the on-slaught of communism continues. They are tinkering with our military security against attack, as well as with our safeguards against internal subversion.

The least that can be said is that the men around President Johnson stand for a new way of life for the United States; and they make clear—and allow to be officially expressed—their fundamental lack of confidence in our nation despite its wonderful achievements, unique in all history.

Why did President Kennedy hand-pick these men? Why does President Johnson champion them, front for them and retain them?

There is no flat answer. We know that JFK turned abruptly to the Left after his 1956 rejection in Chicago. Before that he had made it clear he knew what was going on. He had publicly blamed "the Lattimores" and others of that ilk for the loss of China to the Reds. He had spoken out disparagingly of the ADA; had even contributed personally to Richard M. Nixon's campaign for the Senate against Party-liner Helen Gahagan Douglas; and had straddled the McCarthy issue. But after his rejection at Chicago, he voted down the line in the Senate for ADA policies, and after that he never opposed ADA on anything.

Perhaps John F. Kennedy thought he was using this group, rather than they him. Certainly he learned to depend upon them for much of his work. President Johnson, by keeping them in the fold, allows them to continue to execute their policies.

There is some reason to think that the quick, hard blows at the very start of the New Frontier—the Bay of Pigs, Laos, the Berlin Wall, the cruel meeting Khrushchev forced at Vienna

—coming in hammerlike succession, drove its leaders away from hard realities into the comfortable ivory tower of "advanced thinkers," into the New Frontier's never-never land.

Theodore Sorenson, Kennedy's Presidential aide who drafted his prize-winning *Profiles in Courage* and who was Kennedy's administrative assistant in the Senate, is an old-line ADAer and a man whose thinking runs along with that of the rest of the Inner Circle. President Kennedy always enjoyed his relaxation and these "eager beavers" were prepared to do, and did do, his routine work for him. Surely Kennedy willingly permitted his Inner Circle to play its all-encompassing role; and Lyndon Johnson, as President of the United States, has the power and organization to brush such characters summarily out of the way.

It was Sorenson who wrote a series of eight articles based on his Columbia University Speranza Lectures, advising the President on the day-to-day operations of the White House office. He concluded that "overruling advisers carries risks," that there is "no sure test of a good adviser" and that the important factor of politics rears its ugly head in Presidential decision-making. The Johnson advisers and their role in our government are proofs of all three of these conclusions.

Perhaps President Johnson feels that he needs these men to help him win the liberal vote in the big cities where elections can be decided. Perhaps he is afraid to buck the press claque they influence and which cooperates with them. He knows this claque has destroyed other prominent politicians. Perhaps he feels that, as the first President from the Confederacy since the Civil War, he can ignore the South and get its vote anyway. Perhaps the glorification of John F. Kennedy by TV and the rest of the news media after Kennedy's assassination have made it, in his eyes, too dangerous to discard the advisers who set JFK's policies.

The fact remains that these men whom we never elected, today have an overwhelming and highly dangerous influence on our lives and futures. We have a duty to ourselves and to our descendants to take a careful look at them and at their policies, and then to make known our views on them.

For, under the American system, we have a way of ridding ourselves of these men, even if President Johnson—when faced with overwhelming public demand for their dismissal—refuses to do so. We Americans are still at this moment—and perhaps for the last moment—the masters of our own destiny. We can vote our views—or can we?

THE END

INDEX